Early Childhood Education
in
Historical Perspective

Third Edition

D. Keith Osborn

Education Associates
A division of The Daye Press, Inc.

Library of Congress Cataloging-in-Publication Data

Osborn, D. Keith.
  Early childhood education in historical perspective
/D. Keith Osborn. — 3rd ed.
  Includes bibliographical references.
  ISBN 0-918772-22-2
  1.Education, Preschool--History. 2.Education, Preschool
  United States--History. 3. Education, Preschool--Biblio-
  graphy. I. Title.
  LB1140.2.08 1991   90-23294
    372.21'09--dc20   CIP

Send mail orders to:

Daye Press, Inc. Box 389 .. Athens, GA 30603 *or:*
Education Associates.. Box 8021 .. Athens, GA 30603

© 1991 by Daye Press, Inc.

Printed in the United States of America
10 9 8 7 6 5 4 3 2 1

ISBN # 0-918772-22-2   Text Edition

DEDICATION

I would like to dedicate this book to a friend of all early childhood educators — and a friend of mine. A constant source of inspiration and a person who deeply cares for children, James L. Hymes, Jr.

ACKNOWLEDGMENTS

There are always many persons to thank in a work like this. One could not attempt a history without the help of many librarians. I am particularly appreciative of the librarians at the University of Georgia and the Library of Congress. After the first edition, a number of people offered criticisms and suggestions. I am especially indebted to Dorothy Hewes, Jimmy Hymes, Alice Keliher, Flemmie Kittrell, Barbara Taylor, Judy Williston, and Phyllis Young.

The two major professional organizations that impact on the early childhood field are ACEI and NAEYC. The staffs at both headquarters were always ready to provide "one more fact." I would specifically like to acknowledge Lucy Prete Martin, editor of CHILDHOOD EDUCATION, Polly Greenberg, editor of YOUNG CHILDREN, Mary Anne Dooley, NAEYC Affiliate Groups, and Pat Spahr, NAEYC Information Service

In gathering information from the various states (see Part II), I received assistance from a number of NAEYC state presidents, ECE state specialists, and state librarians. I would like to acknowledge their help and interest. A list of individuals who helped with the state information is listed at the end of Part II. I also wish to acknowledge suggestions and assistance from Stephanie Bales, Wanda Callaham, George Stanic, and Steve White.

Not everyone who offered help, suggestions, and criticisms will agree with my interpretation "of the facts." Readers may find some dates at variance with other reference sources. Every effort was made to study original documents to determine the correct date. In cases of variance, the most probable date was chosen. In cases of error or differences in interpretation of certain events, I alone am responsible for the material included here. I must admit being ever mindful of Alistair Cooke's admonition, "Social history is never written by that 'objective reporter,' but always by a single human being confined more than he knows by the tether of his own experience."

Photo Credits: Cover, "Kinderspiele" by Pieter Bruegel, reprinted by permission from Kunsthistorisches Museum, Vienna. Photos "Doffer Boy," "Dinner Toters," and "Phenix Kindergarten," reprinted by permission from the Lewis Hine Collection, Hargrett Rare Book and Manuscript Library, University of Georgia. Susan Blow and Patty Smith Hill courtesy of ACEI. Maria Montessori courtesy of Sheryl Sweet. Kaiser photos courtesy of Jimmy Hymes. Merrill-Palmer photos from author's private collection. The medievel tapestry design was drawn by Alan H. Zubay, Jr.

INTRODUCTION TO THE FIRST EDITION

A sign at the National Archives says, "The past is prologue." When James Hymes and I were working in Washington on Project Head Start we realized the truth of this statement. Bryan, Montessori, and others had programs for children of the poor fifty years before Head Start. In 1908, the British government found that children under six were in dire need of good health care. Abigail Eliot and Edna Noble White had emphasized the importance of working with parents; Wellman had suggested that preschool programs could change I.Q.

Most of the "innovations" of Head Start (the advisory committee, training pamphlets, consultants, public participation, comprehensive services and a strong parent program) can be found in the WPA and Lanham Act nurseries. Even the war nurseries showed that "soft money" can be cut off on short notice.

Forty years before Nimnicht and McAfee, the Iowa preschool used "interest centers." One hundred years before Bandura, Susan Blow spoke of the importance of modeling. Prior to Freud, several individuals noted the effect of the early years on later development — including Aristotle, Plato, and Locke. Two centuries prior to the British Infant School, the British philosopher, Edmund Burke, emphasized allowing the child to investigate at his own rate — as opposed to memorizing a few "barren and lifeless facts."

The purpose of this book is to give the student an overview of factors which contributed to the early childhood movement. Until this century, the years of childhood have been, on the whole, a most unhappy period of life. In Greek and Roman times, infanticide was practiced. While the beginning of Christianity did curb infanticide, this practice continued into the 19th century. The view of the child as a miniature adult, allowed the western world to exploit children during the Industrial Revolution. Prior to the 18th century, the attitude of spare the rod and spoil the child caused most children to be, in reality, battered, abused children.

The student may find some dates at variance with other reference sources. Every effort was made to study original documents to determine the correct date. In cases of variance, the most probable date was chosen.

October 1975   D. Keith Osborn

INTRODUCTION TO THE THIRD EDITION

Since writing the first edition of this book, many events have taken place which have greatly influenced the early childhood field. The federal court decisions which have affected children, their parents and their teachers. Public Law 94-142 and the concept of mainstreaming have had an impact. Another major influence has been the women's movement and its effect on sex roles of children and our manner of teaching.

During this period we have also seen a growing awareness of the problems of child abuse, of inadequate facilities in day care, and the pernicious problems created when children use alcohol and drugs.

The earlier editions have been used as a text in over 100 colleges and universities. A number of students and professional colleagues have made suggestions for improving this text. In accordance with their wishes, I have enlarged the material between antiquity and the beginning of cities to show the approach to child rearing in the dawning days of pre-civilization. I have also enlarged the material concerning early kindergartens and the works of Froebel. Thanks to the work of Charles Cunningham, I have included more material on the role of Blacks in the early childhood movement. There are many threads in the early childhood tapestry — and I have tried to show how they are woven together.

Following the earlier editions of *Early Childhood Education in Historical Perspective,* a number of persons asked for specific historical references to ECE activities on a "state by state" basis. In response to this request, Part II of this text contains historical information on all the states and the District of Columbia. In most cases, this material will show the first kindergarten and nursery school in the state. The reference section has been considerably enlarged and contains over four hundred entries.

I am constantly impressed at how many "seemingly new concepts" have their origins in an earlier time. While Piaget emphasized the importance of play and active involvement, so did Commenius, Locke, and Rousseau. The very recent "invention," the infant mobile, was suggested to parents by Froebel. However, it appears that mobiles were originally employed by the early Egyptians and later by the Greeks.

Once again, I wish to acknowledge the helpful criticisms and encouragement of my wife, Dr. Janie D. Osborn.

dko

February 1991

v

Early Childhood Education in Historical Perspective

Social history is never written by that "objective reporter," but always by a single human being confined more than he knows by the tether of his own experience.

Alistair Cooke

WHERE ARE THE CHILDREN? Prior to the 1970s historians seemed to exhibit little interest in the role of children or the place of ordinary families in academic historical study. DeMause (1974, p. 1) states: "Historians have concentrated so much on the noisy sandbox of history with its fantastic castles and magnificent battles, that they generally ignored what was going on in the homes around the playground." Laslett (1965, p. 104) notes: " ... crowds and crowds of little children are strangely missing from the written record ... There is something strangely mysterious about the silence of all these multitudes of babes in arms, toddlers, and adolescents." This book attempts to provide the reader with some insight into early childhood education and child rearing practices throughout history.

180 MILLION BC MELANODON. Where did child rearing and early childhood education really begin? The first mammals began to appear about 180 million BC, during the Mesozoic Era. The melanodon, a lemur-like animal, is one example of these early mammals. Unlike earlier species, the mammal did not lay eggs in the environment and then desert them. Instead the mammalian female carried her eggs internally. Because of this hereditary feature, the female would have a much smaller litter and would nurse her offspring following birth. In this manner, some sort of commitment to child rearing was established. In many ways, these rather primitive actions represented the earliest beginnings of a family life pattern and ultimately lead to a human commitment to nurture and raise its offspring.

TWO MILLION BC EDUCATION AND CHILD REARING IN PREHISTORIC TIMES. It is impossible to place an exact date on the origin of modern man. There were many stages from our apelike ancestors to early *Homo sapiens.* Evidence of early man can be seen in East Africa on the edge of the Serengeti Plain in Tanzania (Leakey & Lewin, 1978). In China, 500,000 BC, there is evidence of a type of prehistoric human being called Peking man.

Note: The material presented in the remainder of this section is largely speculative. The theoretical assumptions concerning the rearing of the prehistoric child are based on the writer's hypotheses. The theory is based on assumptions from the field of paleoanthropology plus anthropological studies of modern-day hunting and gathering tribes. For the interested reader, there are several excellent sources concerning the origin of man in the *Reference* section of this book. For the casual reader, a delightful book by Panati (1984) is highly recommended. More technical references include: Ardney (1970), Attenborough (1977), Johanson and Edey (1980), Leakey and Lewin (1977, 1978), Pei (1966), Ponnamperuma (1972), and Williams (1975).

While no formal school existed, there is evidence that the essential characteristics of the educational process were taking place. All societies appear to have engaged in some form of informal education which would prepare offspring for the physical and social environment.

Nearly two million years ago, Africa contained a small population of manlike creatures (*Australopithecus* and *Paranthropus)* with brains not much larger than apes. These prehumans walked upright and lived on the ground. Observations of animals today would suggest that these creatures operated mostly from instincts and were highly nurturant in terms of their young. Simple learning took place via imitation and reinforcement. In these instances, a reinforcement might be a slap or a screech.

About one million years ago, *Homo erectus,* the first persons of our own genus appeared. The cranial capacity of these individuals extended into the lower range of *Homo sapiens.* From existing evidence, there is no way to determine if *Homo erectus* used spoken language. We do know that *Homo erectus* led a communal life and possessed knowledge of the use of fire. We believe that this group of

2

people was highly nurturant. The scant evidence which exists suggests to the author that the prehistoric child was generally desired, nurtured, and cared for. Early nomadic groups were usually very small and children were probably not too bothersome. Child rearing methods were largely instinctual.

However, some training was taking place. In its most primitive form, early education involved learning how to hunt and gather food and how to construct simple shelter for protection from the elements. This early training was, for the most part, unconscious and occurred in the form of observational learning. Strapped, or cradled to the mother's back, the neonate was fed on demand. The infant actually participated, albeit passively, in gathering foods for the family and tribe. This practice of cradling would continue into the second year of life. Then, when the child could walk, he continued to tag along with his mother and learned the art of gathering via imitative behavior. The young child would acquire other tribal rituals via observation and participation in community activities. Because of the simplicity of life in the hunting and gathering era, children became almost entirely self-sufficient (in terms of gathering) by four or five years of age.

In a society of gatherers, the time period needed for education was short in duration. In some types of gathering activity, a child of six to eight years of age would be on equal footing with the adults. In other instances, a youngster might actually be a better "producer" than many older adults in the group. Later, when animals were added to nomadic tribes in order to provide a more consistent source of food, children served as keepers of the flock. Thus, even young children were producers and assets to the tribal community. In early primitive societies, a fifteen-year-old would be considered an adult. In addition, a person of twenty to thirty years of age might well show the ravages of illness and disease. This individual would be considered an "older person" who no longer possessed outstanding hunting and gathering skills and who, in actual fact, might be a burden to the group.

Thus, early in life, young children would no longer need nurturing or parental control. In addition, it seems quite possible that youngsters could gain adult status since they were suitable providers who could make substantial and meaningful contributions to the life of the tribe.

3

We could use the term "migratory workers" to describe *Homo erectus*. They roamed the countryside and lived on game and fruits. Some evidence suggests that they may have developed the early rudiments of a spoken language. We have very little knowledge of their way of life and do not know what finally became of this group of early humans. The culture of the *Homo erectus* finally disappeared about two or three hundred thousand years ago and gave way to other forms of human existence.

The first significant step toward a higher civilization probably occurred thousands of years ago as man learned to communicate more effectively with his companions. While no record exists of these early interactions, it seems quite probable that during a hunt the leader would employ grunts and simple hand signals as a means of directing the other hunters. Another possibility is that speech began with spontaneous exclamations like joy, despair, fear, anger, and surprise. From these early crude methods of communicating, man finally derived spoken language.

As language became increasingly sophisticated, the more complex primitive societies developed ceremonies, religious chants, incantations and dances. Through imitation children learned the language, the customs, the simple folkways and mores of the tribe. Through these rituals children learned how to appeal to their gods in times of stress. There is evidence to suggest that some of the more complicated ceremonies were consciously taught in a formal way to some of the male children in the society. In certain instances this early schooling was selective and sons of the chief were taught specific ceremonial tasks.

As specialization developed in tribal groups, some boys learned to be witchdoctors, garden magicians, medicine men, and warriors. The girls learned simple domestic duties and increased their skills in gathering berries and other foods. All children learned dances and ceremonies for times of trouble like death, famine, and drought and for good times like the harvest, the killing of a large animal or a victory in warfare.

In many ancient societies some form of initiation ceremony was conducted which served an educational purpose. These rites occurred when the child was ten to thirteen years of age. The initiation might last a few days or continue for months or even years. The purposes of the initiation varied from one group to another. Generally, the purpose of an initiation rite was to: a) provide specific skills — like hunting, gardening, cooking, and food preservation; b) teach values like honoring the chiefs and elders, bravery, endurance, and obedience; (c) teach dances and ceremonies; and d) serve as a rite of passage in which the child became an adult.

Anthropological evidence from contemporary primitive tribal groups would suggest that prehistoric children were generally desired, nurtured, and cared for. As indicated above, even when they were very young, children probably participated on an equal footing with adults in early primitive societies.

8000 BC THE ADVENT OF FARMING. One of the salient characteristics of an advancing and more highly complex type of civilization was the change from food gathering societies to societies which produced their own foods. The historical record shows evidence of systematic food production through planting and harvesting crops in the Middle East about 8,000 BC. During this period goats and sheep were domesticated by these early farmers. Records also indicate that in southeast Asia and Mexico, people began raising crops about 7,000 BC.

7000 BC HIGHER CIVILIZATIONS AND EARLY VILLAGES. Historical records suggest the earliest indication of ancient civilizations can be found in Egypt and Sumer. This latter civilization was located in Mesopotamia.

Even before the establishment of early villages and towns, there is evidence that tribes would often settle in one place for an extended period of time. A tribal group might locate near a source of water — like a river or an oasis. Often a group would locate on a small hill — which would give them the "high ground" in the event of an enemy attack. Tribes would also settle near caves for protection during inclement weather. In addition, a cave might be used as a tribal burial ground. There is evidence to show that some of the early tribes would return to the same area each year to conduct religious ceremonies and honor their dead. However, sooner or later, adverse conditions would cause the group to assume its nomadic ways. By 6000 BC, some tribal groups had begun to herd cattle.

The advent of farming allowed people to remain in the same location for extended periods of time. As farming villages developed, some forms of permanence began to appear. Small buildings were erected. Tribes of hunters and gatherers would assemble at a village and exchange berries and furs for vegetables. Persons from other villages would come and trade with their counterparts. Certain individuals were designated to establish rules and regulations and other persons were appointed to guard against attack from rival tribes.

The ancient land of Mesopotamia, located in what is now eastern Syria, southeastern Turkey, and most of Iraq, is the region in which many of these early villages were established. This area, known as the *Fertile Crescent*, is a crescent shaped region, located between the Mediterranean Sea and the tip of the Persian Gulf. The area stretches between the Tigris and Euphrates Rivers. It was in this region that the Sumerian civilization was established.

6000 BC JERICHO, THE FIRST CITY. Archaeological evidence indicates that Jericho, located in Jordan and just north of the Dead Sea, is the oldest city in existence. Jericho enjoys a mild climate and many crops (both fruits and vegetables) can be grown year-round.

Some archaeologists date the beginnings of modern civilization and cities about 5000 BC, with the Sumerians who established early communities in the *Fertile Crescent*. The Sumerians used irrigation techniques and herded cattle. They created the world's first alphabetic writing system based on the old Egyptian system of hieroglyphics.

By 3500 BC, archaeological records indicate that a number of villages were in existence in areas of the middle east. With time, these primitive villages grew larger and more complicated in scope and purpose. As these changes took place, the village atmosphere gave way and began to take on the characteristics of cities and city life. By 3000 BC, Sumerian cities had beautiful palaces and temples. Most of the cities were walled for protection against invaders. Some of the Sumerian cities grew into city states. For a discussion of the change in history from village to city, see Good and Teller in the *Reference Section*

4000 BC EGYPTIAN CULTURE. Along the Nile River valley in eastern Africa, the culture of ancient Egypt was established. While few ancient civilizations gave women rights, Egypt was the exception. Women could own property and buy and sell goods. They also had the legal right to obtain a divorce. However, the father was definitely head of the household and could punish his wife. Evidence suggests that Egyptian children were wanted and nurtured. A number of ancient toys still exist from this period including balls, dolls, and board games.

3000 BC MINOAN CULTURE. The first civilization in the area of Greece occurred on the island of Crete. This early culture was called the Minoan culture after King Minos, the ruler of Crete.

3000 BC YANGSHAO CULTURE. There is evidence that stone age cultures had begun in China about 10,000 BC. From these early beginnings a distinct Chinese way of life, the Yangshao, emerged about 3000 BC. From this historic group another culture, the Longshan, developed which spread over most of China. The Longshan lived in walled villages, cultivated crops, and raised animals. From the Longshan culture China's first dynasty, the Shang, arose *See 1700 BC, Early Chinese Education.* During this period, Chinese women had few, if any, rights. Infanticide was a common practice, particularly among females.

3000 BC THE RISE OF SCHOOLING. The complexity of the new cities gave rise to a wide variety of services and vocations. It was not long until some type of formal schooling was needed to meet the demands of the city.

In the cities of Sumer, a number of institutions were developed because of the vast trading network which was being created. As business increased, persons specializing in writing were needed to keep accurate records. The necessity of keeping accounts created the need for bookkeeping skills. As the demand for scribes and accountants increased, schools were developed to meet this need. Since Sumerian writing was difficult to master, a long training period was needed. The first students were males who came exclusively from upper class families.

Panati (1984, pp. 152-153) gives an excellent description of the early Sumer schools: "The head of a Sumerian school was the *ummia* (expert), though he was also known as the 'school father' and a student was called 'school son.' ... Early schools had several 'men in charge of drawing' ... and at least one disciplinarian or 'man in charge of the whip,' who kept track of attendance and maintained classroom order ... students attended classes daily from sunrise to sunset, and vacations at a particular school were left to the headmaster's discretion. Education usually began at childhood and ran into early adulthood and encompassed a variety of religious, economic, administrative, and literary subjects ... women did not attend school."

In Egypt, schools for scribes were being established for children from the upper classes. Scribal schools were operated in the palace of the king, temples, and some government agencies. Subjects taught in these schools included reading, literature, geography, and mathematics. However, the main subject to be mastered was writing. This skill was learned by copying business accounts and letters. Since the Egyptian language was written in hieroglyphics — a system which consisted of over 800 characters and symbols, the skill of writing was very difficult to master. Unlike many ancient cultures, Egyptian girls from well-to-do families were sometimes allowed to attend these early schools. *See, Children of the Bible.*

EARLY CHILD REARING PRACTICES: TWO POINTS OF VIEW. While the melanodon made a commitment to nurture and care for its young, ancient historical documents suggest that this commitment to young children was indeed tenuous. Few records exist which describe early urban life and child rearing practices during this period. It seems likely that as specialization occurred, some persons would find themselves unemployed and without the skills necessary to survive in these early cities. We do know that the large majority of the population was poor and lived in dire poverty. In many instances, food and shelter were difficult to acquire. It appears likely that under these conditions children would become more of a burden than an asset. In prehistoric non-specialized cultures, children could effectively compete; in the rather specialized city environment they were largely ineffective as producers for the family.

Only recently have historians begun to seriously investigate ancient child rearing practices. How children fared during this era

8

has been a source of some discussion by historians who have studied this particular time frame. As is the case with many theoretical assumptions, there are two differing points of view concerning child rearing during this historic period.

Lloyd DeMause, a psychohistorian, reports that the further one goes back in history, the lower the level of child care and the more likely children were to be abandoned, beaten, terrorized, and sexually abused. Like DeMause, there is a group of historians who believe that babies were seen as the unavoidable result of sexual relations and infanticide was a common practice in most ancient cultures (DeMause, 1974).

A second opinion is offered by other writers. For example, French (1977) states that a study of the historical record suggests a different conclusion. She believes that the answer lies in a careful study of beliefs about children in a cultural context and has looked for evidence of the child's influence on others. She agrees that there was some infanticide, but believes that the general mode of child rearing during this period was nurturant.

Pollock (1983) studied records dating from the sixteenth century and concludes that children have always been seen as different from adults. However, when one views the way many children were treated during early Greek and Roman periods and during the Middle Ages, children could hardly be seen as being the objects of nurturant parents. During the Industrial Revolution (e.g., working 14 hours a day, six days a week) or during the period of American slavery (when Black children were treated exactly like their elders — beaten, made to work long hours, separated from one's mother and other family members, barely fed, and treated as items of real property), it is difficult to defend the thesis that children were always seen as different from adults.

Regardless of the point of view which the reader takes, the historical evidence suggests that in the more complex cultural setting of the villages and cities, infants and young children could be viewed as relatively helpless and incapable of directing their own affairs. It is during this period that we observe some formal education, usually a school for highly privileged young males, which taught reading and writing. Professions, like being a scribe, were carefully guarded occupations and generally passed on from father to son.

CHILDREN OF THE BIBLE. The Bible provides some insight into the Jewish child during Biblical times. The Old Testament suggests a strong family group and a view that children were God's gift. Barrenness was an indication of His displeasure. For parents, children represented honor and pride (Ps. 144:12), and males were particularly desired. The educative task of the parents was instruction and discipline. There are several examples of severe punishment and extreme child abuse. For instance, "Do not withhold discipline from a child; if you beat him with a rod, he will not die" (Prov. 23:13) Historical references indicate that Jewish males were taught to read in order to be able to read and understand the Torah. In the Jewish tradition, the son would normally follow the father's vocation, and his training would be provided by the father.

The New Testament provides a different interpretation of both God and of children. There are several references to children as symbols for regeneration of the spirit and as naive and unspoiled. In many ways their dependency makes them receptive to receiving God's comfort and love. "Unless you turn and become like children, you will never enter the kingdom of heaven" (Matt. 18:3). "Let the children come unto me and do not hinder them, for such belongs the kingdom of heaven" (Matt. 19:14). However, there are still references in the New Testament which would also show that parents need to be firm and employ firm discipline. "Children obey your parents in the Lord, for this is right" (Eph. 6:1).

1700 BC EARLY CHINESE EDUCATION. Education in China can be traced to the earliest beginnings of her civilization. According to Kuo (1915), children received training via modeling from the family and the tribal group. There is some evidence that, as early as 2300 BC, a more formal education had been begun. During the Shang dynasty (1766-1122 BC), a definite school system emerged. A system of writing was established and a minister of education was appointed. Old records show that only males were educated during this period. Historical evidence shows that females were viewed as having little value. Until the recent Communist Revolution, a husband could divorce his wife on the grounds that she did not produce any male children. In many cases females were killed at birth since they were viewed as useless.

During the Shang dynasty there were two types of educational institutions: Siao Hsueh (lower education) and Ta Hsueh (higher education). Lower education was provided to commoners and consisted of teaching manners, customs, and laws of the land. Higher education was for princes, the sons of nobles and high government officials. In addition, higher education was also provided for the intellectually gifted sons of commoners.

The Shang kingdom instituted the practice of a competitive examination system. Boys of common descent who were the most qualified, were provided with a higher education by the state. These young men were then educated to work as civil service officers. After completion of their education, they were assigned jobs with the state. However, even after being employed, workers were examined every third year and, based on their test scores, either promoted or dismissed from service.

700 BC GREEK CITY STATES. Ancient Greece was divided into a number of city states. The ancient Greeks were the first group of people to develop a democratic form of government and historians regard the Greeks as the founders of Western civilization. Greek philosophers were concerned about corruption in politics and sought to devise ways of child rearing and education that would assure selection of better governing officials.

Most of the sources relating to child rearing in ancient Greece were written by men of social status. These writings usually make reference to "well-to-do" youngsters. Generally the Greeks viewed children as objects of affection and as important family members. Nevertheless we do see concern for strong discipline. For example: "Now of all wild young things, a boy is the most difficult to handle ... he is the craftiest, most mischievous, and unruliest of brutes" (Laws. Bk. 7:808).

Records indicate that infanticide was practiced in ancient Greece, at least on a limited scale. The practice of infanticide (usually by exposure) was, for the most part, restricted to female babies. Greek families during this period were usually small and often limited to one daughter. Life was relatively simple, but it was also extremely difficult. The famous historian, Herodotus, said, "In Greek homes, poverty is always a guest."

The attitude of this period is seen in the writing of Plato and Aristotle. Plato discussed regulating sexual relations in order to produce the "most perfect" human beings. Aristotle, on the other hand, was concerned with over-population. In his pronouncements, Aristotle pointed out that lack of population control led to poverty strickened families and suggested that population should be limited by law. Aristotle also suggested that abortion would be a preferable method for control over the Greek practices of exposure and abandonment.

It is interesting to note that both Aristotle and Plato spoke of the need to educate the child prior to the age of six. Aristotle said that training should begin early and that recognition should be given to the fact that each child possessed specific talents and skills. Aristotle would appear to be the first person to detail the idea of individual differences in children. Plato suggested that since most parents were unfit for child rearing, youngsters should be separated from parents and educated by the state. While never implemented, Plato suggested that children should be reared in state nurseries. In contrast to the prevailing Athenian opinion, Plato believed that women should be allowed to pursue all the educational rights given to male citizens. He believed that some women were fit to serve as rulers and be among the philosophical elite.

While a few of the Greek city states did make some provision for the education of females, most educational training in Greece was limited to men. The type of education varied depending upon the particular city state. In Sparta, for example, education emphasized physical development and gymnastics. Spartan children were severely beaten if they disobeyed their schoolmasters. The pupils were also trained to undergo extreme privation. Thus, the statement, "a Spartan existence." Reading and writing were not emphasized in Spartan schools and most of the adults of Sparta were ignorant.

In sharp contrast, the city of Athens emphasized perfecting the individual talents of their male children. It was expected that boys from wealthy homes would develop their own individual skills. In Athens, school began when the child reached the age of six. The young student was guided in his instruction by a trusted household slave — called a *pedagogos*. The method of instruction was primarily through memorization. As indicated above, Plato's idea of equal education for both sexes was never implemented and women in

Athens had no legal or economic rights. Historic records indicate that only a few girls from "well-to-do" Athenian homes were educated by tutors.

500 BC CONFUCIUS (551-479 BC). Confucius was the most influential philosopher in Chinese history and, until the Communist revolution in 1949, was the single most important influence on Chinese thought. For most of the history of China, Confucianism represented the official government philosophy. His teachings stressed the need to develop moral character and personal responsibility. Confucius believed that people could improve themselves through study. He also believed in a well ordered society in which parents rule their children; men rule women; and educated rulers guided the state.

400 AD ROME. The child rearing practices in Greece continued under Roman rule and doubtless influenced the attitudes of Romans in rearing their children. Romulus and Remus, the mythical founders of the Roman Empire, were abandoned children. Both Seneca and Pliny the Elder viewed the practice of infanticide and exposure as necessary means of population control. In some instances parents apparently did not wish to dispose of their children by exposure and resorted to the practice of *potting*. In potting, the parent placed the infant in a large basket or urn and left the container in a public place. Sometimes expensive ornaments were placed with the child as an inducement for someone to "adopt" the youngster. An excellent example of potting is found in the *Bible* (Exodus, Chapter 2), in the case of Moses.

Schools were established in Rome about 250 BC and initially followed the Greek tradition. In early Roman schools it was not unusual to have a Greek slave as a teacher. In general, the Roman approach to education was conservative and limited to the upper classes. Teachers were very strict and the use of corporal punishment was common.

CHRISTIANITY AND INFANTICIDE. The rise of Christianity caused a decisive change in attitudes toward infanticide. Early Christian philosophers viewed the newborn child as possessing a soul and denounced infanticide as a pagan practice and murder. The Christian view held that the enjoyment of children was an integral part of family life.

In 318 AD, Emperor Constantine declared that killing a child was a crime. Later Emperor Augustus offered a stipend to any family who would rear a foundling. By 400 AD, Christian churches were demanding that infanticide and abandonment be stopped. Village homes, ordered by the Council of Nicene, were established to care for orphans.

The Theodosian Code (ca. 322 AD) shows concern for young children. The code states, "To restrain the hands of parents from infanticide and turn their hopes to the better ... a parent should report if he has an offspring which, on account of poverty he is unable to rear, there shall be no delay in issuing food and clothing, since the rearing of a newborn infant cannot tolerate delay ..."

During the Middle Ages, a distinction was made between infanticide and exposure. Infanticide (willful disposal of children) was punishable by law. On the other hand, if the parent claimed the death was accidental there was no punishment.

As a result, a common form of infant death during the Middle Ages was *overlaying*. Overlaying supposedly occurred when an infant died of suffocation while laying in bed with its parents. Since it was almost impossible to prove intent, this crime generally went unpunished. During this period of history, the usual penalty for infanticide was a year of penance. Overlaying became such a problem that in 1500, the Bishop of Fiesole set fines for parents who kept babies in bed with them. An Austrian law (1784) prohibited children under five from sleeping with their parents.

A quote from a civil authority during the Middle Ages perhaps reflects the prevailing view of society in general: "Parents who commit infanticide are to be congratulated!" In the 1700s several other methods became commonplace — the use of opiates, starvation, and dunking a youngster in very cold water. A medical doctor of that period wrote: "Dunking is a good method of control. Some children may die as a result of dunking — but mothers should not feel concern or guilt, since dunking is a very successful method of discipline" (DeMause, 1974).

In an effort to curb infanticide, large cities in Europe established foundling homes. Several of these institutions were quite large. St. Petersburg, Russia, had a "home" with 25,000 children. The London Hospital admitted nearly 15,000 children during a four year period. Considering the huge task of providing good health care, it is perhaps understandable that the mortality rate was high (often 30-40%) during this period despite the best efforts of the professional staff.

In order to make leaving a child at a hospital more convenient, Napoleon (1811) decreed that every hospital in France be equipped with a turntable "la tour." The mother could place her child on one side, ring a bell, and have a nurse turn the table and take the child. In this fashion, the mother could leave the infant without being identified or detected.

During the Industrial Revolution, working mothers often left their newborn children with wet nurses who were actually hired for the purpose of disposing of infants. This practice was known as "baby farming" and the nurses were called "killer nurses" or "angel makers."

While Christianity was a major influence in attitude change, the practice of infanticide was still occurred with relative frequency until this century. In 1895, missionaries to China were appalled that infants were often thrown into the streets and allowed to die of exposure.

Finally in response to public opinion, largely from church groups and physicians, the first comprehensive law was passed. *See 1872, Infant Life Protection Act.* Perhaps the modern counterpart of infanticide is the battered child syndrome. Since the early 1960s, all states have enacted child abuse legislation. *See 1963, Colorado.*

600 AD FIRST CHILDREN'S BOOKS. If the Greeks or Romans wrote poetry or stories exclusively for use by children, none of these pieces of literature survived through the Middle Ages. Textbooks written in England by Saint Aldhelm, Bishop of Sherborne, are believed to be the first books for children. These books were written in question and answer form. Textbooks followed this style for nearly 1,000 years.

400-1600 AD THE MIDDLE AGES. The period between the decline of the Roman Empire and the rise of modern civilization is termed the Middle Ages. Historians disagree on the exact dating for this period and dates will vary from 400-1600 AD.

In ancient Greece and pre-Christian Rome, pagan practices were generally followed in all areas of society. A number of contemporary philosophers of that era severely criticized many of the early writers for their low moral standards. Quintilian, the famous Roman educator said, "The Greeks are licentious in many of their writings and I am loath to interpret Horace in certain passages." Several of the early Greek plays would be termed "hard core pornography" today.

Under these circumstances it is not surprising that the values found in early Christian homes and the ideas taught in pagan schools would be in conflict. During the second and third centuries, in order to overcome the influence of pagan school teachings, instruction was often given privately in Christian homes. In the third century efforts were made to dissolve pagan schools and establish Christian schools throughout the empire. In 313 AD, Constantine declared Christianity the official religion of the Roman Empire and Christian schools began to expand and flourish (Edict of Milan). The purpose of the early Christian schools was to teach children to read the word of God and to prepare them for church membership. In the year 529 A.D, Justinian closed the schools of philosophy in Athens because he felt their teachings were pagan and issued an edict (Edict of Justinian) calling for the closing of all non Christian schools in the empire.

With the fall of the Roman Empire (476 AD) and the rise of Christianity, much of the knowledge of the old world was lost. For several centuries the church discouraged secular books and most of the historic learnings, writings, and cultural activities were destroyed and completely lost during the period of the Dark Ages. Had it not been for the early monasteries and the great library of Alexandria, most of the documents from the early Greek philosophers and writers would have been lost forever.

This period was an extremely difficult time for young and old. Except for the lords and the clergy, the majority of the population of Europe consisted of peasants and farmers. This group was extremely

16

poor and possessed few civil rights. For the most part, poor families spent their entire lives tilling the fields of their master — the feudal lord. Peasants lived in crude huts and existed primarily on dark bread, cabbage, turnips, and a few other vegetables. The rarely had meat. Since the game belonged to the lord of the manor, peasants were prohibited from hunting and fishing. War, disease, and famine kept the population small. The average life span during this period was about thirty years. Most persons were too poor to travel and seldom ventured more than five to ten miles from their birthplace. Only a few children received schooling and most of the skills of the ancient world were lost. One can gain insight into the culture's view of children by studying works of art during this period. Children were pictured as miniature adults possessing adult mannerisms and mature facial features (See illustration on page 18).

Since there was a high incidence of infant mortality, little value was placed on the young child. Quoting from *Le Caquet de l'accouchee*, Aries (1962, p. 38) provides additional insight concerning this period: "We have a neighbor standing at the bedside of a woman who has just given birth, the mother of five 'little brats,' and calming her fears with these words: 'Before the children are old enough to bother you, you will have lost half of them, or perhaps all of them.' " People could not allow themselves to become too attached to something that was regarded as a highly probable loss. In many cases, this attitude existed into the 17th and 18th centuries.

SCHOOLS IN THE MIDDLE AGES. During the final years of the empire, the Roman army could no longer protect their cities and towns. These were largely destroyed by the invading Germanic barbarians from the northern parts of Europe. The conquerors divided the remnants of the empire into numerous small kingdoms and manors.

Faced with lawlessness and total anarchy, the general population deserted the villages and towns and fled to the manors to seek protection from the local king or lord. In this atmosphere of fear and destruction, city schools ceased to exist.

The only educational force to remain during the early part of the middle ages was the monastery. Monasteries founded schools for the relatively small number of boys who intended to become monks.

Figure 1. Tapestry design from the Middle Ages, ca. 1000 AD.

We can gain insight into a culture's view of its children by studying works of art. In this medieval tapestry children were pictured as miniature adults possessing adult mannerisms and mature facial features.

These schools were also available to the very rich in the surrounding area. Students were kept under severe conditions and discipline was very strict. The curriculum usually consisted of the seven liberal arts as outlined by a medieval scholar, Martianus Capella, author of *The Marriage of Philology and Mercury.* These subjects, entitled the seven ways to knowledge included: grammar, rhetoric, dialectic, arithmetic, geometry, astronomy, and music. The first three ways to knowledge were called the *trivium*; the last four subjects were named the *quadrivium.* This material was not taught in the language of the area, but rather utilized Latin as the language of the schools.

In the latter part of the Middle Ages (the late 1300s and early 1400s) the Renaissance period began. During this period commerce commenced to develop and small towns began to flourish once more. Skilled crafts and specialized occupations began to develop to meet the needs of these new communities. *See 1423, The Invention of Printing.* This need gave rise to a new group of citizens — a type of middle class. In order to protect themselves from the excessive demands of the local lords, these skilled laborers began to organize themselves into guilds — much like our labor unions today. These guilds offered training to young boys. The training was divided into three stages: apprentice, journeyman, and master craftsman. Training was often begun as early as six or seven years of age, and lasted for eight to ten years. Two examples of children who learned crafts in this fashion were Leonardo de Vinci, who apprenticed under Verrocchio, and Michaelangelo, who first apprenticed with the artist, Ghirlandajo, and later with the sculptor, Donatello.

During the period of the Renaissance, a group of classical humanists developed. These scholars emphasized the Greek and Roman classics and stressed the importance of the human experience. This group believed that the role of education was to create good, well rounded citizens. In the period between 1400 and 1500, the humanists developed a number of schools patterned after the early Greek gymnasiums. These schools stressed good manners, body building, and a general liberal arts curriculum. These institutions were the forerunners of the secondary schools which offered young boys and men a general program of study based on Greek and Latin.

In the late thirteenth century, several cities in Germany developed city schools with the permission of the Roman Church. However, the church would not permit these schools to teach Latin so they used the local language or vernacular. Usually these schools taught writing, arithmetic, bookkeeping, and other practical subjects. The invention of movable type made printing materials more available and many persons wished to learn to read and to write. By the 1500s, schools were fairly common throughout Europe. While vernacular schools were being demanded by the common people, there was an increasing demand for more Latin schools by the wealthy class. This demand for more schools and more knowledge helped greatly in creating the need for universities which began to develop during this period.

1000 AD THE FIRST EUROPEAN UNIVERSITY. Most historians agree that the first university in Europe was established in Bologna, Italy, about the year 1000. (*Note:* There were earlier universities in the Arab world. The oldest operating university in the world is the University of Al-Azhar. It was established in Cairo in the year 970.) Initially the spread of universities was slow but the Renaissance period saw the rapid development of these institutions. By 1400, a number of universities had been established largely to teach the professions of theology, medicine, and law. Some of these universities began to depart from traditional theological instruction. This group of scholars, the classical humanists, helped create a revival in ancient Greek and Roman learning. This reawakening of interest led to our modern concept of a college liberal arts curriculum.

1423 THE INVENTION OF PRINTING. Actually printing was invented in China shortly after the birth of Christ. However, this invention did not make its way to Europe and was not discovered in the Western world until the fifteenth century. The year, 1423, represents the earliest printing on wooden blocks. Prior to this event, all books were reproduced by hand — usually in the monasteries of that period.

1439 THE INVENTION OF MOVABLE TYPE. During the 1400s, there was an increasing demand for more Latin and vernacular schools. With this rise in demand came the need for more books in the field of education. Block printing helped fill this need. Even then, however, printing was relatively slow.

In 1439, Johannes Gutenberg, a German printer, invented movable type. This invention enabled a printer to create completely new pages of printing in a short period of time. Whereas it often took a monk several days to produce a single page of script, Gutenberg's printing press could produce 300 copies of a single page in one day. Then the type could be dismantled and reset to create another page of new material.

Many persons viewed the printing process as a "Satanic Art" which came from the devil. Nevertheless, printing spread throughout Europe and the price of books became relatively inexpensive. By the early 1500s, there were nearly 2,000 printing establishments in Europe and more than three million books had been produced. This rapid influx of information helped to spread the idea of the Renaissance and brought an end to the Middle Ages.

1440 VITTORINO de FELTRE. An Italian educator and classical humanist, Vittorino de Feltre, emphasized the importance of poetry, dance, and games for young children. De Feltre believed that schools should recognize the "whole" child and, in sharp contrast to other schools during that era, his program alternated between work and play periods.

ca. 1442 THE HORNBOOK. The invention of printing helped in the creation of a small "book" for children. The hornbook was actually a single sheet of paper attached to a wooden board with a handle. The paper was covered with a thin sheet of cow's horn for protection. Hornbooks were small in size — about 3" x 4". The "book" usually consisted of the alphabet, vowels and consonants, the Lord's Prayer, and/or some biblical verse. Early shipments to the American Colonies often included hornbooks for young children. In her book, *Antiques of American Childhood,* McClinton tells of a child (ca. 1691) of two and a half years of age going to school carrying his hornbook. These books were very popular with the early colonists and remained in use as late as the early 1800s. For the interested student, Folmsbee's, *A Little History of the Hornbook,* is recommended.

1600 CHRISTIANITY AND EDUCATION. As we have seen, Christianity played an important role in infanticide. If the infant had a soul, then the practice of infanticide was tantamount to murder. We have also seen that Christianity played an important role in education during the Middle Ages. Had it not been for the archives in the monasteries, much of the learning of the old world would have been lost.

In another way, Christianity also had a profound influence on education. Learning to read was important because Christians needed to read the Bible. All groups of the clergy emphasized the importance of education but there were two radically different points of view presented as the reason for this need. One view held that the child was basically evil and bad and, therefore, doomed to hell and damnation. For example in *A Godly Form of Household Government* (1621), we read:

"The young child which lieth in the cradle is both wayward and full of affection; and though his body be small, yet he hath a wrongdoing heart and it inclined to evil ... if this spark be suffered to increase, it will rage over and burn down the whole house. For we are charged and become good, not by birth, but by education."

The opposing point of view saw the child as a *tabula rasa* — a blank slate. This point of view can best be seen in Earle's *Microcosmography* (1628). Earle states:

"The child is a small letter, yet the best copy of Adam ... His soul is yet a white paper unscribbled with observations and he knows no evil."

In both instances, however, the road to salvation was via the same pathway — education. This education was needed to save the child from corruption and from the evils of sin.

1600 CHILD REARING AND EDUCATION IN THE NEW WORLD. The coming of the Renaissance caused dramatic changes throughout Europe and swept away a thousand years of customs and beliefs. As we have seen, education underwent vast changes and a spirit of adventure and curiosity prevailed. The discovery of America fitted perfectly into this new era. The early colonists came to America to establish a "new beginning." Their culture would be dramatically different from Europe. They would change their lifestyle and their concept of education. They would move from the European type of community to a wilderness environment. Life in America was harsh and so was child rearing. DeMause states that most children in the New World could be considered abused children in terms of the strong discipline and hard work which they had to endure.

Educational historians have noted some differences in terms of child rearing and education in the various colonies. While not wishing to oversimplify, some regional differences did occur and one can discern different general patterns in New England, the Middle, and the Southern Colonies.

In New England the government was theocentric; that is, church, state, and education were closely tied together. While children were loved, their parents believed that they needed a strong style of discipline. Since children were born ignorant and sinful, the role of the parent involved filling the child's mind with knowledge and biblical truths.

As a result, in Puritan New England there was a major emphasis on learning to read — particularly, learning to read the Bible. In 1642, the Massachusetts Bay Colony passed a law requiring parents to teach their children to read. In 1647, Massachusetts passed the "Old Deluder Satan Act," which required that every town with fifty householders maintain a school in order to "thwart ye olde deluder Satan who has conspired to keep men from the knowledge of the Scriptures." Town schools taught religion and were publicly supported.

Problems with religion in England caused the Puritans to venture forth and these Puritans often spoke of the New World migration as a blessing for their children. Cotton Mather told his congregation:

"Was it not with respect unto posterity that our fathers came unto this wilderness, that they might train up a generation for Christ?" Mather also added, "It was for your sakes, especially that your fathers ventured their lives upon the rude waves of the vast ocean to come to America."

In Colonial times, discipline was harsh and children were expected to obey immediately and without question. Respect for parents was mandatory and the Biblical commandment to "Honor thy father and mother" was considered a fundamental precept. Parents were usually addressed as: "honored sir," "honored madam," or "esteemed parent." In Puritan New England when a child spoke to his parents, he stood up. When he saw his parents approaching, he went out to meet them and bowed to them.

In *The History of Childhood*, DeMause reports that it was considered a capital crime for a child over sixteen to "curse or smite his natural father or mother." John Calvin, the great Protestant minister, said: "Those who violate the parental authority by contempt or rebellion are not men but monsters. Therefore the Lord commands all those who are disobedient to their parents to be put to death." *Note*: There are no reports of this punishment having ever been carried out.

Young infants were not expected to cry or make noise. The Puritan household was a quiet place and children were to "be seen and not heard." Children quickly learned that they would receive nothing if they cried. *The Harmony of the Gospels* (1678) notes: "Withhold not correction from the child, for if thou beatest him with the rod he will not die. Thou shall beat him with the rod and deliver his soul from hell."

Colonial parents loved and respected their children, but they did not display much overt affection. Generally the Puritan family did not show many outward emotions. Greenleaf (1978, p. 89) reports one father saying, "Fondness and familiarity breeds and causeth contempt and irreverence in children."

Discipline was also taught in school as illustrated in *The New England Primer*. In the alphabet section of the primer, the following couplets appear:

(F)   "The idle Fool —
        is whipt at school."

(J)   "Job feels the rod —
        yet blesses God."

Historians have noted a different lifestyle in the Middle Colonies. While Puritans shared a common language and a common set of religious beliefs, the Middle Colonies were characterized by linguistic, religious, and cultural pluralism. In terms of religions the Middle Colonies had representation from the Lutherans, the Society of Friends, the Dutch Reformed Church, Roman Catholics, plus Baptist and Jewish faiths. Most of these religious groups established and supported their own schools. As a result, a greater degree of religious and educational freedom existed and more variations in education were permitted. While colonists in this area certainly accepted the reality of sinfulness, they seemed to place a higher value on the power of reason. Parents in this category were more likely to believe that parental love and discipline were more persuasive than the threat of Satan, fire, and brimstone. As a general rule, schools in this area were not state supported and, as a result, only about 10% of the children attended schools.

Some early immigrants in the Middle Colonies were young children who were brought to America as indentured servants. They worked on farms or as apprentices to repay for their passage to the New World.

In the Southern Colonies children of plantation owners and aristocrats attended private schools or had tutors. A few schools in the Southern Colonies were run by ministers in order to "catechize and to teach." Poorer parents, who could not afford to send their children to school, would, when possible, teach their children how to read and write. We say, "when possible," since most poor colonists were illiterate.

The South did have a type of secondary school, the Academy, which remained quite popular from the 1600s into the twentieth century. Generally the Academy was not designed as a college preparatory school. Rather, these schools were private and the curriculum was fashioned to enable young men to learn writing, bookkeeping, and related skills designed to help them in farming and business. *See, Education in the Rural South.*

Like Puritan New England, discipline was firm in the Southern Colonies. In the early 1700s, John Wesley served as a pastor in Georgia, and cautioned parents not to "indulge their children lest they spoil them." He remarked that if the parent gave a child what he cried for; the parent was, in effect paying the child for crying and would only promote further crying. (*Note:* While Wesley never heard of reinforcement theory, he was an excellent observer of human behavior.) Greven (1973, p. 93) quotes Susanna Wesley, John Wesley's mother, as saying: "The first thing to be done is to conquer their (the children's) will and bring them to obedient temper."

1600 CHILDREN AS ECONOMIC TOOLS. In Colonial America some children received an education by serving as apprentices. Under this system young boys were "bound out" to learn a trade from master craftsman. The master promised to provide food, clothing, and lodging and to teach the youngster the skills and secrets of his craft. In some instances girls were "bound out" to serve as house-keepers, cooks, maids, or seamstresses.

The New World had definite commercial overtones. While many persons saw America as a way to establish religious freedom and a new life, others recognized this country as a land of commercial opportunity.

In the New World many people were needed to settle the land and establish communities. In New England children worked the land with their parents. Children were a definite economic asset and families of eight to twelve were quite common. A large family was also consistent with the Christian ethic, "Be fruitful and multiply."

Bossard and Boll (1966, p. 502) quote from *The New England Plantation* (1629): "Little children, by setting of corne, may earne much more than their own maintenance." Bremner (Volume 1, p. 3) quotes from an early book on colonization that: "Even boys and girls twelve to fourteene yeeres may bee kept from idleness in making a thousand kindes of trifling things which will bee good merchandise for that country."

While New England colonies were settled primarily by families searching for religious freedom, the Middle-Atlantic colonies were often settled by individuals more interested in the New World as a business venture. Children as young as ten years of age were recruited from London and sent to America to work as indentured servants. From 1618, and for many years thereafter, the Virginia Company requested large numbers of orphan children to be shipped to the colonies from England.

The Lord Mayor of London acceded to this request and in 1620, the Privy Council of Great Britain granted the Virginia Company the power and authority to coerce children to come to America. In 1620, the Privy Council minutes read:

"The City (London) deserveth thanks for redeeming so many poor souls service." (Since a number of children did not actually wish to go to America, the City of London was granted the authority to) "...receive and carry children against their wills ... If any of these children shall be found obstinate to resist or disobey ... they shall be imprisoned or punished and shipped to the Virginia Company." *Note:* Parts of the above passage were paraphrased for clarity.

1600 COLONIAL CHILDREN AT PLAY. Colonial children spent only a small fraction of their time in school. Most waking hours were spent in work. However, while times were hard, records do show that colonial children did engage in some recreation. Whenever possible colonists combined work and play. Often families would gather together to share a common task and, at the same time, have contests or other forms of recreation. Early activities included building a church or community center, raising a barn, or harvesting a crop together. Games included hop scotch, foot races, arm wrestling, bag races, hide and seek, blindman's bluff, spelling bees, and group singing. Toys were relatively few and, for the most part, homemade. Boys usually had knives, marbles, and tops. Girls usually played with dolls and housekeeping items.

1619 FIRST BLACKS IN AMERICA. The first Blacks in Colonial America settled in the Virginia Colony in 1619. These early settlers were not slaves, but arrived in America as indentured servants occupying the same status as accorded the Europeans who came to the colonies under similar circumstances.

1620-1865 CHILDREN IN ENSLAVEMENT. Although the first Black settlers were indentured servants it was not long before Blacks were brought to the New World as slaves. Slavery existed mainly in the Southern part of the colonies and by 1860, there were about four million slaves in America. Statistics are not available to show how many of these persons were young children.

In most states the children of slaves were not viewed as human beings, but rather as real property of the owner. From an 1809 legal opinion (South Carolina, M'Lain vs. Elder) "This law applies to the young of slaves, because as objects of property, they stand on the same footing as other animals." In cases of illegitimate children and mixed marriages (example: free mother; slave father), the children were viewed as bastards and slaves; the courts holding that a slave spouse was incapable of contracting for a marriage.

During the Revolutionary War (1775-1783) many Northerners turned against slavery believing that the United States was formed to protect the natural rights of individuals. By the early 1800s, most northern slave owners had freed their slaves. In the U.S. Census of 1820, there were 763,747 Black children under fourteen years of age. About 94,000 were free children; the rest were in slavery. As mentioned earlier, the exact number of slave children at the end of the Civil War is unknown.

Living conditions for slave children varied considerably but were generally poor. Often the only clothing worn by young children was a tow sack shirt or dress. In his autobiography Frederick Douglass (1855, pp. 84-85) recalled:

"I was kept almost naked — no shoes, no stockings, no jacket, no trousers; nothing on but a coarse tow linen shirt reaching only to my knees." Douglass described mealtimes for slave children on a Maryland plantation: "Our food was boiled corn mush. It was put into a large wooden trough, and set down on the ground. The children were then called, like so many pigs ... they would devour the mush ... he who ate the fastest, got the most; he that was strongest got the best place, and few left the trough satisfied."

While marriages were not recognized by law, many slaves had the ceremony performed. In spite of this marriage, the master might sell the father or mother and the family unit would be broken. Frederick Douglass, cited above, was separated from his mother at an early age and then saw her on only one occasion during the remainder of her life. There are instances where the master would threaten to sell the husband and wife separately. This practice was used to keep the slaves "in line."

Because of the high economic value of young women and children, there was a certain amount of care given to infants and the young. A pregnant woman was often given light work until the baby arrived and given some time off during the early nursing period. After a short interval, the mother returned to the fields. If there was not a person available to care for the newborn, it was taken to the field and placed by a fence or under a tree.

Olmstead (1861) described a nursery on a plantation in South Carolina (ca. 1850). Infants and small children were left in a small cabin while the mothers worked in the fields nearby. An older woman was left in charge and assisted by several young girls, eight to ten years of age. The infants, for the most part, lay on the cabin floor or the porch — and once or twice daily the mother would come in from the fields to nurse the baby. Children of toddler age played on the porch or in the yard and, at times, the older girls might lead the group in singing and dancing.

As children got older they were left to themselves and often played in the fields or the creeks. Usually they passed the time playing simple games such as hide and seek. When children reached the age of five or six they were sometimes organized into work groups and assigned simple tasks around the plantation. These tasks included drawing and carrying water, herding cows, feeding the chickens and pigs, picking berries, and weeding the garden. At twelve years, children were assigned to the fields and expected to perform one-quarter of the workload of an able-bodied adult. *Note*: For the history buff: There are several "first person" passages on children in slavery presented in Bremner (1970), Volume 1.

1658   JOHN COMENIUS (1592-1670). A Czech educator, Comenius designed the first children's textbook, *Orbis Pictus*, (Visible World) which used illustrations. In 1628, Comenius wrote, *The School of Infancy*. In this book he described the "school of the mother's lap," where the child from birth to six could learn the rudiments of all knowledge. Like the classical humanist philosophers, Comenius believed in a broad general education. The reader is referred to Braun and Edwards for writings by Comenius and other philosophers like Locke and Rousseau.

1690   THE NEW ENGLAND PRIMER. Originally written by a Boston printer, Benjamin Harris, *The New England Primer*, was a small book of eighty-eight pages. It was written in rhyme and concerned Christian doctrine. The sole purpose of reading during this period was the acquisition of religious knowledge. Books were illustrated with startling realism, depicting the glory of heaven and the terrors of hell. The Primer was popular; more than five million copies were sold during the hundred years that it was used as a textbook for young children. About 1770, Benjamin Collins introduced the *Battledore*, a three-leaved "booklet," made of heavy card stock and folded to pocket size. It contained short didactic stories, attractive woodcuts, alphabets and numerals — but not direct religious teaching. Battledores received their name from the children who read them first and then used the booklet as a type of shuttlecock paddle. The battledore and the New England Primer continued in use as late as the mid-nineteenth century.

1690 JOHN LOCKE (1632-1704). John Locke was an English philosopher whose writing had a great influence on political science and education. Locke attended the University of Oxford and studied medicine. He received his bachelor's degree but never completed the full qualifications for the doctorate. His writings on education were greatly influenced by his background in medical science.

Three of Locke's works have had a great impact on the field of education: *Essay Concerning Human Understanding* (1690), *Some Thoughts Concerning Education* (1693) and *On the Conduct of Understanding* (1705). Locke placed very little stock on one of the contemporary ideas of the time — that is, that intelligence was innate and placed in the mind at birth. Locke believed that individuals acquired concepts as the result of their experience.

Throughout his discussions, Locke approached the student as a physician would examine a patient. He saw the student as an individual case which needed a separate diagnosis. Locke, then, was the first person after Aristotle to really discuss the idea of individual differences in children. Previous scholars had assumed that education was a process in which the same subject areas were taught in the same way to all children, thereby producing a uniform cultural product. By combining the philosophies of education and medicine, Locke pointed out that there could be no true education which did not take the nature of the learner into consideration.

At least two hundred years prior to Freud, Locke noted the importance of early experience believing that, "little or almost insensible impressions on tender infants have very important lasting consequences."

This English philosopher saw the advantages of play and felt that play was a method of learning for the child. He felt that the child learned much quicker when doing something he enjoyed. In discussing play he said, "Nothing appears to me to give children so much becoming confidence."

In his book, *Some Thoughts Concerning Education,* he emphasized the importance of "natural" education as opposed to the harsh discipline of the 1600s. Locke felt the need for freedom was a necessary condition for education. He stated, "Children have as much a mind to show that they are free, that they are absolute and independent, as any of the proudest of grown men. As a result, they should seldom be put to doing those things that you (the teacher) have an inclination for them to do."

In actual practice, Locke's philosophy was not in such a permissive mode. He felt that upper class parents treated their children too gingerly and were too tender and indulgent. He suggested a simple diet, with very strict rules governing eating behavior. He also stated that crying was not to be indulged and suggested strict and exacting toilet training. Thus, it seems apparent that Locke really did not perceive the practical consequences of his own theoretical position. His concepts seemed to be based more on adult needs rather than the child's abilities and capabilities.

1697 MOTHER GOOSE TALES. One of the most famous collections of stories, *Contes de Ma Mere l' Oye,* appeared in France in 1697. Charles Perrault is credited with collecting the stories which included: "Little Red Riding Hood," "Sleeping Beauty," "Cinderella," and "Puss in Boots." In 1729, R. Samber translated the tales of *Mother Goose* into English, and discovered the child as a potential consumer of books. Although *Mother Goose* is usually associated with rhymes, she first appeared as a teller of tales.

1700-1850 THE INDUSTRIAL REVOLUTION. This period, the time of the Industrial Revolution, resulted in a dramatic change in the lives of children, families, cities, and entire nations. Before 1700, most "industries" utilized the *domestic system*— a process by which manufactured goods were produced by families in a home setting. Actually very little manufacturing was carried on in this manner since most families made the products they needed. Prior to the Industrial Revolution, 90% of all persons were engaged in farming, contrasted to 2% today. Before the Industrial Revolution most children were at home and worked beside their parents. The Industrial Revolution separated home and work. In many instances, children and women were the principal workers in a factory.

The Industrial Revolution began in England in 1709 with the first coke furnaces used to smelt iron ore. In 1719, a silk factory opened in Derby, England, employing young children. The invention of the flying shuttle (1733); the roller spinner (1738); and the spinning jenny (1769), revolutionized the textile industry. As cotton factories were rapidly built, the owners looked to women and children to serve as workers. In 1730, England had one textile mill; by 1780, there were over 120 mills in operation. The major city for these mills was Manchester, England, which grew from a city of 15,000 in 1750 to 250,000 in 1830.

Working conditions for children were unbelievably poor. Many children under ten years of age were deformed by working long hours or crippled by unsafe machines. In addition to working many hours daily, the children were given little food and the factories were poorly ventilated. Sanitation conditions were usually nonexistent. Following wide outbreaks of illness in 1784, the Manchester city council passed a resolution prohibiting children from working at night or over ten hours a day. In 1802, the *Sir Robert Peel Act* was passed which prohibited children from working more than twelve hours per day, prohibited night work, and required ventilation in factories. Unfortunately the resolution of 1784 and the Peel Act were never enforced and conditions remained unchanged.

The Factory Act of 1833 in England prohibited children under nine years of age from working in mills or mines. For some reason, perhaps political pressure, the silk mills were exempt. Children nine to twelve years of age could not work more than forty-eight hours per week and children 13 to 18 years old could not work more than twelve hours a day. The 1833 Act also provided for some schooling for factory children but, for the most part, this act was never enforced.

During the hearings of the Factory Act of 1833, the manufacturers summoned several witnesses in favor of child labor. One physician stated that, "even twenty-three hours of work a day was not too much for a child."

In a biographical study, Gaines (1974) tells the story of typical child workers in an English factory during this period. The children slept fifty to a room and were locked in at night. Breakfast was water-porridge and an oat cake. The cake was usually taken to the mill since children were not served the noonday meal. On some occasions children worked sixteen hours without rest. If children slowed down in their work they were kicked, cuffed, or beaten. When a youngster became ill, he worked until he fell down. He was then placed in a wheelbarrow and transported back to his barracks.

In the United States, child labor was an important social problem into the early twentieth century. Like Great Britain, children as young as five or six years of age worked in factories for as long as sixteen hours a day.

Osborn and Osborn (1975) conducted interviews with some ex-child labor workers. These persons had worked in textile mills around 1900 to 1910. In describing conditions during that era one of these early workers said:

"It was really not so bad. We were never treated like the children in England. We were never beaten or mistreated. My daddy brought our lunch to the mill every day and he wouldn't let them hurt us …after all we were his meal ticket!"

"Also … times were hard after the war (the Civil War). My daddy didn't hardly make five dollars in a whole year. This man from the mill come up to the farm and told daddy that we kids could make a quarter to fifty cents a day. We made more in a month than daddy made in a year … and they give us this nice house for two dollars a month. We really was better off in the mill. We would go to work every morning at six and have a half-hour for lunch and work till six that evening … Boy, I really liked Saturdays!"

(Interviewer): "You probably did like Saturdays, since you had the day off!"

"No, you don't understand. We worked on Saturdays, but we got off at four o'clock!!"

Note: In the textile mill cited above, all children, regardless of age, worked over sixty hours per week.

In 1836, Massachusetts passed the first child labor law in the United States. This law prohibited children under fifteen from working in the factory unless they had three months of schooling during the previous year. This law was seldom enforced.

In 1916, the U.S. Congress passed the first child labor law — which set up an eight hour day and forty-eight hour week. *See 1916, Federal Child Labor Law.*

1700-1900 EDUCATION IN THE RURAL SOUTH. During the colonial days, few persons in the rural South received an education. Mandeville in his *Essay on Charity and Charity Schools*, said that in order to make society happy, "It is necessary for large numbers of people to remain ignorant as well as poor since knowledge only enlarges and multiplies desires ... nothing should be taught free except at church." Indeed, for the most part, education did revolve around the church and much of the instruction was religious in nature.

According to Cremin (1970), except for the children of plantation owners, few others were educated. Since the owners of plantations comprised only ten percent of the total population, few people received any education.

In the early 1700s, some Germans and Moravians settled in Georgia and the Carolinas and established schools for their own children.

In 1735, Charles Delamotte conducted the first regular school in the colony of Georgia. Delamotte had come to Georgia with John Wesley to carry on missionary work with the Indians. He brought 500 Bibles, 100 primers, 70 spellers, 300 hornbooks, and over 1,000 different books for adults. After a short period of time, Delamotte felt that the work with the Indians was impractical and he established a school for children in Savannah. He taught them to, "read, write, and cast accounts" (Joiner, 1979, p. 8).

In some rural areas of the South, "field schools" were established for the children who lived nearby. The curriculum was composed of teaching the three Rs and little else. Youngsters were usually taught by an older child who could read and write. In describing these schools Joiner (*op. cit.*, p. 24) states they were, "Local and modest in their claims, transient, and short-lived."

As mentioned earlier, in some areas of the South a type of secondary school did exist. These schools were termed, "Academies." Generally the academy was not designed as a college preparatory school. While some academies did teach Latin and the classics, the curriculum was usually fashioned to enable young men to learn reading, writing, and bookkeeping to help them in business and farming. Some of the academies were co-educational and girls received training in the three Rs. However, little attention was paid to young girls since the "female mind would never enter the business world."

During the years of reconstruction, following the Civil War, the financial problems which beset the South contributed to the slow movement in education. For the most part, public education did not come to the South until the 1870s to 1890s.

The level of teaching was poor. The Georgia Department of Education Annual Report (1896) stated: "Rural teachers are barely literate and their appointment to the school is primarily based on political reasons." It should be pointed out that white teachers were usually paid about $30.00 monthly for a three month school year. Black teachers were usually paid half that amount.

Discipline was very strict and a schoolmaster's reputation depended upon his ability to maintain order. Whipping was considered the best punishment. One common practice was the "circus way." Children were marched in a circle and whipped as they passed the teacher.

The post Civil War schools were usually log cabins with puncheon seats, placed in a circle on a dirt floor. Since there were few textbooks, children learned their lessons by rote and recited them before the class. One teacher observed that few children attended schools regularly. Rather, most became discouraged and quit.

1701 THE SCHOOL OF GOOD MANNERS. A book printed in London which gives some insight into child rearing in the early 1700s. The book cautions children to: "Sing not, hum not, wriggle not."

1744 JOHN NEWBERY. Newbery was the first English publisher of children's books. Publications included *A Pretty Little Pocketbook* (1744) and *Goody Two Shoes* (1765). Since 1922, the Newbery Medal has been awarded by the American Library Association (ALA) for the most distinguished contribution to American children's literature.

1762 JEAN JACQUE ROUSSEAU (1712-1778). A French philosopher during the Age of Reason. Rousseau was one of the first writers to support the movement of romanticism. This point of view held that feeling was more important than reason and that spontaneity, self indulgence, and impulsive behavior was more important than discipline.

Rousseau's own childhood was extremely tragic. Shortly after his birth, Rousseau's mother died. The father blamed his son for the mother's death and abandoned him. Rousseau was only ten years of age at the time. He was sent to live with a minister who generally mistreated him, accused him of lying, and beat him severely. The pastor's sister also beat Rousseau often. It is not surprising that, as an adult, Rousseau was unstable, often unpredictable, and suffered from severe emotional distress.

Rousseau felt that man was not social by nature. He felt that people were good only when they lived in a natural state without the corrupting evils of society. He felt that society brought forth the evil in persons and created feelings of hatred and aggression. Rousseau believed that people should be placed in small communities which were completely controlled. He derived a system for behavior modification and control which is similar to contemporary psychological learning theories.

Rousseau believed that the school curriculum should display a direct relationship to the interests of children. Perhaps thinking of his own childhood, he felt that strong discipline and strict lessons were inappropriate. He believed that children should be treated with sympathy and compassion. In his book, *Emile*, (1762), Rousseau discussed the importance of beginning a child's education at birth, saying, "Since children are born good — and society has corrupted them — the goal of education must be to protect the child from the evils of society." Emile was a hypothetical child who was educated by a tutor and breast fed by his mother. Emile was reared in a country untouched by any of society's evils. Kessen (1965) has edited portions of Emile which give the reader a comprehensive view into Rousseau's philosophy.

Rousseau and his mistress, Therese, had five illegitimate children. In spite of his theories about the need for sympathy and compassion, each child was taken by the mid-wife to a foundling hospital. Rousseau justified these actions by saying that he was suffering from a terminal illness and would soon die. He also added, "If Therese's family brought these children up, they would all become 'little monsters'." In spite of his concern about an early death, Rousseau was 66 years of age when he died.

1782 FRIEDRICH FROEBEL: THE EARLY YEARS. Friedrich Froebel was born in Oberweissbach, Germany, in 1782 and died in 1852, at the age of seventy. Froebel was the originator of the kindergarten concept plus many other innovations in the field of early childhood education.

Froebel's early life was extremely difficult. His mother died when he was only nine months of age. His father, a busy pastor in a large church, devoted little attention to his young son. In his later years, Froebel would comment upon this situation stating that he was, "a stranger to my father throughout his entire life." During the first few years, Froebel was primarily cared for by his older brothers.

When he was four years old, his father remarried and, initially, he was well received by his stepmother. Following the birth of another child, however, the stepmother began neglecting young Friedrich and the relationship fell apart.

This early experience would prove to have a profound effect on Froebel in later life. In his writings, he emphasized the importance of the mother in the early life of the child. He also wrote of the "earliest wickedness" as the neglect of young children by their parents. Like

Rousseau, he felt children were basically good. However, through neglect, children would fail to realize their potential and this failure would lead to lying, deceit, and other problems.

As a youngster, Froebel had so much difficulty in learning to read that he was considered stupid and he was not permitted to attend the regular boys' school. Instead, he attended the village girls' school (Herford 1904). At ten he was sent to Switzerland to live with his aunt and uncle. In describing this experience, Froebel noted: "As austerity reigned in my father's house, so here was kindness and benevolence. There I encountered mistrust, here I was trusted. There I was under strict restraint, here I had liberty" (Downs, 1978, p. 14). Froebel stayed with these relatives until he was fourteen.

Upon returning home the strained relationship between he and his parents was so great that he was apprenticed to a forester. In this two year apprenticeship he studied forestry, surveying, agriculture, and botany. This work in nature would affect Froebel's views of children, their growth, and development. Describing this experience Froebel said: "My religious life now changed to a religious communion with nature …in the last half-year I lived entirely amongst and with my plants, which drew me towards them and fascinated me." Throughout the remainder of his life, Froebel would view his ideas in a total Gestalt of God and nature.

As a young man Froebel attended the University of Jena. Unfortunately, due to a lack of funds, he was unable to complete his degree. During the next few years he held several jobs including draftsman, bookkeeper, and clerk in the forestry department of a large country estate. In 1805, he encountered Dr. Anton Gruener, a disciple of Pestalozzi, who offered him a teaching position. Prior to taking up his teaching duties, Froebel did go to Yverdon and observe in Pestalozzi's school.

His first class in Dr. Gruener's school was a group of forty boys ranging in age from nine to eleven. Froebel thoroughly enjoyed this experience and later wrote: "It seemed as if I had found something I had never known, but always longed for, always missed; as if my life had at last discovered its native element. I felt as happy as the fish in the water, the bird in the air" (Downs, op. cit., p. 20). Froebel stayed with Dr. Gruener for two years. In 1808, he went to Yverdon and worked for two years under the direction of Pestalozzi.

1787 DIETERICH TIEDEMANN published a biography on the behavior of his infant son. Earlier, in 1774, Pestalozzi kept a record on his attempts to educate his four year old son. Parts of this diary were published in 1828. Darwin also kept a biography of his son (1840) and this account was published in 1877. While there are obvious research limitations to these biographies, they do represent a serious systematic attempt to record the growth, development, and behavior of infants and young children.

ca 1790 PHILLIPPE PINEL. In the 1700s, mentally ill patients were usually placed in chains and kept in dungeons. Starvation and torture were common practices and rehabilitation seldom occurred. Pinel, a French physician, became director of a Paris mental institution about 1790. One of his first acts as director was to remove the patients' chains and allow them to exercise in an open courtyard. This treatment, while primitive, resulted in several cures. Although the conditions which Pinel found generally continued in other institutions for the next one hundred years, he had pointed the way toward modern psychiatry.

1796 EDWARD JENNER developed vaccination as a means of preventing smallpox. Jenner successfully vaccinated an eight year old boy, James Phipps. Prior to this discovery, many children died from this disease.

1801 JOHANN HEINRICH PESTALOZZI (1746 - 1827). Pestalozzi was a Swiss educator whose theories formed the basis for many practices in modern education. His theories have had a decided impact on the field of early childhood education. Pestalozzi was greatly influenced by the romantic philosophers of his day. Rousseau's writings were of particular interest to him. Like Rousseau, Pestalozzi felt that education should be based on the natural development of children. However, in testing these principles with his own son, Pestalozzi discovered some definite shortcomings in Rousseau's theories. At the age of eleven his son, Jacobli, could not read or write. As a result of this failure, Pestalozzi felt that Rousseau had neglected to articulate the principles needed to teach basic skills to children.

Pestalozzi studied law at the University of Zurich. However, he discontinued his studies because of poor health. He moved to a farm at Neihof and began to perform experiments in the field of agriculture. When the farm began to fail, Pestalozzi decided to convert the farm into a school and implement some of his own theories on education. He opened the school in 1774 for the poor children in the surrounding area.

The young Swiss educator felt that every person, regardless of status in life, had the right to an education. He felt that everyone was capable of learning and that all persons should have the right to develop skills which would make them successful and enable them to fulfill their own potential. Since Pestalozzi felt that children were active by nature, he provided them with a variety of exercises which met educational, moral, and vocational needs. His curriculum included reading, writing, and arithmetic. His approach to the three Rs was primarily oral. The students did not use textbooks. Teaching was generally done by having the pupils repeat material in unison until the material had been mastered. The children were also taught music via the imitative method. In addition, boys learned the practical skills of farming and girls were taught gardening and housekeeping.

Unfortunately this school failed. During the next few years Pestalozzi refined his teaching philosophy and accepted several other teaching positions. Then, in 1801, Pestalozzi opened a school in Yverdon. In this same year he published, *How Gertrude Teaches Her Children.* This book is considered a classic in education. In the period from 1801 until his death in 1827, Pestalozzi consolidated his theories and performed his most creative work. During this period he also concentrated on instructing teachers in his methods.

Pestalozzi (1911, pp. 11-12) said, "The aim of all instruction is the development of human nature by the harmonious cultivation of its powers and talents and the promotion of manliness of life." More than 100 years before Piaget, Pestalozzi felt that children learned best through self-discovery, stating: "Before the child learns, he must experience something for himself and gain his own impressions." He also said (1951, p. ix): "Life shapes us and the life that shapes us in not a matter of words, but action."

Pestalozzi believed that children were capable of pacing themselves and that, in general, they could provide their own direction and goals. His theories placed great emphasis on the importance of the individual and his teachers were instructed to respect the rights and individuality of each child.

Pestalozzi's school at Yverdon became a mecca for educators in the early 1800s. Many Europeans and Americans came to observe these innovative practices. The school was visited by the famous British industrialist, Robert Owen, and the German philosopher, Johann Herbart. As a young man, Friedrich Froebel was a student and later a teacher in the school at Yverdon.

The interested student is referred to a small handbook which contains some aphorisms by Pestalozzi, with an introduction by William H. Kilpatrick. *See Pestalozzi, 1951.*

1802 ORIGINAL CHILD LABOR LAW. In 1802, the British Parliament passed the first law regulating child labor. The law was specifically targeted toward pauper children, e.g., children on public charity. Youngsters under the age of nine were prevented from working in cotton mills. Children under fourteen were not permitted to work more than twelve hours a day and could not work at night. In 1819, this law was enlarged to apply to all children. The law was not enforced.

1804 ORIGINAL POEMS FOR INFANT MINDS by Jane and Anne Taylor. Unlike other literature of this era, these poems were written in a manner which would be of interest to young children. One of the Taylors' best known poems was "Twinkle, Twinkle Little Star."

1808 JOHANN FRIEDRICH HERBART (1776-1841) is known as the "founder of modern educational psychology." Herbart was a German philosopher and psychologist who had tremendous influence on education from the middle 1800s to the early 1900s. Herbart was the first person to base the study of education in the tenants of ethics and psychology (Felkin & Felkin, 1895).

Herbart visited Pestalozzi's school and was greatly influenced by his theories. Like Pestalozzi, Herbart felt that children learned best through real experiences. He felt that education should not be so concerned with "seeing and hearing" things as "touching, handling and experiencing" things. He also stressed the importance of motivation and interest. He believed that the teacher's role was to arouse interest and stimulate pupils to participate in various activities.

Herbart stated that there were four stages in teaching: (a) The teacher should present new information to the pupil.(b) Help the student to analyze and evaluate the new material and to compare this material with previously learned information. (c) IIncorporate the new material and thereby devise some principle or generalizations related to the new information. (d) Help the pupil apply the information to new situations and/or use the material in problem solving situations.

In 1808, Herbart became lecturer of philosophy and education at the University of Konigsberg. Here he wrote his treatise, *Outlines of Educational Doctrine.* Herbart's philosophy did not become popular until the 1860s—years after his death. Through Herbart's philosophy, American education began to look at the teacher's role, motivation, and the importance of giving children a variety of real experiences.

1812 FIRST FORMAL PLAYGROUND. Influenced by the writings of Rousseau, Gutsmuth, a German educator and gymnast, introduced outdoor play and exercise training. According to Frost and Wortham (1988), the Jahn Gymnastic Association adapted the ideas of Gutsmuth and formed the first system of school play in 1812. The first formal playgrounds in America appeared in 1886 at the Boston sandgartens and launched the playground movement. The article by Frost and Wortham, cited above, and the article by Wortham (1985) provides the reader with an extensive description of the evolution of the American playground.

1815 EARLY PARENT GROUPS. As communities grew along the Eastern seaboard of the United States, life became more comfortable. In several cities, minister's wives began to establish parent groups. The earliest group was established in 1815 in Portland, Maine. These groups were called "Maternal Associations" and dealt with religious and moral training of children. In 1832, the first magazine for parents appeared entitled, *Mother's Magazine.* Two other periodicals followed, *Parent's Magazine* (1840) and *Mother's Assistant* (1841).

1821 JEAN MARC ITARD wrote, *Treatise on Diseases of the Ear* which made an important contribution to education of the deaf. Itard felt mental deficiency was an educational problem, not a mental one and combined pedagogy and medicine. Itard made the first practical attempts at experimental psychology and greatly influenced Montessori.

1822 ROBERT OWEN AND NEW HARMONY (1771-1858). Robert Owen was a reformer during the Industrial Revolution. Owen was a combination businessman, philanthropist, and visionary. He improved working conditions in the mills and transformed schools and general living conditions for mill workers. Owen, strongly influenced by Pestalozzi, is generally credited with the establishment of the first infant school in England, the forerunner of the modern day nursery school (Gesell, 1924; Spodek, 1985).

In 1799, Owen was co-owner and manager of the New Lanark Mills in Lancaster, England. Unlike most mill owners, however, Owen showed great concern for his young workers — five hundred pauper children. Owen encouraged these young employees to attend school at the close of each workday. However, since the child workers were between the ages of four and ten — and worked fourteen hours daily — it became obvious to Owen that the schooling did not do "any real good." In 1815, he began to develop his concept of an "Infant School." His school received children "at one year or as soon as they could walk." Children between the ages of six and twelve attended the infant school daily. Although the concept of the infant school was controversial, the movement began to spread throughout England. In 1824, the London Infant School Society was founded. By 1835, there were over 150 infant schools in England. According to Adamson (1930), from 1824 onwards, schools for children under seven years of age formed an integral part of English primary education.

Owen came to America in the early 1820s. He established a cooperative community in New Harmony, Indiana, in the Spring of 1822. As a part of the community, Owen established an infant school and a day care center. The infant school in New Harmony enrolled children as young as eighteen months of age. In the New Harmony mills, Owen prohibited children from working until they could at least read and write. Children under twelve were limited to six hours of work per day; children over twelve years of age worked twelve to fourteen hours daily. In terms of modern standards, these work conditions were quite strict and abusive. However, Owen should be viewed as a reformer since the common practice in mills was for children five years of age to work fourteen hours daily without any lunch break and no provision for their education. *See Industrial Revolution.* Due to a good deal of internal bickering and strife, the cooperative community experiment failed and was abandoned in 1827. Owen's son, Robert Dale, became a member of the U.S. Congress (1843-1847) and was a pioneer in advocating birth control and universal education.

1833 FELDMAN, a German physician, did an observational study of thirty-five infants in the area of locomotion. Dennis (1949, p. 228) translates part of this study as follows: "If you inquire at what time children attain the faculty of walking ... six were able to walk at the 11th and 12th month ... the rest required thirteen months and one in eighteen months." This study probably represents the first systematic study in the growth and development of infants.

1826-1837 FROEBEL DEVELOPS THE FIRST KINDERGARTEN. Friedrich Froebel described a system of kindergarten education in his book, *Education of Man* (1826). This system, a child's garden — where children would grow and develop, outlined education for children between the ages of three and six years. Froebel also outlined suggestions for mothers which would develop the faculties of infants.

The kindergarten was designed to train children in habits of cleanliness and neatness, courtesy, punctuality, and deference toward others. It also emphasized language, numbers, forms, and eye-hand coordination.

Froebel believed the child should develop impulses which came from within. The role of the teacher was to "cooperate with nature" and guide the child as these impulses developed. He emphasized allowing children to choose activities of interest to them. Froebel developed a variety of curriculum materials which he called "gifts and occupations." *See next section, Gifts and Occupations.*

Froebel's philosophy had a strong religious base. The gifts were said to be "gifts from God." In the area of social studies, Froebel wanted children to learn the sources of evil in civilization and the methods for eradicating evil. Froebel's central theme was man's unity with God and the idea that man is an active, creative being. "What is to be taught to the child," Froebel said, "is something which already exists, something which humanity already possesses. But a new thought at once blesses its creator, and enriches all humanity, and each life which actualized its own possibilities gives to the world what might have been lost forever."

It is difficult to place an exact date on the "first" kindergarten since Froebel experimented with parts of the program for several years. The most generally accepted date is 1837. Two cities in Germany, Blankenburg and Keilhau, are mentioned as the site of the first kindergarten.

In later years, Johannes Barop, a school principal from Keilhau, claimed he helped Froebel select the original site at Blankenburg. In his reminiscences, Barop said:

"In 1837, Froebel and his wife came to Keilhau once more, and there the idea of the kindergarten burst upon him." Froebel went to Berlin to get some materials for his gifts and occupations. Barop continues:

"When Froebel came back from Berlin the idea of an institution for little children was fully formed in him. I rented a locality in the neighboring town of Blankenburg. For a long time he could find no name for his cause. Middendorf and I were one day walking to Blankenburg with Froebel over the Steiger Pass. (NOTE: Middendorf was a longtime friend and associate of Froebel.) He kept on repeating, 'Oh, if I could only find a name for my youngest child.' Blankenburg lay at our feet and he walked moodily toward the village. Suddenly he stood still as if riveted to the spot, and his eyes grew wonderfully bright. Then he shouted to the mountain so it echoed to the four winds, 'Eureka, Kindergarten shall the institution be called'" (Boldt & Eichler, 1982, pp. 94-95).

Froebel explained the concept "as in a garden under God's favor, and by the care of a skilled, intelligent gardener. Growing plants are cultivated in accordance with Nature's laws, so here, in our child-garden, our kindergarten shall be the noblest of all growing things, men (that is children, the germs and shoots of humanity) be cultivated in accordance with the laws of their own being, of God and of Nature."

Froebel's autobiography (1889) is a classic. In addition, an excellent short discussion of Froebel can be found in Weber (1969), chapters one to four.

FROEBEL'S GIFTS AND OCCUPATIONS. Froebel spent over fifteen years perfecting his concept of the gifts and the occupations — the heart of his kindergarten curriculum. While the materials were practical in use, there was a great deal of symbolism.

Froebel's thoughts on the gifts: The following quotes from Froebel's *Reminiscences* will give the reader a feeling for the gifts and their purpose in the curriculum.

"The A,B,C of things must precede the A,B,C of words, and give to the words (abstractions) their true foundations. It is because these foundations fail so often in the present time that there are so few men who think independently."

"Perception is the beginning and preliminary condition for thinking."

"Every child brings with him into the world the natural disposition to see correctly what is before him; the truth."

"The linking together which is everywhere seen, and which holds the Universe in its wholeness and unity ... the eye perceives ... these first impressions are the root fibres for the understanding that is developed later."

"The correct perception is a preparation for correct knowing and thinking."

The Gifts: The gifts represent symbolic ideas in concrete form. Originally Froebel felt that the first gift should be given to the infant at about four months of life. Froebel said, "As soon as the child enters the world he begins to receive impressions through the senses, and these first impressions are lasting ones."

Gift #1: The first gift consists of six soft woolen balls colored in six standard colors derived from the spectrum — red, orange, yellow, green, blue, and violet. The balls were to be provided with strings for use in various motions. Froebel chose the ball as the first gift because it was the simplest shape and the one from which all others were subsequently derived. He said, "It is the shape most easily grasped by the hand as well as the mind. It is an object which, viewed from all directions, always makes the same impression." Froebel said that as soon as the child started noticing objects (about four months) the ball should be given to him. "It may be suspended over the cradle while the baby is asleep, and he will discover it on awakening." Froebel felt that the first gift (of the six colored balls) was the only gift the child would need during the first year of life.

Preceding Erikson's formulation of the sense of trust by nearly one hundred years, Froebel noted, "A little child learns to love his playthings. It is natural for him to love and trust that with which he is surrounded. It depends upon those who have the care of him, whether this love is fostered, or fear and distrust are allowed to come in and leave lasting and harmful impressions."

Symbolically the ball showed the child the unity of God. The ball was seen as a perfect form. Froebel wrote songs to be sung to the child with each gift. Later kindergarten teachers would design other songs and activities to use with each gift. Following mastery of the first gift, the child was given the second gift. While ideally, the child would be given the first gift during the early months of his life — in practical fact, most youngsters did not experience the first gift until their entry into kindergarten.

Gift #2: Froebel's second gift consists of a wooden sphere, cube, and cylinder — two inches in diameter. The first gift suggests unity; the second suggests variety and emphasizes contrasts. The most important characteristic of this gift is that it contrasts forms and leads to distinguishing different objects. Froebel felt that the child should receive this gift in the second year of life.

The second gift — when used in connection with the first gift would show the child the difference between soft and hard, rough and smooth, light and heavy. It was suggested that the mother (or the teacher) encourage experimentation on the part of the child so that he could perceive these differences. Froebel felt that it was extremely important that the child be allowed to explore and see these contrasts for himself.

Froebel attached great symbolism to the second gift. Others would later attach even more symbolic significance to this gift. For example, Wiggin (1895) compared the cube to the mineral kingdom and said it represented the inorganic. The cylinder, the vegetable kingdom, and represented the organic. The sphere, the heavenly kingdom, and it represented unity. Another kindergartner said that the ball (with its easy mobility) was representative of infancy. The cylinder (half-steady, turbulent) of adolescence and childhood. The cube (firm, solid) of the firm character of adulthood. Still another suggested that the child would perceive the cube as "rest," the cylinder as "growth," and the sphere as "perfection." Hailmann suggested that the second gift be given to the child in the form of beads. He felt that the single pieces of this gift would not hold the interest of the young child.

Gifts #3, 4, 5, and 6: The building gifts: The first and second gifts were undivided units. Gifts 3 to 6 are divided units and their significance lies in the relationship of the parts to one another, and to the whole. These gifts help the child to develop constructive powers. The child was encouraged to build structures with these materials. In kindergarten magazines of the late 1800s, there are many line drawings of structures which the child could duplicate with these gifts.

The third gift is a wooden cube measuring two inches. It is divided once in height, breadth, and thickness —thus eight one inch cubes are produced. The child could go from the undivided to the separate parts and still see the idea of unity. Wiggin points out that the third gift, "satisfies the child's growing desire for new and independent activity and for the exercise of analysis and synthesis." The terms, "analysis and synthesis," refer to taking things apart and putting them back together.

The fourth gift is a two inch cube divided once vertically in its height and three times horizontally. This gives six "bricks" one inch wide and two inches long. It possess some of the dimensions of the third gift but it is unlike it in division. In the third gift the parts are like each other and like the whole. In the fourth gift the parts are like each other but unlike the whole.

The fifth gift is a three-inch cube. It is divided equally twice in each dimension to produce twenty-seven, one inch cubes. Three of these are divided in half by a diagonal cut; three are divided into quarters. In all there are 39 pieces. Gift number five extends the child's horizons and offers the child increasing comparisons plus the chance to see a wide variety of differences. With gifts 3, 4, and 5 combined; the child has almost limitless ways in which to combine the gifts. Since gift five introduces some triangles — we have all the basic forms of architecture in the first five gifts. Froebel suggested that the child not be given the fifth gift until he was five years of age.

By the fifth gift, we can see that Froebel has moved from simple to complex; from unity to variety; from the whole to its parts; from easy manipulation to more difficult manipulation.

Froebel felt that the building gifts could be used with children as old as 10 to 12 years of age. He pointed out that with these gifts the child would get a variety of experiences in mathematics — since the blocks would teach addition, subtraction, multiplication, division, and fractions.

The sixth gift is a three-inch block divided by various cuts to produce 36 pieces. This gift is an extension of gift #4 and deals with multiples of two and three. Basically the sixth gift gives the child additional materials and adds to the architectural forms. Froebel points out that with the addition of the sixth gift, the child can duplicate all the architectural forms of Egypt, Greece, and Rome. Frank Lloyd Wright, the famous architect, once said that he began his interest in his profession while using Froebelian blocks as a child.

In discussing the use of the first six gifts in the kindergarten curriculum, Kate Wiggin, in her book on the gifts (1895, p. 122) said, "We must not be too anxious to resolve these gifts into the routine of lessons; especially with our younger pupils ... play is the natural, the appropriate business and occupation of the child left to his own resources, and we must strive to turn our lessons into that channel —only thus shall we reach the highest measure of true success."

Gifts #7, 8, 9, and 10: Moving to the abstract. The first six gifts illustrated the solid; the seventh gift begins a move toward more abstract forms.

Gift seven is a series of colored square and triangular tablets (about one inch thick). They could be constructed of wood or pasteboard. In the American version of the Froebelian kindergarten, some teachers began introducing circles and oblongs with the seventh gift. This change occurred about 1885 to 1890. With the seventh gift the child begins the study of planes.

The eighth gift was a series of wooden staffs of varying lengths. The modern day equivalent of these wooden sticks are Cuisenaire rods. The laying of sticks in different positions was seen as preparation for drawing exercises. Children would also receive experience in making angles, triangles, and other polygons. In addition, youngsters would begin to have an awareness of fractions.

The ninth gift was a group of whole circles one, two, and three inches in diameter. These circles were made of copper or metal wire and soldered together to form the correct size. When combined with the eighth gift, the child could place the rods across the circles to form half-circles, quadrants, and segments.

The tenth gift was represented by many natural objects. The tenth gift was a point. Froebel suggested using beads, beans, peas, pebbles, leaves, buds of flowers or seeds. By the tenth gift we can see that Froebel has moved from the solid to the divided solid; to the plane, the line and finally, the point. He has also moved from the solid to the abstract. In doing so, he laid the groundwork for drawing, mathematics, and geometry.

Froebel said that in devising these gifts he was leading the child early in life to the practical knowledge of things about him. To inculcate the love of industry, helpfulness, independence of thought and action, neatness, accuracy, economy, beauty, harmony, and truth.

In his *Reminiscences* (p. 73) Froebel said, "I give children a guide for creating, and because it is the law according to which they, as creatures of God, have themselves been created, they can easily apply it. It is born with them."

A Comparison between the Gifts and Occupations. The gifts were seen by Froebel as concrete materials to be manipulated, while the occupations were manipulative activities to be performed. Wiggin states that the chief connection between gifts and occupations is that the impression made through the gifts is converted to occupations.

In essence the occupations turn the ideas of the gifts into practical use — the child achieves an end product with the occupations. There are four major points of contrast: (a) The gifts are analytic, the occupations synthetic. (b) In the gifts there is investigation, combination, and rearrangement of certain definite material — but no change in form. Occupations are modified, reshaped, and transformed. (c) The results of the gifts are transitory; the results of the occupations are permanent. (d) Gifts go from solid to line to point. The occupations go in the reverse — from point to line to solid.

The Occupations: All of the occupations will not be presented in this book. Writers divide the occupations differently but generally there are ten occupations. Wiggin's book on the occupations is a definitive treatment of the total subject. To give the reader a "flavor" of these materials, some of the occupations are presented below.

The first occupation was perforating. Thus, Froebel started where the gifts had finished — with a point. The child was given a needle (in a handle) and presented designs which he could punch in a piece of cardboard. In the second occupation, sewing, the child sewed colored bits of yarn into a cardboard perforated with holes to form a design. Drawing was also used as an occupation. There was linear drawing done on dotted paper, called a tracing occupation. Later the child could draw "freehand." Other occupations included paper twisting, slat interlacing, weaving, paper cutting, pease work, and clay modeling.

The curriculum of the Froebelian gifts and occupations was a major departure from most of the education of the day. Froebel wrote: "What the child tries to represent, he begins to understand."

1836 FIRST CHILD LABOR LAW IN THE U.S. In the 1830s, nearly 50% of all factory workers were children. In 1836, the state of Massachusetts passed a law prohibiting children from working in factories unless they had attended school for three months in the preceding year. This law was seldom enforced.

1846 EDOUARD SEGUIN. A pupil of Itard, Seguin published his classic work, *Traitement Moral des Idiots*, in 1846. Seguin combined medicine and education. He felt that the most effective therapy for many feeble-minded children would be education. He believed that the entire system should be focused on preparing all individuals for the world and for life. In his book, Seguin (1866, p. 98) wrote:

"Each student must have an education to support his strengths and strengthen his weaknesses. Education must deal with the activity of the body before the mental functions." In another passage (*op. cit.*, p. 33) he observed: "Respect of individuality is the first test of a teacher. At first sight all children look much alike; at the second their countless differences appear like countless obstacles; but better viewed, these differences resolve themselves into groups easily understood and manageable." Warning against forgetting to educate the "whole child" Seguin (*op. cit.*, p. 95) said, "Ordinary education is so much preoccupied with mind that it forgets the body altogether and leaves ... (this training) to chance." Montessori stated that she derived her concepts of child development from Seguin.

1853 NEW YORK CHILDREN'S AID SOCIETY was established because of its concern for vagrant children in New York City. The society established a Sunday School and taught children to read and write. This group also made arrangements to send homeless children to live and work with farm families.

1855 HENRY BARNARD AND THE AMERICAN JOURNAL OF EDUCATION. The first educational journal in the U.S. was established by Barnard. It seems quite likely that through this journal the American educational community first learned of the kindergarten movement.

Barnard's contribution to the cause of kindergarten was so great that he has been referred to as the "Father of the American Kindergarten." Barnard first saw Froebel's ideas at an exhibit in London in 1854. He was so impressed by this curriculum that he published an article entitled, *Froebel's System of Infant Gardens* (July 1856). This was the first article on the kindergarten to appear in America. In the next few years *The American Journal of Education*, published many articles on kindergartens, including articles on mother play and several articles by Susan Blow, Mary Mann, and Elizabeth Peabody.

Barnard was a charter member of the American Froebel Union and early advocate of women kindergarten teachers. He believed, "the motherly instinct of female teachers can constitute a powerful force for checking 'the passions of men,' which threaten to turn class against class, section against section." Barnard also stated that kindergarten: " ...is by far the most original, attractive, and philosophical form of infant development the world has yet seen."

Barnard was influenced by Rousseau and drew inspiration from the liberalism of the French Revolution. To him schools were agencies of social change. He felt that education was an inherent right and that it should be available to all citizens. He believed that education was a force which could cure social and moral ills and create a just and prosperous society. He also felt that education should do more than teach the three Rs. Rather, it should be a source of enrichment for the child and the progress of society.

Barnard's philosophy and the Froebelian system were in close harmony. A complete revolution in educational thought on the part of Americans would be necessary before the philosophical approach of the kindergarten could hope to be recognized and accepted. Along with Elizabeth Peabody, Barnard was instrumental in making this point of view known to educators and the general public.

1856 FIRST U.S. KINDERGARTEN. Carl and Margarethe Schurz came to America from Germany in 1852, and soon settled in Watertown, Wisconsin. Relying on Froebel's philosophy, Margarethe established the first kindergarten in America in 1856 in her own home. Her own daughter, Agathe, was enrolled in this German speaking kindergarten. There is a detailed description of the Watertown kindergarten in *History of the Kindergarten Movement in the Mid-Western States*, ACEI (1938).

Mr. Schurz was an active statesman who travelled around the country giving speeches. It was on one of these trips that Margarethe and Agathe met Elizabeth Peabody in 1859. Snyder (1972) describes this historic meeting which was to influence the direction of the development of kindergartens in the United States.

53

1858 EARLY GERMAN KINDERGARTENS. In 1858, the second German speaking kindergarten opened in Columbus, Ohio. It was operated by Ms. Caroline Frankenburg. Vandewalker cites ten German speaking kindergartens in the U.S. by 1870.

The European Revolution of 1848 had caused many well-to-do Germans to come to the U.S. In the decades of 1850 and 1860, they established many bilingual private schools in communities in which they settled. There were private schools and/or kindergartens in Detroit, Milwaukee, Louisville, and Newark.

1859 ELIZABETH PALMER PEABODY (1804-1894). Peabody began her teaching career at the age of sixteen. During her lifetime she established several independent schools. Unfortunately, due to financial problems, most of these schools failed after a relatively short period of time. In addition to her teaching, Peabody authored several books and numerous articles, letters, and essays. She is generally credited with being the first female lecturer in the United States.

Peabody did not take up the cause of kindergarten until late in life. Prior to that time she had championed the cause of the Blacks and the betterment of the Indian.

Peabody first became aware of kindergartens through Barnard's reports. She also read an account of kindergartens which appeared in the *Christian Examiner* in 1859. However, a chance meeting with Margarethe and Agathe Schurz "fanned her interest into a flame of enthusiasm" (Vandewalker, 1908). Peabody was so impressed with Agathe, she decided to focus on the kindergarten. She became a self-appointed spokesperson for kindergartens, and opened the first English speaking American kindergarten in Boston in 1860.

In 1862, Peabody published an article about kindergartens which appeared in the *Atlantic Monthly*. In 1863, she published the first American textbook on the kindergarten with Mary Mann. *See 1863, First American Kindergarten Text.*.

Peabody soon began to realize that she did not understand the Froebelian philosophy in depth and in 1867, she went to Europe to engage in additional study. While in Europe, Peabody observed and worked with many outstanding persons in the field. These included Frau Louise Froebel and Emma Christiana Marwedel. Marwedel had been a student of Froebel's and one of the most capable interpreters of that philosophy. Peabody also visited kindergartens in England and in Italy. When she returned to the United States she revised her kindergarten text.

During the next few years, Peabody traversed the United States several times spreading the philosophical tenets of Froebel through lecturing, writing, and individual discussion with some of America's educational leaders. Her goal was to establish kindergartens from coast to coast and to set up a number of kindergarten training institutions. She was instrumental in getting school superintendent William Harris to organize the first public school kindergarten in the United States in St. Louis, Missouri.

1860 - 1930 RISE IN POPULATION. There was a dramatic rise in child population from 17 million in 1860 to 48 million by 1930. Thus, as children became more visible, their needs became more apparent. In addition, more adults were available to devote time to care and rear children. These factors, coupled with the rising opposition toward child labor and the increasing awareness of the need for education, helped to change attitudes concerning the role of the child in society.

1860 COMPULSORY ATTENDANCE IN SCHOOL. In the early settlements in America, the family was primarily responsible for the education of its children. Parents taught their children the alphabet plus reading and writing skills. In 1634, Benjamin Syms endowed the first free school in the Virginia colony. In 1635, the Boston Latin School was founded. The Massachusetts School Law of 1647, required towns of over fifty households to employ a school master to teach basic reading skills. While shop owners and masters were expected to educate their apprentices, this practice was haphazard at best. In 1836, Massachusetts passed the first compulsory attendance school laws and by 1860, seven states had similar requirements. However, none of these states had any penalty for non-attendance and no provisions were made for enforcing the law. Note in Table I that, with the exception of Pennsylvania, all of the states listed are in New England. *See 1600, Children in the New World.*

TABLE I

COMPULSORY SCHOOL ATTENDANCE LAWS
RIOR TO 1860

State	Year	Upper Age	Required
M A	1836	15	3 months
M A	1858	12	4 months
VT	1837	(discretionary)	
RI	1840	12	3 months
CT	1842	15	3 months
NH	1846	12	3 months
NH	1848	12	6 months
ME	1847	12	3 months
P A	1849	13	3 months

1619 TO 1860 BLACK EDUCATION PRIOR TO 1860. A portion of the material which follows is excerpted from Cunningham and Osborn (1979).

The first Blacks in colonial America settled in the Virginia Colony in 1619. The first Blacks to arrive in Virginia were indentured servants. Between 1619 and 1860, three distinct types of educational facilities for Blacks emerged: Formal schools, Sabbath schools, and Clandestine schools.

Formal schools: In 1620, the Virginia Colony established a public school for "Negroes and Indians." No records exist describing the curriculum of this school and its personnel. As settlers in the colonies began to import slaves, the status of Blacks changed dramatically. By 1640, the importation of slaves had become commonplace, and no further provision was made for their education on any systematic basis (Quarles & Fishel, 1976).

In 1740, a school was established in Charleston, South Carolina, by Hugh Bryan, a wealthy Presbyterian minister, who wished to develop religious leadership among Blacks. In 1750, the Reverend Thomas Bacon, an ex-slave, established an integrated school for poor children in Maryland. By 1755, several formal schools had been started in Virginia. In 1798, a private school for Blacks was established in Massachusetts. In 1852, Boston established a Negro primary school. *The Negro Yearbook* (1931-32) lists twenty-four examples of formal Black schools prior to 1860.

Sabbath Schools. A second major educational facility for Blacks was the Sabbath school established at the turn of the nineteenth century. These schools were a vital part of the religious lives of many slaves. In addition to providing religious instruction, church Sunday schools also provided training in literacy skills. Prior to 1800, plantation owners, themselves very religious, often lent support and official sanction to the Sabbath school, and this type of institution was allowed to operate in some parts of the South. A large segment of the slave population benefited from this form of education through learning to read the Bible, reciting catechisms, and memorizing Bible verses.

In the early 1800s, however, small groups of slaves began to rebel against their owners. Fear spread throughout many areas of the South, and plantation owners began reprisals. Since education was viewed as a breeding ground for revolution and discontent, southern states began enacting laws that prohibited Formal schools and Sabbath schools. By 1830, Black schools were limited to oral instruction. By 1840, historical records indicate only fifteen schools serving Blacks remained in operation in the entire South.

Between 1834 and 1835, Frederick Douglass established two Sabbath schools. His description of these schools provides the reader with some insight into the operation of the Sabbath school. The passages which follow are paraphrased from his book, *My Bondage and My Freedom.* The excerpts are from pages 124 and 162 to 165.

"The whole community — with but a single exception, among the whites — frowned upon everything like imparting instruction either to slaves or to free colored persons. That single exception, a pious young man, named Wilson, asked me, one day if I would like to assist him in teaching a little Sabbath school at the house of a free colored man, named James Mitchell. The idea was to me a delightful one, and I told him I would gladly devote as much of my Sabbaths as I could command, to that most laudable work. Mr. Wilson soon mustered up a dozen old spelling books and a few testaments; and we commenced operations with some twenty scholars in our Sunday school. Here, thought I, is something worth living for; here is an excellent chance for usefulness; I shall soon have the company of young friends, lovers of knowledge ... Our first Sabbath passed delightfully, and I spent the week after very joyously. At our second meeting, I learned that there was some objection to the existence of the Sabbath school; and sure enough, we had scarcely got to work, simply teaching a few colored children how to read the gospel of the Son of God — when in rushed a mob ... armed with sticks and other missiles, drove us off, and commanded us never to meet for such a purpose again. One of the mob told me, that if I did not look out I should get as many balls (bullets) into me as Nat Turner did into him. Thus ended the infant Sabbath school in the town of St. Michael's."

About a year later, Douglass was acquired by another slaveowner at a nearby farm. "I found myself in a congenial society, at Mr. Freeland's. There were Henry and John Harris, Handy Caldwell, and Sandy Jenkins. The Harris boys were brothers and belonged to Mr. Freeland. They were both remarkably bright though neither of them could read. I had not been long at Freeland's before I was up to my old tricks. I began to address my companions on the subject of education, and the advantages of intelligence over ignorance, as far as I dared, I tried to show the agency of ignorance in keeping men in slavery. As summer came on ... I wanted a Sabbath school to exercise my gifts and to impart the little knowledge of letters which I possessed, to my brother slaves. A house was hardly necessary in the summer; I could hold my school under the shade of an old oak tree, as well as anywhere else. The thing was, to get the scholars, and to have them thoroughly imbued with the desire to learn. I secured Henry and John for my purposes and the contagion spread. I was not long in bringing around thirty young men who enrolled themselves gladly in my Sabbath school, and who were willing to meet me regularly, under the trees or elsewhere, for the purpose of learning to read. It was surprising with what ease they provided themselves with spelling books. These were mostly the cast off books of their young masters or mistresses. All were impressed with the necessity of keeping the matter as private as possible, for the fate of the St. Michael's attempt was notorious, and fresh in the minds of all. Our pious masters, at St. Michael's, must not know that a few of their dusky brothers were learning to read the word of God, lest they should come down upon us with the lash and chain. The slaveholders of St. Michael's, like slaveholders elsewhere, would always prefer to see slaves engaged in degrading sports, rather than see them acting like moral and accountable beings. The purpose of improving the mind was esteemed a most dangerous nuisance, to be instantly stopped."

I have had various employments in my short life; but I look back to none with more satisfaction, that to that afforded by my Sunday school. An attachment, deep and lasting, sprung up between me and my pupils. Besides my Sunday school, I devoted three evenings per week to my fellow slaves. Let the reader reflect upon the fact that slaves hid in barns, in the woods, in fields, in order to learn to read the Holy Bible. Those dear souls, who came to my Sabbath school came not because it was popular — for they risked having forty lashes laid on their naked backs. Every moment spent in school was under the threat of punishment."

Clandestine Schools. The laws against Formal and Sabbath schools gave rise to a third major educational facility for Blacks — the Clandestine or midnight school. Since these facilities existed in secret and under great security, it is impossible to cite exact statistics on the number of clandestine schools in operation. Descriptions do exist that recount the danger and fear of discovery experienced by teachers and pupils. There is an account of one such school in Lerner's *Black Women in White America.* Susie King Taylor, who later served as a nurse in the Civil War, described the fear of reprisal and related how she would sneak to Widow Woodhouse's Clandestine school to learn to read and write.

One might reasonably assume that many of these schools were quite informal in curriculum and, due to the danger involved, short-lived. However, Bullock (1967) describes a midnight school in Savannah, Georgia, which was founded in 1838 by a Ms. Deaveraux. This school was still in operation when federal troops captured the city in 1864.

1863 FIRST AMERICAN KINDERGARTEN TEXT was published in New York and written by Mary Mann and Elizabeth Peabody, entitled, *The Moral Culture of Infancy and Kindergarten.* Mary Mann was a sister of Elizabeth Peabody and the wife of the famous educator, Horace Mann. In discussing the teacher's role, the authors said that the teacher should be a friend to the child, rather than a judge or accuser. They also pointed out that there should be no punishment in the kindergarten. "It is often better, instead of

59

blaming a child for a shortcoming, to pity and sympathize ... In a hopeful voice, mention it as something the child did not intend to do and suggest, perhaps, how it can be avoided in the future."

The book closely followed Froebelian philosophy and emphasized moral training and the use of "object lessons." For example, (p. 32): "When the children were assembled the first day ... I said, 'Come and I will show you what is beautiful. It is a rose fully blown. Now say the words —all of you — after me;' and I said again, 'It is a rose fully blown.' They all repeated these words with glad voices ... After it was all over, I said, 'What did God make the rose for?' They all smiled, as if conscious of knowing; and one, more courageous than the rest said, 'To give us pleasure.' "

1865 ALICE IN WONDERLAND was published in 1865 by Lewis Carroll, an Oxford mathematics professor. It is considered the first English masterpiece for children. *Alice*, and its sequel, *Through the Looking Glass*, were unique in their nonsensical content, and were written solely for pleasurable reading. *Alice in Wonderland*, thus launched the literature of fantasy and nonsense with illustrations that carried out the theme.

1865 BLACK SCHOOLS IN THE RECONSTRUCTION YEARS. Prior to the Civil War, education was severely limited for Blacks. During the reconstruction years following the Civil War, a number of schools were established which enabled many Blacks to pursue an education.

By 1866, over 79 private schools for Blacks had been established. By 1876, at the end of the period of reconstruction, there were 1,075 Black public schools and 121 Black private schools.

Between 1865 and 1890, several Black colleges and universities were founded including: Atlanta University (1865), Fisk University (1865), Morehouse College (1867), Hampton Institute (1868), Meharry Medical College (1876), Jackson State College (1877), Tuskegee Institute (1881), Spelman College (1881), and Florida A & M University (1887).

In 1890, the Second Morrill Land Grant Act was passed providing additional funding for 17 Black institutions. Since the

Morrill Act specifically created funds for agriculture and mechanical and domestic arts, these colleges played an integral part in developing the fields of family life and child development — usually in departments of Home Economics.

In 1873, the Butler School, located on the campus of Hampton Institute, admitted five-year-old children. The Butler School was affiliated with the local school system and served as a free school for Blacks. While no record exists of any curriculum for five-year-olds, it seems doubtful that a kindergarten program, in the Froebelian mode, was utilized.

In 1883, Lucy Laney, a former slave and member of Hampton's first graduating class, established a nursery and day school for Black children in Augusta, Georgia. Initially her plan was to provide mothers in the community a program of enrichment for their children. Unfortunately, as the years progressed, Ms. Laney devoted more attention to the education of older children and the day nursery idea was abandoned by 1887.

During the post Civil War years, there were a few examples of integrated schools in the U.S. Generally, however, if the schools accepted Blacks at all, it was on a strict quota basis. Billingsley and Giovannoni (1972) noted that while Blacks were sometimes admitted to the upper grades, they were often excluded from kindergartens. Thus, as the early childhood education movement began to grow and expand in the years following the Civil War, it grew along separate color lines. Excluded by whites, Black communities began to establish their own kindergartens, day care centers, and teacher training programs.

1867 U.S. OFFICE OF EDUCATION was established by Congress. Henry Barnard was the first Commissioner of Education. Barnard had been Secretary of the Board of Education for the State of Connecticut and edited the *American Journal of Education*. In 1868, while U.S. Commissioner of Education, Barnard reported on Froebel's kindergarten to the Congress. Later, in 1880, he published *Kindergarten and Child Culture Papers*. This book was an outstanding treatise on the subject of the kindergarten.

1868 EARLY KINDERGARTEN TRAINING SCHOOLS. The first training school for kindergartners was founded in Boston by Ms. Matilde Kriege. Other early training centers included one in New York City, established in 1872, by Professor John Kraus and Maria Kraus-Boelte. William and Eudora Hailmann established a training school in Milwaukee in 1873. Emma Marwedel founded a school in Washington, D. C. in 1872, and Susan Blow began in-service training for her public school teachers in 1873.

1870-1900 EDUCATION ON THE PRAIRIE. While the kindergarten movement would grow and develop in the decades following the Civil War, this growth would take place primarily in big cities on the eastern seaboard and large cities in the far west. However, in rural areas of the south and midwest, and in the sparsely populated areas of the west — little would be known of the kindergarten movement and the changes which were occurring in the entire field of education.

In some of the states an attempt would be made to establish a state department of education, but in general these departments were ineffective and carried little influence in terms of education at the local level.

In the little towns which developed on the prairie, a small schoolhouse was often erected. This building, made of logs, puncheon floors, and stick chimneys, also served as the community meeting house. In some areas, the school building was decorated further to attract new settlers. Many families journeyed along the prairie and finally settled where they found the best schools. In this manner, the towns with the best schools attracted the most new families.

Most of the prairie school teachers were young men with five or six years of education. They engaged in teaching to earn extra money. School terms were usually six months long and conducted in the winter. Discipline was usually very strict and whippings were common. Schools taught the three Rs and most of the instruction was through recitation. Writing was taught to children between the ages of seven to twelve. A piece of slate was used for the children to compute problems in arithmetic. School books were scarce on the prairie. Books were usually borrowed from local families.

1870 THE UNITED STATES GETS READY FOR THE KIN-DERGARTEN. The years from 1856-1870 served as an introductory period for kindergartens. However, growth was slow and, in 1870, there were only eleven kindergartens in the United States. With the exception of Peabody's school in Boston, all the kindergartens were German speaking.

The decade of the 1870s would change many attitudes about education and focus on new directions. By 1870, the Civil War had been over for five years and as the nation rebuilt, many fortunes were made. As a result there was a rise in industry and the beginnings of a strong middle class. America seemed ready to forget the war and to forget the early Puritan era and its strictness and abhorrence of anything pleasurable. Instead there seemed to be a new appreciation of education and the arts. There also seemed to be a new concern for others and a "passion" for social services was begun.

The rise in wealth and industry also meant a need for more advanced training and an increased interest in higher education. More colleges and normal schools came into existence. In addition, the last two states east of the Mississippi River established public school systems. Georgia, the last of the thirteen original colonies, did so in 1870. Tennessee adopted a public school system in 1873. Many educators were saying that education should be more than the three Rs and the kindergarten seemed to contribute to this new dimension.

Froebel's philosophy — the religious and spiritual emphasis; the love of beauty; the importance of childhood — all seemed to fit perfectly into the mood of the new post-war America.

In this environment, the kindergarten found acceptance and began to grow. In 1870, Susan Pollock founded a kindergarten in Washington, D.C. and, in that same year, another was formed in Cleveland, Ohio. In 1872, John Kraus and Maria Kraus-Boelte started an English speaking kindergarten in New York City. The first public school kindergarten was begun in St. Louis under the direction of Susan Blow in 1873. Alice Putnam established a kindergarten in Chicago in 1874. In that same year, the Hailmanns started a school in Milwaukee. In the next two years, there were kindergartens established in several cities including Philadelphia, Cincinnati, and Indianapolis. In the west programs were begun in Denver, Los Angeles, and San Francisco.

In 1870, there was one English speaking kindergarten in the United States; by 1880, there were over 400 kindergartens in thirty states.

1870 THE NATIONAL EDUCATION ASSOCIATION was founded in 1870. In the early years, this organization placed a great emphasis on the value of the kindergarten. At its first national convention, William Hailmann of Louisville, Kentucky, delivered a paper entitled: *Adaptation of Froebel's System of Education to American Institutions.*

1870 MEN IN THE AMERICAN KINDERGARTEN MOVEMENT. In spite of the fact that the kindergarten was conceived by Friedrich Froebel, we usually associate women with the kindergarten movement. In its earliest beginnings there were several men in the United States who taught in teacher training centers, lectured, and wrote about the importance of the kindergarten experience for young children. This text mentions two prominent contributors in detail. *See 1855, Henry Barnard and 1873, William T. Harris.*

Other early men pioneers include: William Hailmann, the principal of the German-English Academy of Louisville. In addition, Hailmann wrote numerous articles on the kindergarten. In 1874, he and his wife, Eudora, moved to Milwaukee where he assumed the presidency of a German-English Academy. The following year they established an English speaking kindergarten and held bilingual training classes for teachers. In 1880, Eudora, organized the first kindergarten in the United States connected with a normal school at Oshkosh, Wisconsin. The Hailmanns were also responsible for many other innovations. In a letter to the author, Hewes (1981) stated: "The Hailmann's introduced the doll house, small tables, and chairs for group activities, the sand table, and wooden lentils at the Friends of Froebel meeting in 1882." The reader is also referred to the microfilm publication by Hewes (1975) which presents the story of Hailmann, "a nineteenth century humanist and educational pioneer of the Froebelian system," who exerted considerable influence on today's liberal advocates of the open classroom.

Between 1874 and 1880, Colonel Francis Parker emphasized the value of child study and helped influence the establishment of child study associations (Baker, 1937). In 1880, Colonel Parker was

64

the first person to utilize the Froebelian philosophy as part of the curriculum of an elementary school. This approach of ingrafting the Froebelian philosophy into the primary grades was known as "The Qunicy Movement." His book, *Talks on Teaching* (1883), was considered a classic in its day and a great influence on education. In the 1880s, both Parker and Hailmann taught courses in kindergarten education at the Cook County Normal School in Illinois.

Maria Boelte, a pupil of Froebel's came to the United States in the early 1870s. She married John Kraus, a professor in New York City. Kraus was already a proponent of the kindergarten movement and, together with his wife, they founded a training school in New York in 1872. Professor Kraus died in 1896 and his wife continued operation of the school into the 1900s. Susan Blow, the first public school kindergarten teacher in the United States, attended the Kraus training school and worked under the supervision of Ms. Kraus-Boelte. Adolph Douai, established a kindergarten at the German-English Academy in Newark in 1861.

In the 1870s, Felix Adler, the well known foe of child labor, made an extensive lecture tour throughout the United States. In his speeches he offered the kindergarten as an educational alternative. The lectures influenced the establishment of kindergartens in several cities including Denver, Los Angeles, and San Francisco.

It should be pointed out that while these men supported the kindergarten movement, they did not serve as kindergarten teachers. While William Harris often visited Susan Blow's classes and played with the children, these men generally felt that teaching should be left to women who were "gentle," "inspired by God," and "innately suited" to work with children at such a tender age.

1871 MILTON BRADLEY COMPANY manufactured Froebel's gifts and occupations for American schools and was the first commercial concern to sell materials specifically for kindergartens.

1873 WILLIAM T. HARRIS was Superintendent of the St. Louis public schools. Strongly influenced by Elizabeth Peabody and Susan Blow, Harris decided to establish an experimental kindergarten program in the Des Peres School during the 1872-73 academic year.

The program was so successful that the following year the program was expanded to include the Divoll and Everett Schools in St. Louis. Students who had been trained by Susan Blow, served as directors in these schools.

In his annual report (1875), Harris spoke glowingly of the experiment and added: "It was hoped that children of the very poor would be brought to the kindergarten, inasmuch as the peculiar power of the new institution to elevate, and regenerate as it were ... and where its influences were most needed. Cleanliness, manual skills, taste in ornament and design, politeness and courtesy, are the very virtues needing cultivation first among the indigent. But, as in all educational matters, the intelligent and well-to-do were foremost in appreciating the kindergarten."

In a report for the American Social Science Foundation (1880), Harris cited several potential problems with kindergarten and emphasized the importance of having trained teachers: (a) The danger of too little discipline (causing overbearing children to become tyrants). (b) The danger of too much flattery by the teacher (which cultivates conceit). (c) The danger of over-stimulation (emphasizing that quiet periods are important in the learning situation). (d) The danger of eye strain. (e) The danger of repression (crushing individuality). (f) The danger of remaining in kindergarten for several years, letting the golden moment for beginning the definite acquisition of knowledge slip away.

1873 SUSAN BLOW (1843-1916). FIRST PUBLIC SCHOOL KINDERGARTEN. Susan Blow was director of the first public school kindergarten opened by Dr. William Harris, Superintendent of the St. Louis public schools. Her teacher trainees worked in the kindergarten in the morning and studied theory in the afternoon. Both programs were closely coordinated between theory and practice. In addition, in order to expand the knowledge of her teachers, Ms. Blow presented an advanced course on great literature.

In 1871, Blow approached Dr. Harris and offered to teach the kindergarten without pay. He agreed to this arrangement and she went to New York to study the philosophy of Froebel under the supervision of Maria Kraus-Boelte.

In her annual report to Superintendent Harris, Susan Blow observed the following advantages of kindergarten (Paraphrased from Bremner, 1971, p. 1456).

Kindergarten children submit more readily to school discipline than children received directly into the primary school. The average intelligence of kindergarten pupils is greatly superior to children who enter primary school without previous kindergarten training. They observe accurately, seize ideas rapidly, and work independently. Thus far, promoted pupils have led every class into which they have been received. Kindergarten children show a special aptitude for arithmetic and natural science and have a quick comprehension of language.

These were precisely the results which Froebel's followers claimed should follow the correct application of his system. Note that Blow's observations precede the findings of Wellman by more than fifty years. *See 1932, The Wellman-Goodenough Controversy.*

Susan Blow noted a potential problem which subsequent kindergarten teachers have encountered, "There is the argument urged in many quarters, that the comparative freedom of the kindergarten tends to unfit pupils for the regular school." When William Harris resigned in 1880, the St. Louis Board of Education placed the kindergarten under the elementary grade supervisors. Blow feared the more formal influence of elementary education and she and her supporters resigned their positions.

Under Blow's influence many new and innovative ideas were initiated through the kindergarten in America. She shared Froebel's deep feelings for the importance of motherhood, and the far reaching effects that the mother-child relationship could have. As a result she instituted home visiting and mother's meetings. Her curriculum also included excursions and field trips, the use of collateral materials, nature study, and gardens.

Since she was the leading proponent of Froebel in America, Susan Blow served as conservative sub-committee chairperson of IKU's Committee of Nineteen. *See 1903, Committee of Nineteen.* She wrote five books and presented innumerable papers and lectures defining Froebelian principles and philosophy. Patty Smith Hill, the liberal sub-committee chairperson of IKU, and Blow jointly lectured

Susan E. Blow

at Teachers' College, Columbia from 1905-1909. Snyder (1972) has excellent chapters on Susan Blow and Patty Smith Hill. In volume I, numbers 5 & 6 of the journal *Kindergarten and the First Grade*, there are several tributes to Ms. Blow. These tributes and a short article by Patty Hill (1916, pp. 241-242) provide added insight into Susan Blow's role in the American kindergarten movement. One of the most touching tributes comes from a former student in the first public school kindergarten (Curtis & Tappan, 1916, p. 237):

"One day I was suddenly seized with a fit of homesickness, and Miss Susie in her gentle, loving fashion took me on her lap and told me a little story about two small buckets, one behind each eye, that turned over and spilled out the water for tears when I wanted to cry ... afterwards Mr. Harris came into the room and carried me around the room on his shoulder to divert me. Then on another occasion we were all invited to Miss Susie's home to a party; the ice cream was frozen like a big white hen and lots of little yellow chickens. When I was given a little chicken my delight was so great that I carried it around the house until it melted all over my blue sash but I could not be persuaded to give it up until Miss Susie herself took me to her room and induced me to let her wash off what was left of the ice cream."

Note for history buffs: Was the first public school kindergarten established in St. Louis in 1873? *The Kindergarten Centennial* (ACEI, 1937) makes reference to a public school kindergarten in Boston in 1870 and states it was "discontinued after a few years of existence." The U.S. Commissioner of Education Report for 1870 does not list this kindergarten, but does list a "public kindergarten" in Boston in 1873. *See Figure 2, p. 71.* In addition, Hafer (1938, p. 68) states: "Although no record survives, there is evidence that at least an experimental effort to establish free kindergartens in New York City was made as early as 1871." As evidence, Hafer quotes a college record from 1902 by Dr. Thomas Hunter (first president of Hunter College), "It is not generally known that the first free public kindergarten in the United States was established in 1871 as a department of the Normal College." (Normal College was later renamed Hunter College.) However, other than this statement by President Hunter, there appears to be no extant record of this particular kindergarten. Certainly, it does not appear to be a *bona fide* "public school kindergarten" in the sense of the kindergartens established in St. Louis in 1873. Most authorities accept the Des

Peres Kindergarten (1872-73 academic school year) as the first public school kindergarten in the United States.

1873 ST. NICHOLAS MAGAZINE FOR CHILDREN. Mary Dodge was the first editor of the monthly magazine, *St. Nicholas,* which was the best known children's periodical of that era. It did not sermonize to readers and maintained a high quality of fiction. The magazine ceased to be published in 1940.

1873 THE BUTLER SCHOOL (HAMPTON INSTITUTE) AND EARLY LABORATORY KINDERGARTEN PROGRAMS FOR BLACKS. In 1873, the Butler School, located on the campus of Hampton Institute, admitted five year old Black children to their program. While it seems doubtful that these children were taught via a kindergarten curriculum, the Butler School was a harbinger of "new education" for the Black child. In 1879, Ms. Frances Bullard, a pupil of Colonel Frances Parker, came to Butler and "introduced his innovative methods." Since Parker was experimenting with "ingrafting" at that time, it seems highly probable that Froebelian methods were used in the elementary curriculum of the Butler School. *See 1880, Ingrafting the Kindergarten Curriculum.*

By 1893, Hampton Institute had a kindergarten training school and offered child care courses to its students. The Butler Kindergarten was established as a laboratory program and used an adaptation of Huntington's concept of the "kitchen garden" — a curriculum designed to introduce children to the domestic industry. This curriculum had many elements of Montessori's "practical life" materials. At the turn of the century, Tuskegee Institute operated a kindergarten along lines similar to the Hampton program. Tuskegee also had a parent program and taught the care and feeding of infants and general childrearing information.

In the early 1900s, Howard University and Atlanta University offered students a program of study along traditional academic lines. In 1902, Howard University awarded 13 kindergarten diplomas. Atlanta University's program was strongly oriented toward Froebelian philosophy in the early 1900s. The curriculum consisted of courses such as Froebelian Gifts, Froebelian Occupations, Froebel's Mother Play, Kindergarten Theory, and Nature Study. In addition, students

TABLE XXVI.—Statistics of Kindergärten for 1873; from replies to inquiries by the United States Bureau of Education.

Number	Name of conductor.	Name of teacher.	Post-office.	When founded.	Public or private.	How connected or supervised.	Number of teachers.	Number of pupils.	Between what ages.	Hours per day.	Days per week.	Weeks in session.	Weeks in year.
	1	2	3	4	5	6	7	8	9	10	11	12	13
1	W. N. Hailman	Miss Eliza Vidall and Miss Julia Dietsch	Louisville, Ky		Private		2	47	4-7	4	5		40
2	Miss H. F. Sawyer	Miss H. F. Sawyer	Louisville, Ky	1872	Private		1	15	4-8	3½	5		40
3	Mary I. Jones	Mrs. O'Donnell	Baltimore, Md		Private	Mount Vernon Institute	2	17	3-8	3	5		40
4	Miss Alma Kriege	Miss Mary Garland	96 Chestnut street, Boston, Mass		Private		1	20	3½-7	3	5		40
5	Annie C. Rust	Annie C. Rust	113 Pembroke street, Boston, Mass		Private		1	12	3-7	4	6		36
6	Harriet J. Viaux	Harriet J. Viaux	Boston, Mass		Private	Public Kindergarten	1	57	3-6	3	5		40
7		Miss Martha L. Stearns	Fitchburg, Mass		Private		1	13	3-7	3	5	10	
8	Miss M. J. Hersey	Miss M. J. Hersey	Melrose, Mass	1872	Private		1	11	4-6	4	5	10	40
9	Miss M. C. Peabody	Miss M. C. Peabody	26 Seventh street, New Bedford, Mass		Private		1	13	3-7	3	5	10	40
10	Lucy B. Hunt	Lucy B. Hunt	Northampton, Mass		Private		2	17	4-13	4	5	10	40
11	Nathaniel I. Allen	Charlotte W. Thurston	West Newton, Mass		Private	West Newton English and Classical School	2	14	2-8	3½	5	12	38
12	Mrs. Anna B. Knox	Mrs. Anna B. Knox	No. 1 Elm street, Worcester, Mass	1870	Private		1	14	3-7	3	5		40
13	Alice Matthews	Alice Matthews	Yarmouth, Mass	1872	Private		1	10	3-6	3	6	13	39
14	Miss Nellie Hahn	Miss Nellie Hahn	Detroit, Mich		Private	German-American Seminary	1	30	4-6	4	5		44
15	Fanny M. Richards	Fanny M. Richards	Detroit, Mich		Private	Everett School	1	36	4-7	3	5		40
16	Miss M. D. Hyde	Miss M. D. Hyde	Grand Rapids, Mich		Private		3	21	3-8	3	5		40
17	Miss Susie E. Blow	Miss Susie E. Blow	St. Louis, Mo	1873	Public	Public schools of St. Louis	1	42	4-7	3½	5	11	40
18	Thomas J. Klaud	Miss Louise Luther	Hoboken, N. J	1873	Private	Hoboken Academy	2	42	4-6	4	4		44
19	Miss Emma F. Plumley	Miss Emma F. Plumley	Metuchen, N. J		Private	Mothers' Kindergarten Association	3	30	5-7	3	5	11	40
20	Miss Julia G. Smith	Miss Julia G. Smith	Montclair, N. J		Private	German-English Society School under Newark School Associat'n	3	19		3	5	10	40
21	Dr. Adolph Douai	Miss Mary Douai	29 Liberty street, Newark, N. J		Private	German-English School, Beacon st.	3	100	3½-7	3	5	10	49
22	Ida Leichhardt	Ida Leichhardt	31 Green street, Newark, N. J		Private		3	85	3-7	5	5		48
23	Miss Kate S. French	Miss Kate S. French	New Brunswick, N. J		Private		2	20	3-8	4	5	10	40
24	John Lockwood		139, 141 South Oxford street, Brooklyn, N. Y		Private	With Lockwood's new academy	1	19	4-6	3	5		40
25	Mrs. A. W. Longfellow and Mrs. I. S. Cragin.	Mrs. A. W. Longfellow and two assistants.	158 Remsen street, Brooklyn, N. Y		Private		3	34	3-7	4	5		40
26	Miss M. A. E. Phillips, principal of institute.	Miss M. A. E. Phillips	26 East Fiftieth street, New York	1873	Private	D'Aerts' Institute	1	13	3-8	3	5	20	40
27	Mr. Gebhard	Miss Helen Douai	Eighty-fifth st, between Third and Lexington aves., New York City.	1873		German-English Society-School	1	30	4-7	5	5		44

Figure 2. Report of the U.S. Commissioner of Education, 1873.

were involved in observation and participation in kindergartens throughout the city of Atlanta.

1873 KINDERGARTEN MESSENGER, the first magazine in the United States exclusively devoted to kindergarten practices. This magazine was founded by Elizabeth Peabody. The magazine was short lived and, in 1877, Peabody discontinued its publication. *The New England Journal of Education* assumed part of the *Messenger's* function and placed a kindergarten section in the journal.

1873 TYPICAL FIRST GRADE CURRICULUM. While the kindergarten movement was growing, it was still slow in influencing the education of the day. In most cities and small one-room country schools, discipline was very strict and the curriculum was based on the three Rs. The following curriculum for a first grade is taken from the annual report of a small Southern town in 1873.

"At the end of the school term all pupils will stand an examination to determine if they are fit to advance in their standing. Any student who fails the written and oral examination conducted by the school board, the superintendent and the principal will be retained in grade" ... the report continues ... "The curriculum for the first grade will be as follows: Pupils will be taught from the Black Board, Charts and Readers, the Elements of Reading; Writing in script with pencil, simple sentences from the board; Spelling by sound and letter; Numbers to 10 inclusive; Roman numerals to 'L'. The first forty pages of *McGuffey's Reader* by rote; calisthenics and moral object lessons."

Note that the curriculum does not include any art, music or similar activities. By the late 1880s and 1890s, the impact of the kindergarten would be felt and changes in the curriculum apparent. *See 1880, Ingrafting the Kindergarten Curriculum.*

1876 PHILADELPHIA CENTENNIAL EXPOSITION. In celebration of its 100th year as a nation, a centennial exposition was held in Philadelphia. One of the outstanding attractions of the fair was the kindergarten exhibit. In addition to displaying books and materials, a kindergarten was in daily operation. This event gave thousands of persons the opportunity to observe this new system of education and to hear lectures on its philosophy. The exhibit proved so popular that the idea was repeated at later expositions in the last quarter of the nineteenth century. Two kindergarten classrooms were in operation at the Columbian Exposition in Chicago (1893) and at the Southeastern Exposition in Atlanta (1895).

1878 COLOR ILLUSTRATIONS IN CHILDREN'S BOOKS. Randolph Caldecott, *John Gilpin's Ride*, and Kate Greenaway, *Under the Window*, employed watercolor to illustrate children's books in a lively and humorous manner. The costumes of their characters influenced children's fashions throughout the entire world. Each year, since 1938, the ALA has awarded the Caldecott Medal for the year's outstanding children's picture book.

1879 THE FIRST PSYCHOLOGICAL LABORATORY was established in Leipzig, Germany, by Wilhelm Wundt. The studies by Darwin were having a tremendous impact on the scientific world of the late 1800s. The field of psychology became more like the biological sciences, adopting their scientific approach in the study of man. Wundt's laboratory would train many of the world's psychologists in the systematic study of human beings. This systematic approach to the study of human beings would be "transferred" to education and the "new psychology" would have a tremendous impact on all fields associated with human services.

1879 THE NEW PSYCHOLOGY. The biological sciences laid the foundation for the new psychology. This approach to growth recognized that the development of the child falls into several well-marked stages. A number of persons in the field of pedagogy began to feel that, in order to be valid, education should be attuned to these different stages of growth. Some teachers in the kindergarten field felt that education should be based on the interests and activities which reflected these different stages. This group, labelled the "progressives," believed that the kindergarten curriculum should be based on scientific knowledge rather than Froebelian doctrine.

The child study movement was a natural outgrowth of this new psychology and attempted the task of gathering information on the nature and growth of children at different ages and stages.

73

1879 KATE DOUGLAS WIGGIN (1856 - 1923). Kate Wiggin is perhaps best known for her children's writing which includes: *The Story of Patsy* and *Rebecca of Sunnybrook Farm*. However, Wiggin was also a prominent kindergarten educator and potent force in the kindergarten movement for nearly forty years.

In all, Wiggin wrote nearly fifty books. However, her writing style is now considered old fashioned and few of her novels are read today. Wiggin wrote of an idyllic childhood — with a comfortable home in a beautiful bucolic setting with woods to romp in and tender animals. Usually her stories contained loving parents and a happy family life.

When Wiggin was about twenty she met Caroline Severance, a friend of Elizabeth Peabody. Severance convinced Wiggin that kindergartening was "her calling" and Wiggin attended the kindergarten training school in Los Angeles under the direction of Emma Marwedel. After a year of study, Wiggin opened a private kindergarten in Santa Barbara. However, Felix Adler convinced her to open a free kindergarten in San Francisco. In 1879, Wiggin opened the famed Silver Street School, the first free kindergarten west of the Rockies.

During this period, Wiggin travelled east and spent several weeks with Peabody and Harris. Upon her return, she opened a training school for teachers in conjunction with the kindergarten. This school remained in operation until the great earthquake in 1906. During that period over 400 teachers received training.

In 1880, Wiggin helped to establish the California Froebel Society and was its first president. She was also active in the Golden State Kindergarten Association and was a vanguard in the movement to place kindergartens in the public schools. Snyder (1972) has an excellent chapter on Wiggin and her role in the kindergarten movement.

1880 BEGINNINGS OF PSYCHOANALYSIS. This particular year was chosen since it was the year Josef Breuer worked with the famous case of Anna 0. Anna was diagnosed as having hysteria, and in this case Breuer established catharsis as a therapeutic technique. Freud was an associate of Breuer and greatly influenced by this case. Later, in 1885, Freud went to Paris to study hypnosis under Charcot.

In the years which followed, Freud developed a method for treating individual patients which he named psychoanalysis. In working with his patients, Freud developed a theory of infantile sexuality which greatly influenced the field of early childhood education. *See 1892, Freud Cites the Importance of the Early Years.*

During this period a "new psychology" was being formed which would have both scientific and clinical roots. While these schools of thought disagreed on methods of study, they did provide new insights into the nature of the child and the education process.

1880 INGRAFTING THE KINDERGARTEN CURRICULUM. The Cook County school system, under the guidance of Colonel Francis Parker, began an experiment in 1880 which involved utilizing Froebel's gifts and occupations in the elementary grades. Teachers were also instructed in the philosophy of Froebel. This approach was often referred to as, "Ingrafting the Froebelian approach into the public school." This idea spread and a large number of elementary schools added Froebelian occupations like drawing, slat interlacing, weaving, paper tearing and cutting, and pease work to their curriculum. Also included were gardening and clay modeling. The following passage is excerpted from a report by Parker which shows the influence of Froebel in the grade school:

"This year we altered our curriculum and added drawing and handwork. The first grade children ... worked with kindergarten gifts as designed by Friedrich Froebel ... the sphere, cube, and cylinder ... easily lead to the form work of modeling those gifts in clay and, that in turn, is followed by drawing the modeled objects on the board and slate." The report continues: "We have also included mat weaving, paper folding, tablet laying, cardboard embroideries, pease work, and nature observations of the seasons and the flowers."

Parker also developed strong programs of science and geography in the elementary schools. In 1899, he established the Chicago Institute. This program later merged with the University of Chicago to become the Department of Education at that institution.

1881 SILVER NITRATE PROPHYLAXIS was developed. For years "sore eyes" or ophthalmia was a severe problem for infants and children, particularly those in institutions. In New York state, for example, about 30% of the children in state institutions suffered from ophthalmia and, in many instances, blindness resulted. Today silver nitrate is routinely placed in the eyes of the newborn.

1882 WILLIAM PREYER published an extensive account on the mental development of children from birth to four years of age. This work, *Die Seele des Kindes*, is considered the first scientific study related to children. Dennis cites forty-two other publications prior to 1882, but most of these reports were "baby" biographies. Kessen (1965) has an extensive passage from Preyer's book.

1883 G. STANLEY HALL is considered the "father of the child psychology and child development movement in the United States." He wrote a book, *The Content of Children's Minds*, one of the first scientific studies about children. This book was an extensive investigation to determine the child's familiarity with ordinary objects. The study focused on a description of the child's concepts and contained educational implications for the teacher. Hall was the first psychologist-educator to relate child study experiments to actual teaching. His scientific approach to the study of children was one of the major contributing factors in the ultimate move away from Froebelian philosophy. As Spodek stated: (1982, p. 176): "Hall criticized Froebelian kindergarten theory as being superficial and fantastic—he considered that young children needed large, bold movements rather than the sedentary activities of gifts and occupations and asserted that free play could serve their developmental needs."

In 1889, Hall became the first president of Clark University and made it a major center for research and writing in child study. Nevertheless, in his book Kessen (1965, pp. 149-150) observed that after Hall died "child psychology was sorted into at least half a dozen insulated lines of development, none of which could claim him as founder or seer...Hall has had no descendents, only heirs." Nevertheless, Hall made a lasting impression on the field of education and greatly influenced the nursery-kindergarten movement at the turn of the century.

1884 THE NATIONAL EDUCATION ASSOCIATION established the department of kindergarten education (EKNE). In 1885, NEA made a general recommendation that kindergartens should become a part of all public schools. In 1891, at their annual meeting the following resolution was passed:

"Resolved that we view with pleasure the spread of kindergarten principles and methods and trust that they may be generally introduced into all public schools. To this end, we recommend that the different states secure the necessary legislation that will enable communities to support kindergartens at public expense."

1885 KINDERGARTENS IN JAPAN. The earliest kindergartens in Japan were established by American missionaries. The first kindergarten was founded by the Presbyterian church in the city of Kanazawa. In 1889, the Congregational mission opened a kindergarten at Kobe. The Japan Kindergarten Union was established in 1906. Most of the members of JKU were American and English missionaries. Volumes 1 and 2 of *Childhood Education* have a number of articles concerning these early Japanese kindergartens.

1885 THE PROGRESSIVE MOVEMENT IN EDUCATION. This philosophical approach would exert a great influence on American Education from the late 1800s to the mid-twentieth century. The progressive movement emerged from the belief that traditional schools were not keeping pace with the rapid changes in American life. At the turn of the century this approach was encouraged by John Dewey, G. Stanley Hall, Francis Parker, and William Heard Kilpatrick.

In 1885, traditional schools placed their emphasis on specific subject matter — particularly the three Rs. Teachers were very strict and often whipped children "until the blood flowed." They were the sole authority in the classroom and children sat quietly except during the recitation period.

Proponents in the progressive education movement believed that classrooms should be child-centered and oriented to the interests of children. They believed teachers should recognize individual differences and allow children to progress at their own rate of development.

Some of the major features of the progressive philosophy include: (a) Recognizing individual needs and individual differences in children. (b) Teachers are more attentive to the needs of children. (c) Children learn best when they are highly motivated and have a genuine interest in the material. (d) Learning via rote memory is bad and useless to children. (e) The teacher should be aware of the child's total development: social, physical, intellectual, and emotional. (f) Children learn best when they have direct contact with materials and can manipulate them. (g) Children should be able to obtain information and learn at their own pace.

During the first half of the twentieth century, the progressive movement was a strong force in most American schools. In the 1950s, the movement began to be strongly criticized. A number of persons felt that this approach had failed to sufficiently stress the fundamentals. In 1957, following the flight of Sputnik, schools began to accelerate programs and emphasize math and science courses.

1887   ANNA BRYAN graduated from the Chicago Free Kindergarten Association and opened a training school and kindergarten for the poor in her native Louisville, Kentucky. Patty Smith Hill was a student in Bryan's first training class in Louisville.

Snyder (1972, p. 240) states: "Although the preparation Bryan received at the Chicago Free Kindergarten Association was rigidly Froebelian, her contacts with Alice Putnam and Colonel Parker at the Cook County Normal School were modifying influences. Their teaching and her own liberal spirit made her question much of the training she was receiving." As Principal of the Louisville Kindergarten and Training School, Miss Bryan deviated from Froebelian philosophy and emphasized practical life and problem solving situations. Many persons came to visit the Louisville program in order to observe Bryan's innovative practices.

In 1893 Bryan returned to Chicago to serve as Principal in the training department of her alma mater, the Chicago Free Kindergarten. One of her students was Alice Temple. Upon graduation, Temple worked as a critic teacher under Bryan's direction. Later Temple became head of the Kindergarten Department at the University of Chicago. Bryan, Hill, and Temple along with Dewey and Hall were prime movers in the new progressive movement in the kindergarten.

1887-1938 CHILD LABOR. Prior to 1880, the young child had been viewed as an economic asset by the family. During the colonial period children were needed to serve as apprentices in the various trades or for farming. In the early 1800s, with the advent of the Industrial Revolution , children were recruited to work in mines and factories. *See 1836, First Child Labor Law in the U.S.* Following the Civil War, many mills moved to the South and over 80% of the mill workers were children under fourteen. Because of the poverty in many areas of the South, it was expected that children would help the family by going to the mill or to the mine.

However, several factors emerged to mitigate change: (a) Between 1865 and 1900, population in the United States increased from 32 million to 75 million. Immigration brought many persons to America and adults began competing with children for jobs. (b) The rising labor force began to organize and labor leaders decried child labor on economic grounds. (c) The new child development movement wished to put a stop to child labor for humanitarian reasons. Table II depicts the number of children, ten to fifteen years of age, in the work force.

In referring to Table II, the figures are low since the census did not count children as workers unless they were employed full time. As indicated above, there was a very high percentage of children employed in mill and mine industries. There were also a large number of children under ten years of age employed on a part time basis.

TABLE II

TEN TO FIFTEEN YEAR OLDS
IN THE WORK FORCE
1870 - 1900

Year	Females	Males
1870	191,100 (7%)*	548,102 (19%)*
1880	293,180 (9%)	825,290 (24%)
1900	485,790 (10%)	1,264,411 (26%)

Figures in parenthesis show percent of total child population (10-15 years old) employed during that period.

Doffer boy in Georgia Mill, ca. 1910. This youngster
is about eleven years of age.

Influence of the labor movement: Originally labor leaders criticized child labor on economic grounds. Children were viewed as "unfair competition" since they worked for less pay than adults. However, labor leaders soon recognized the economic argument was not totally effective and joined forces with child development reform groups to attack child labor on humanitarian grounds. In his annual report of 1887, AFL President Samuel Gompers said, "So far as the labor of children is concerned, it is the same sad story; the exploitation of the tender and young, drawn into the factory, into the shop, into the mine ... by the dragnet of modern capitalism ... robbed in their infancy of the means of an education, dwarfed both in mind and body. What may we expect of the future manhood and womanhood in America?"

Child Development Influence: G. Stanley Hall had defined child growth into an age and stage theory. Hall emphasized that outside pressures, work under poor conditions, neglect of education could all serve as factors to impede growth and thus effect the child during a specific stage of development and ultimately have a profound effect on his adult life.

Felix Adler, speaking before the National Child Labor Committee in 1905, echoed the same sentiment: "First infancy, then childhood, then early youth; and during all that period he must remain dependent on the protection of adults. If that period is curtailed the end of nature in this highest type of living being — man, is thwarted. It is for this reason that premature toil is such a curse. The child must develop physically, and to do so, it must play; the child must develop mentally, and to do so it must be sent to school."

During the early 1900s, opposition to child labor attracted many proponents. Ministers, women's groups, social workers, consumer groups all joined with labor reformers and the child development specialists to crusade against child labor. In 1912, President Theodore Roosevelt emphasized the "conservation of childhood" as an important natural resource.

These concerted actions began to have an effect. In 1900, over 18% of all children 10-15 years of age were gainfully employed; by 1910, the number had been reduced to 12%. In 1916, the Keating Owen Act was passed. By 1920, the figure was about four percent and by 1930, the percentage was only two percent. In 1938, *the Fair*

81

Labor Standards Act was the first enforceable law to set up standards for the employment of minor children.

1887 S.E. CHAILLE published a group of tests for children under three years of age. These tests were arranged in order of difficulty.

1888 CONNECTICUT, INDIANA, AND VERMONT were the first states to enact statewide legislation for the kindergarten.

1888 THE FEDERATION FOR CHILD STUDY was established in New York City because of the belief that "parenthood is an art, a science, and a vocation." The movement spread rapidly as other cities established chapters to encourage parents and professionals to study children. Groups held discussions on such topics as discipline, nutrition, and habit training. By 1920, there were over 75 chapters throughout the United States. In 1923, the Federation started the journal, *Child Study*. The first editor was Sidonie Gruenberg. The journal advisory board included Felix Adler, John Dewey, Patty Smith Hill, and Edward Thorndike. Two years later in 1925, the group changed its name to the *Child Study Association of America*.

1888 DISCIPLINE IN THE SCHOOLS. A study in Boston revealed that there were 23,000 boys in the elementary grades. Discipline was so harsh that 18,600 cases of flogging were reported that year. Throughout the country a number of educators spoke out against such harsh treatment of children. One educator said, "The boys in Boston would be better off in the sweat shops!" Another commented: "I have known an Arab's forty of teachers whose attitude toward boys, and whose avowed principle of controlling them is by severe beatings. I believe we should expose them to indictment for inhumanity before the common courts."

1890 CHILDREN'S AID SOCIETY was organized in Chicago "to improve the condition of poor and destitute children."

1890-1950 CHILD REARING PRACTICES. By analyzing articles from popular women's magazines, Stendler (1950) determined major child training procedures used between 1890-1950. She reports three major schools of thought during this period. 1890-1900: A highly sentimental approach to child rearing. 1910-1930: A rigid, disciplinary approach. 1930-1950: Understanding of a child and self regulation. Stendler notes a change in emphasis from moral (character) development to personality development during this period.

A study by Osborn and Osborn (1975) of farm children at the turn of the century would question Stendler's conclusion for the era, 1890-1900; e.g., a highly sentimental approach to child rearing was employed. The Osborns found that farm children were reared via a strong disciplinary approach. It is probable that the women's magazines studied by Stendler reflected urban families, or idealized family values, and were not an accurate measure of rural American values.

In any event, child rearing was undergoing change. People in all walks of life were beginning to take up the cause of children — their education and welfare. In contrast, De Mause reports that prior to the late 1800s, historical evidence showed that a large percentage of children would have been termed "battered children" by today's standards.

1890 BLACK WOMEN'S CLUBS. Following the Civil War, Black women slowly acquired organizational skills and experience in decision making through their churches and secret societies. However, it was not until the 1890s that these skills came to fruition with the establishment of women's clubs. The following material is excerpted from Cunningham, 1976; and Cunningham & Osborn, 1979.

Josephine Yates, a prominent Black educator during that period noted (1905, p. 293): "Colored women ... began to feel the need of concerted and well directed effort for the purpose of raising to a higher plane — home, moral and civil life." An issue that all Black women had in common was a concern for child care and education. Lerner (1974, p. 159) points out that "frequently women's clubs were formed in order to provide kindergartens, nursery and day care centers for Black children."

In 1896, the National Association of Colored Women (NACW) was established with Mary Church Terrel as president. A staunch supporter of early childhood education, Terrel established a kindergarten section of NACW. The first head of this department was Haydee Campbell. Campbell was a graduate of Oberlin College and the supervising principal of kindergartens for Black children in the St. Louis school system.

Historical records would appear to indicate that Haydee Campbell was the first Black to receive formal training in early childhood education. It seems very probable that following her work at Oberlin, she trained under the supervision of Susan Blow, or her associates, in the St. Louis kindergarten training program. Majors (1893, p. 329) reported that Campbell applied for the position of supervising principal amid intense competition with several whites: "but with courage undaunted took the examination and to the surprise of the board of examiners, the white applicants, and the city of St. Louis, she captured the position with the highest average percentage ever made."

Following the national NACW convention of 1896, Anna Murray, one of the group's leaders, returned to her home in Washington, D.C. and worked to obtain federal funds for the establishment of kindergartens in that city. An article by Murray in the 1900 issue of the *Southern Workman*, describes her efforts on behalf of kindergartens in the nation's capitol. Murray's efforts were successful and this funding appears to be the first instance when federal funds were provided to give direct assistance to kindergartens and the kindergarten movement.

One of NACW's major goals was to establish kindergartens in all sections of the South. In 1896, Murray established the first kindergarten training school for Blacks and successfully recruited students from Tuskegee, Atlanta University, Shaw University in North Carolina plus women from South Carolina and Louisiana. After studying in Washington with Murray, the graduates returned South to "take this gospel of the regeneration of the race back to the Southland and in due time, with experience, be able to make it a part of the normal training in Southern schools" (Murray, 1900, p. 56).

There is little doubt that, in several states, the first kindergartens were Black-sponsored NACW programs. Records in the *Kindergarten*

Review indicate a number of Black kindergartens throughout the South. Alabama had Black kindergartens in Calhoun, Opelika, and Tuskegee; Georgia in Atlanta, Augusta, Columbus, and Savannah; South Carolina in Anderson, Charleston, and Orangeburg. In the early 1900s, there was at least one Black kindergarten in the states of Kentucky, Louisiana, Mississippi, Tennessee, and Texas.

One notable example was the Gate City Free Kindergarten Association in Atlanta. In 1905, the Gate City Association opened four kindergartens in that city. Teacher training was provided by Gertrude Ware, Superintendent of Kindergarten Training at Atlanta University.

Other well-known programs sponsored by NACW included the Phyllis Wheatly Club of New Orleans. In addition to sponsoring a kindergarten, the Wheatly Club developed a teacher training program. The city of New York had at least three separate programs in the early 1900s: the Walton Kindergarten; the New York Kindergarten Club; and the Hope Day Nursery (Cunningham, 1976).

1890 EUGENE FIELD. Often called the "poet of childhood," Eugene Field published several poetry books for children. His poetry illustrated the make-believe world of children and included such poems as, "Little Boy Blue," "Wynken, Blynken and Nod," and "The Sugar Plum Tree." A great deal of controversy has arisen concerning Field and his concern for children. Some critics felt he actually cared little for children personally; others felt "he loved children and studied them with sympathy and sentiments of tenderness."

Commenting on the importance of writing for young children Field said, "It is pretty clear ... that we are not going to have any literature in this country of ours until our children are encouraged in the reading of fairy tales. For many years we have been altogether too practical to develop a decent literature."

1890 EARLY KINDERGARTEN MAGAZINES AND PERIODI-CALS. The first kindergarten magazine has been mentioned earlier in the text — Peabody's *Kindergarten Messenger*, which began publication in 1873. In 1877, the Hailmanns began publication of *The New Education*. In 1888, Alice and Cora Stockham started *The*

Kindergarten Magazine. Contributors to this magazine included Elizabeth Peabody, William Hailmann, Alice Putnam, and Francis Parker. This magazine presented many articles on Froebel's gifts and occupations, leaders in the field, and news related to kindergarten associations around the country.

In 1892, Amalie and Andrea Hofer acquired the *Kindergarten Magazine* and it merged with the Kindergarten Literature Company. For ECE history buffs, the special section in each issue entitled, *Potpourri,* contains information on early kindergarten departments, clubs and associations.

In 1890, *The Kindergarten News* was established by the Buffalo Free Kindergarten Association, with Lois Allen as editor. This magazine was taken over by the Milton Bradley Company in 1897 and publication continued for years as *The Kindergarten Review.* First editors of *The Review* were Emilie and Laura Poulsson. In 1916, Mae Murray established *Kindergarten and the First Grade* as a successor to the *Review.* These periodicals made a great contribution to the field of early childhood education. The serious student interested in the history and development of the kindergarten movement will find these magazines a rich resource since they contain news and information of the movement plus conveying the "flavor" of the times.

1892 INTERNATIONAL KINDERGARTEN UNION. In Saratoga Springs, New York, thirty kindergartners* met together to establish an organization concerned with the promotion of kindergartens. The group set forth four major purposes: (a) To disseminate knowledge of the kindergarten movement throughout the world. (b) To bring into active cooperation all kindergarten interests. (c) To promote the establishment of kindergartens. (d) To elevate the standard of professional training for kindergartners.

Ms. Sarah Stewart, a kindergarten principal of her own private school, is generally considered to be the primary mover and founder of IKU. Ms. Stewart graduated from Mount Holyoke Seminary. She taught kindergartens in Illinois, Pennsylvania, and the State Normal

- - - - - - - - - -

* In the early days of the kindergarten movement, the teacher was referred to as a "kindergartner."

86

School in Whitewater, Wisconsin. She visited Froebelian schools in Europe and was a staunch defender of the Froebelian philosophy.

The establishment of IKU indicates a change in direction for the kindergarten movement. In its earliest days, the leaders looked for "young women who just loved little children." In her biography Baylor (1965, p. 13) reports that Elizabeth Peabody would search for "fine young women" and whenever she saw an attractive girl she would stop her and say, "My dear, you must take up kindergartening." In contrast to this approach, Stewart said, "We are no longer in the experimental stage ... the time is past when anybody can teach little children ... The kindergartner must now take her place with other professional teachers." Stewart cited the need for training and for a closer association with other areas of education.

1892   FREUD CITES THE IMPORTANCE OF THE EARLY YEARS. In a footnote to a translation of Charcot's *Poliklinische Vortrage*, Freud cites the importance of early experiences in contributing to later mental illness. Through Freud's work educators learned that many behavior and learning problems which occur during the school years may be indications of unresolved conflicts in early childhood. Initially kindergarten educators paid little attention to the theories of Freud. Rather, they found much wider acceptance from persons in the fields of child development and nursery school education. This group found that Freud's emphasis on the first five years of life fit perfectly into their own theories on the growth and development of young children. It also gave added importance to the need for providing training and education to the parents of young children. The Walton School was strongly influenced by Freudian psychology as was the Merrill-Palmer Institute. Perhaps Abigail Eliot's background in social work, coupled with the general multi-disciplinary approach taken by nursery educators, made Freud's theory of infantile sexuality more acceptable to the preschool movement.

1893 COLUMBIAN EXPOSITION. In celebration of the 400th year of the discovery of America by Christopher Columbus, a World's Fair was held in Chicago. Two kindergarten classrooms were in operation at the fair. One, located in the Children's Building, was sponsored by several organizations, including IKU. The second kindergarten was sponsored by Illinois kindergartners and was located in the Illinois State Building. In addition to "live" classroom presentations, lectures were given on child rearing and kindergarten philosophy. Nearly one million people observed the kindergarten and attended the lectures. Vandewalker cites this exposition as one of the primary reasons for the rapid growth of the kindergarten in the decade of the 1890s. In 1880, there were 400 kindergartens in the U.S. At the turn of the century there were over 5,000 kindergartens in the country. In citing the importance of the Chicago Fair, Vandewalker (1908, p. 147) said:

"A difference in attitude toward the type of education which the kindergarten represents was clearly discernible during the years immediately following the Chicago Exposition. The evidences of kindergarten progress which the exposition afforded were (clearly) unmistakable, the approval accorded kindergarten by the leading educators at the Educational Congresses was so marked ... that even the most skeptical could not fail to be impressed." There is also a detailed description of the Columbian Exposition in the *Kindergarten Magazine,* in volumes 5 and 6 (1892, 1893).

INDUSTRY OPERATED KINDERGARTENS. Long before the Kaiser War Nurseries (1943), some businesses provided a variety of family services for their employees. In the late 1800s and early 1900s, several business organizations operated kindergartens for the children of their workers. The reason usually cited for the operation of these kindergartens was to help improve and strengthen the family. Generally owners believed that if the family was happy, workers would be more productive.

In 1892, the Colorado Fuel and Iron Company operated a kindergarten in one of their mining camps. This proved to be so successful that by 1900, the company had thirteen kindergartens in operation. Other companies operating kindergartens included the Illinois Steel Mills in Joliet and the Bardeen Paper Company in Otsego, Michigan.

Several southern mills operated kindergartens including the Exposition cotton mills of Atlanta, the Richland and Olympia mills in Columbia, South Carolina and the Eagle and Phenix Company mills in Columbus, Georgia. *See photo p. 89.* The kindergartens were free to the children of employees. The mills hired the teachers and

88

Photo of the Phenix Mill Kindergarten, Phenix City, Alabama, ca. 1909

paid all expenses. There is an extensive report of two Alabama kindergartens operated by the Phenix mill in the *Kindergarten Review* (1905, pp. 505-506).

In 1899, one of the most extensive family care programs was established by the National Cash Register Company of Dayton, Ohio. This program sponsored mother's clubs, operated a free library, provided cooking classes and nutritional information for mothers plus several kindergartens for the children of workers.

1895 NATIONAL FEDERATION OF AFRO-AMERICAN WOMEN AND NATIONAL LEAGUE OF COLORED WOMEN. These two organizations were established in 1895 by Black women leaders from Boston and Chicago. In 1896, the two organizations merged and formed the *National Association of Colored Women* (NACW). From its inception NACW committed itself to the development of kindergartens and "to study kindergarten methods to be used in the home training of children" (Cunningham, 1976).

1895 G. STANLEY HALL is known at the founder of child psychology in the United States and the person who kindled interest in the importance of child study. In the summer of 1895, Hall conducted a seminar to share child development research with a group of kindergarten teachers. According to Snyder (1972), Hall's criticism of Froebel, coupled with his emphasis on the new psychology, so infuriated the group that most of the teachers left the seminar. Only two teachers, Anna Bryan and Patty Smith Hill, remained. Ms. Smith and Ms. Bryan worked with Dr. Hall that summer learning techniques for the scientific study of children. The summer's work also convinced these teachers of the importance of the multi-disciplinary approach in the study of children.

PATTY SMITH HILL (1868-1946) was one of the pioneers in the kindergarten and nursery school movement in the late 1800s and the early part of the twentieth century.

In 1887, Patty Smith Hill was one of Anna Bryan's first students at the Louisville Kindergarten Training School. While Ms. Bryan's training was strictly Froebelian, she apparently had some reservations concerning Froebelian philosophy. As a result she began to introduce some of her own innovative ideas into the Louisville Training School curriculum. According to Snyder (1972, p. 240), Bryan recognized Hill's "spark of imagination and independent thinking" and encouraged Hill to experiment in new and different avenues of curriculum development. A strong relationship developed between the two as they began to experiment with new procedures and ideas. Before long, visitors came from all over the United States to observe Hill and the Louisville kindergarten. In 1893, Hill exhibited some of her work at the Columbian Exposition. As a result of her Louisville teaching, coupled with the Columbian Exposition exhibit, Hill soon became nationally known as an innovator in kindergarten education.

In 1893, Bryan went to Chicago to serve as principal of the Chicago Free Kindergarten Training Department and Hill assumed the position as director of the Louisville Free Kindergarten Association. She served in that position from 1893-1905.

Following her work with G. Stanley Hall, Hill began to move further from the general philosophy of Froebel. While she followed many of the Froebelian principles, major differences occurred in her insistence on the child's free choice and in using a highly flexible schedule. She continued to use Froebel's gifts although she altered the method of presentation and allowed for much free play and experimentation. For the most part, she discontinued use of Froebel's occupations. In a report written for the *Kindergarten Magazine* (1899) Hill wrote:

"We use the gifts of Froebel ... (while) I do not think that Froebel's gifts offer absolutely perfect or complete opportunities for expression ... it seems to me they come nearer to it than anything yet devised or suggested by others." However, in order to supplement the gifts, Hill provided the children with some realistic materials. She said, "We have found the introduction of small dolls, little wagons, small houses, tiny beds, and many other kinds of furniture greatly enhance the child's interest in the gifts."

Many kindergartens of that era used a "question-answer" or didactic approach to teaching. Responding to these methods, Hill (1899) said:

"We are trying to find some happy means between the extremes of absolutely free play and painful dictation. We agree with Dr. Van Liew that the kindergartner 'should not indulge in painfully exact, analytic dictation exercises;' and, furthermore, as we also believe with him that dictation 'stands as a direct violation of both instinct and spontaneity.' In childhood, we are trying to abolish this method in our work."

Hill (1923, p. 56) said: "Some of the main objectives in kindergarten education are the cultivation of social adjustment (learning to work and play together), habits of purposeful work, self-reliance, and good thinking." Hill's curriculum included nature study, literature, music, games, dolls and doll families, art materials and blocks. Hill once said, "Observe the children and then follow their lead."

Hill was active in the IKU and served as the liberal sub-committee chairperson on the Committee of Nineteen. *See 1903, Committee of Nineteen.* Commenting on this work, Snyder said: (1972, p. 268), "Significant as was all of Patty Smith Hill's committee work, no doubt her most lasting contribution was made on the Committee of Nineteen as chairman of the Liberal sub-committee. Her section of the Committee's publication is a comprehensive and definitive statement of the philosophy that has since largely governed the American kindergarten." The chapter by Hill in the 6th Yearbook of the Society for the Scientific Study of Education discusses the problems which "gave rise to the reactionary movement in kindergarten education." Hill details the major differences between the conservative and progressive groups on such curriculum matters as gifts, occupations, art, play, and literature (Hill, 1907, pp. 67-82).

In 1905, Hill joined the faculty of Teacher's College of Columbia, and became head of the kindergarten department (1910) and a full professor in 1922. In 1929, she was awarded an honorary Lit. D. degree. While at Columbia, she worked closely with John Dewey and William Heard Kilpatrick. When Columbia began "New College," Hill helped to develop the Speyer School, a neighborhood school for immigrants which served the needs of very young children, school age children and their parents.

About 1916, Hill became interested in the nursery school movement which was beginning in England under the direction of the McMillan sisters. She was instrumental in getting Abigail Eliot to go to England to study this new innovation in education. *See 1921, Abigail Eliot.*

Hewes (1976a; 1976b) details Hill's work in the establishment of the Committee on Nursery Schools in the early 1920s. She served as temporary chairperson of this committee until 1926 when Lois Meek Stolz was named chairperson of the committee. This committee which included Abigail Eliot, Edna Noble White, Lucy Gage, Bird Baldwin, Alice Temple, Harriet Johnson, and Arnold Gesell, served as the forerunner to NANE — the National Association for Nursery Education. She also worked in the WPA nursery school movement in the 1930s during the great depression.

At her retirement from Columbia in 1935, Dean James Earl Russell said, "Her students the world around, her gracious presence and personal devotion, all testify to a life of successful accomplishments rarely vouchsafed to any educator."

The biography by Snyder (1972) and the articles by Hewes, *op. cit.*, present many highlights of Hill's work and contributions to the early childhood field. Hewes' article on Hill (1976a) is particularly sensitive and insightful in helping to understand Hill and the early childhood movement during the late 1800s and early 1900s plus events which led to the establishment of NANE.

1896 KINDERGARTEN AND IMMIGRANT CHILDREN. A new wave of immigration began in the 1890s. Prior to this period, 75% of all immigrants came from northern and western Europe. By 1896, over seventy percent of the settlers were coming from southern and eastern Europe. A great deal of hostility and resentment arose toward the new immigrants and some educators viewed the kindergarten movement as a vehicle for social change. Richard Gilder, President of the New York State Kindergarten Association wrote (1903, p. 390):

"You cannot catch your citizen too early in order to make him a good citizen. The kindergarten age marks your earliest opportunity to catch the little Russian, the little Italian, the little Pole, and begin to make a good American citizen out of him ... The children are brought into a new social order — along with a new respect for law and order ... The social uplift is felt — first, by the child; second, by the family; and third, by the neighborhood ...the training will naturally tend to good manners, good morals, and good citizenship in the years to come."

1896 JOHN DEWEY (1859-1952). John Dewey was an American educator and philosopher. One of the founders of the progressive movement, he developed the philosophical idea of pragmatism and was very influential in the kindergarten movement. As Spodek (1982, p. 177) observes, "Both Dewey and Hall lauded the philosophy underlying the Froebelian kindergarten while criticizing the limitations of its practice." *See Table III, p. 96.*

Dworkin (1959, p.18) describes the influences which had a tremendous impact on Dewey's philosophy: "The 1880s and the 1890s saw a coming together of the evolutionary approach in the natural sciences, experimental method in the social sciences and pragmatism in philosophy — in a world of technological transformation and in an atmosphere of social and political reformism."

Dewey believed that information and knowledge would enable the individual to improve the quality of life. He felt that children should experiment and discover information and was opposed to the traditional method of teaching by rote. He believed in the development of the "whole child" — that children should develop manual skills, moral well-being, physical prowess as well as intellectual skill.

We can gain more insight into Dewey's philosophy by examining his "Pedagogic Creed."

"All education proceeds by the participation of the individual in the social consciousness of the race. This process begins unconsciously almost at birth and is continually shaping the individual's powers, saturating his consciousness, forming his habits, training his ideas, and arousing his feelings and emotions. The most formal and technical education in the world cannot safely depart from this general process."

"The only true education comes through the stimulation of the child's powers by the demands of the social situation ...through these demands he is stimulated to act as a member of a unity, to emerge from his original narrowness of action and feeling, and to conceive of himself from the standpoint of the welfare of the group to which he belongs."

"The school is primarily a social institution. Since education is a social process, the school is simply the form of community life which should be most effective in bringing the child the opportunity to share in resources available to him. Therefore, education is a process of living and the school must represent life."

Dewey was at the University of Chicago from 1894-1904. In 1896, he established a laboratory school. The school contained a 4-5 year old group which Dewey called, "Sub-Primary."* Since Dewey differed from Froebel in many ways he may have coined this term rather than use the word, kindergarten. Cagle (1972) has contrasted several general differences between Dewey and Froebel. *See Table III, p. 96.*

In 1904, Dewey went to Columbia University and served there until his retirement in 1930. A co-worker and contemporary of Patty Smith Hill, Dewey was a potent force in the move away from the idealistic, religious philosophy of Froebel to a more scientific pragmatic approach to children.

1897-1905 ALFRED BINET studied individual differences in mental ability and was asked by the French government to design a test to determine feeblemindedness in children. It was hoped that this test could be used to determine children who would have the ability to learn under special education programs. Theodore Simon worked with Binet and together they developed the concept of mental age and I.Q. The Binet-Simon Test was first published in 1905, and was immediately hailed as a great success.

The Binet-Simon Test was first used in America by Henry Goddard, a student of G. Stanley Hall's, at the Vineland Training School in New Jersey in 1910.

- - - - - - - - - - - -

* In the early 1900s there was a group of kindergartners who wanted to change the name Kindergarten to "Sub-Primary," "Pre-Primary," or "Junior Primary" as " ... an outward evidence of the evolution of the new out of the old." However, since most Americans were already familiar with the term, kindergarten, the move to inaugurate a name change was abandoned (Hill, 1925).

TABLE III

DIFFERENCES BETWEEN
JOHN DEWEY AND FRIEDRICH FROEBEL

Category	Froebel	Dewey
Philosophical Base:	Idealism; Symbolism	Pragmatism Scientific Approach Objective
Process:	Unfolding	Potential developed through social interaction.
Play:	Symbolic High structure Gifts and Occupations	Based on everyday interest. Free play along interest of the child.
Teacher Role:	Highly teacher directed	Child-centered; teacher is a stage setter and guide.
Content of materials:	Structured; abstract	Everyday, common materials

1900 CHANGING CHILD REARING PRACTICES: THE CENTURY OF THE CHILD. Ellen Key coined the phrase by stating, "These next hundred years are going to be 'The Century of the Child'." Yet, before this attitude could become a reality, many changes had to occur.

Actually the child born between 1890 and 1910 occupies a unique position in history in several ways. These children were born between two major revolutions: the industrial and the technological. While the airplane, automobile, electric light, and movie would all come to fruition during their childhood, these remarkable discoveries would not be experienced until adulthood.

The turn of the century children were born between two wars. In their childhood they would hear tales of fathers and uncles who fought in the great Civil War. If they lived in southern states, they would grow up hearing tales of the grand old South; and the carpetbaggers and damn Yankees who destroyed it. If they were reared in the border states, they listened to tales of crimes committed by both sides. If they were reared in the West, memories of starving winters and vanishing buffalo herds remained fresh in the minds of their elders. If they were Black or Indian, they would hear horror stories about the white man's atrocities.

The 1890-1910 children also shared several other similarities: most were born to large families; most had two parents; experienced a sibling death in the family; did not finish grade school; and were reared on farms or in small towns. In addition, there was one salient characteristic which would distinguish them from future generations of American children. These children were subjected to long hours of work and all the adult expectations for a mature worker. These "adult-children" represent a vanishing breed — the last group of children in America expected to perform adult tasks in an adult world.

Since the Keating-Owen Bill (Federal Child Labor Law) was not enacted until 1916, the 19th-20th century children were born into a culture which legally permitted gainful employment of the young. Actually to force children to work long hours at hard labor was viewed as economically prudent and morally valuable. The census of 1900 showed that over one-quarter (26%) of all boys and ten percent of all girls between the ages of 10 to 15 years were employed outside the home. In 1900, over one-third of the workers in southern industry were children. In addition, children not employed outside the home were doing adult chores on the family farm.

Between 1909 and 1913, Lewis Hine travelled through the South photographing young workers on farms and in shops. Hine found six and seven year old children carrying midday lunches to young mill workers for a fee of five cents. Often these "dinner toters" would go into the mill during the noon hour and "practice" doffing spools, tying threads, and running the machinery. Children were employed in coal mines and steel mills; even five and six year olds worked in seacoast fishing industries. In the city children shined shoes, sold newspapers, wrapped cigars in sweat shops and worked in stores.

In a dramatic account Florence Kelley (Bremner, 1971, p. 612) describes city children at the turn of the century:

"On any one of the main thoroughfares of Chicago on a morning between 6:30 and 7:30, watch the processions of puny, hungry children filing into the dry goods emporiums to run nine or ten hours and, in holiday seasons, twelve and thirteen hours a day to the cry of 'Cash!' " *Note*: Children were often employed to "make change" before the day of the pneumatic tube or the cash register.

By the 1930s — when these children had become adults — several major changes had taken place in American life. State child labor laws and tight compulsory education legislation had drastically reduced the child labor force. These changes did not occur easily — many parents strongly resisted the laws which would prohibit their children from working.

A father of three boys said, "Damn the federal government. I work hard to get my boys grown to ten years of age. Now, when they are ready to work and support me, the federal government says I got to let them get an education. It ain't right. A kid ought to support his old man and the government ain't got no cause to interfere!"

In spite of much opposition, the laws did have their effect. For example, the 1930 census revealed that less than two percent of the 10-13 year old population was gainfully employed.

It is true that for several centuries some persons had spoken out for the rights of children — but these spokespersons had been few in number. By the beginning of the twentieth century, their numbers had grown sufficiently to draw major attention to the plight of children. After much effort on the part of reformers like Jane Addams and Grace Abbott, the first White House Conference was convened in 1909 and the Children's Bureau established in 1912. However, these occurrences attracted attention only in the large cities; their import was usually lost on small communities and farm families.

Thus, we see an interesting paradox. The children born in the early part of the century — the century of the child — were seldom, and in many cases never, treated as children. Actually these "adult-children" were personages of the past — really reflections of earlier times. For the most part parents reared these children as had their

"Dinner toters" at a Columbus, Georgia mill, ca. 1909.

parents before them. Nevertheless, the groundwork was laid and the century of the child was launched.

1900 KINDERGARTENS AT THE TURN OF THE CENTURY. By 1900, Vandewalker reports that there are over 5,000 kindergartens in the United States. In 1890, six normal schools had kindergarten programs; in 1900 nearly 50 normal schools offered a kindergarten program for prospective teachers. One of the greatest areas of growth occurred in the public schools. In 1890, only six states had public kindergartens. By 1900, there were nearly 400 public school kindergartens and public funds were available for kindergarten in 23 states.

This decade had also seen the Froebelian concept of the kindergarten come under attack. One of the reasons for the criticism of the Froebelian philosophy can be traced to the rapid growth of public school kindergartens. Many public school administrators, versed in the principles of the "new psychology," insisted that kindergartners modify their curriculum to the precepts found in this "modern science." As kindergartners changed their methods of teaching they developed a closer kinship with the public schools.

There was no doubt that education was undergoing change. The role of education as a place for exclusively teaching the three Rs was being questioned and progressive educators saw the school as a place to include the manual and creative arts, as well as the principles of child development. Soon kindergarten principles and activities were introduced (ingrafted) into the elementary curriculum. In many elementary schools a new position, the early education supervisor, was created. The supervisor's task was "to coordinate and unify the work of the kindergarten and the primary grades" (Webster, 1938).

At the turn of the century the opposition to child labor was growing rapidly and persons from all walks of life were demanding that action be taken. Part of this concern would finally give rise to the White House Conferences on Children and Youth.

In all walks of life you could feel the new vitality of America. It was changing rapidly. Woodrow Wilson said, "Throughout all the long hundred years in which they had been building a nation,

100

Americans had shown themselves children of utility, not of beauty ... everything they used showed only the plain unstudied lines of practical serviceability." Wilson spoke of, "The dawn of an artistic renaissance in America, which will put her architects and artists alongside the modern masters of beauty, and redeem the life of the people from its ugly severity."

With its new awareness of child growth and development; with its new interest in leisure and beauty; America would begin to more closely examine its children. Changes were still slow in the small communities and the rural areas — but by the 1920s and 1930s, this would truly become the "century of the child."

1900 THE DOLL CORNER. Following the 1895 summer seminar conducted by G. Stanley Hall, more and more teachers turned to the utilization of psychological methods in helping design their curriculum. In 1900, at the University of Chicago, Alice Temple suggested using larger dolls and a playhouse with furniture and household items. Patty Smith Hill moved away from the Froebelian occupations and suggested changing some of the Froebelian gifts (Hill, 1907). She designed a group of larger blocks which became known as "Patty Hill blocks." Weber (1969) vividly traces the influences of these early leaders on later curriculum changes.

1902 NATIONAL SOCIETY FOR THE STUDY OF EDUCATION. Each year the society publishes a yearbook highlighting an area in education. The first volume appeared in 1902 and discussed principles in the teaching of history. Since its inception, six yearbooks have been specifically devoted to kindergarten, preschool, and early childhood education. The following books will be of particular interest to the "history buff."

1907 Yearbook, Part II, includes articles by Maria Kraus-Boelte, Patty Smith Hill, and Nina Vandewalker. The article by Patty Hill is particularly interesting and discusses in detail the major differences between the progressive and conservative kindergarten groups. *See 1903, Committee of Nineteen.* Vandewalker's article is, for the most part, a summary of her book (Vandewalker, 1908).

1929 Yearbook discusses preschool and parent education. The chairperson of the Yearbook was Lois Meek Stolz and contributors included Bird Baldwin, Patty Hill, Beth Wellman, and Edna Noble White. This volume brings the "new" field of preschool education "up to date." While the first section entitled, "history of the movement" is scanty and at times inaccurate, it does present some material from other countries. Chapter 8 describes several vintage 1920 nursery schools in detail. A number of excellent references are included. The section on research in child development provides the reader with insights into the type of research performed during that era.

1947 Yearbook, Part II, entitled, "Early Childhood Education," has articles by Lois Murphy, Bess Goodykoontz, Neith Headley, Millie Almy, and Lee Vincent. This yearbook will provide the reader with the ambience surrounding the post war years. The history chapter, provides statistics on nursery schools from 1928-1945 and outlines developments during the Great Depression and World War II. There is a section on the legal status of educational services for young children. The chapter by Updegraff, *et al.*, represents an attempt to integrate research and the curriculum. There is a chapter on exceptional children.

1972 Yearbook, Part II, was edited by Ira Gordon and includes articles by Jerome Bruner, Bernard Spodek, and Harold Shane. This volume reflects the post Head Start days and the new emphasis on political, economic and social issues. There is more of a "research flavor" to this yearbook. Irving Sigel has a chapter on developmental theory, Merrill Read on biological bases, plus chapters concerning research strategies, instructional theory, and a chapter by Bruner on a theory of cultural differences.

1903 THE COMMITTEE OF NINETEEN. The International Kindergarten Union was organized in Saratoga Springs, New York, in 1892. The Union was primarily Froebelian in philosophy at the time of its founding. However, differences in philosophy among its members became apparent in the 1898 meeting.

During this period the battlelines were carefully drawn. On the one side were members who saw Froebel as an "inspired savior" of children and who clung to every tenant of his philosophy. Peabody, Blow, and Wiggin were of this persuasion. On the other side were the new group which believed in the new psychology and the philosophy of pragmatism as expounded by Dewey. Writings of the period clearly show the differences in opinion. In 1898, Martha Collins, a teacher at the State Normal School in Mankato, Minnesota, wrote: "If men and women of insight, working in other lines, make important discoveries and reach conclusions which relate more or less directly to our own field of action, we should feel only gratitude when the full import of the new idea is pressed upon us, even though their reception involve the relinquishment of long cherished aims and practices. And here let me say that I believe many kindergartners are making a mistake in clinging so tenaciously to almost every detail of the original plan of infant education as laid down by Froebel."

In the *Kindergarten Magazine* Collins (1898, p. 65) wrote: "I firmly believe that those who resist advancing thought in order to be true to Froebel are themselves his real opponents. I also believe that the future growth of the kindergarten depends greatly upon the attitude of kindergartners toward the results of scientific investigation and psychical research."

In the same issue of the *Kindergarten Magazine*, Patty Smith Hill (1898, p. 136) commented, "Instead of moralizing to the children about goodness and unselfishness in stories and verse ... we are trying to bring about these conditions in a ... more unconscious but practical way." Later in the same article she said, "Much of the responsibility for the easy running of the kindergarten is thrown upon the children."

Showing her decreasing emphasis on Froebel's philosophy, Hill added: "In normal classes we give much time to the study of genetic psychology. We study Froebel only in connection with the history of education ...(we are) diminishing the tendency to idealize Froebel and see him and his great work separate and apart from education as a whole."

By 1903, the controversy within the IKU was so great that the membership decided to issue a statement which would clarify agreements and differences in philosophical positions. Susan Blow, Alice Putnam, and Lucy Wheelock were appointed to organize a committee "to formulate contemporary kindergarten thought." This group became known as the Committee of Nineteen.

The committee reported at annual IKU meetings for ten years, finally publishing a report in 1913. The report indicated that, although the members acknowledged some common philosophical ground, their positions were increasingly disparate. The report, given at the 1909 meeting, was actually three reports, one from each of the subdivisions into which the committee had been divided: Conservative (Froebelian), Liberal (Progressive-Dewey), and Liberal-Conservative (a combination of the other two).

This committee division was indicative of the split among the entire IKU membership, and served as a forerunner of the change in kindergarten philosophy from the traditional Froebelian to the new psychology and the ideas of Dewey and members of the Progressive school of thought. Patty Smith Hill was the leader of the new movement.

In an article entitled, *Changes in Curricula and Method in Kindergarten Education*, Hill (1925, p. 99) again recalls the philosophical differences between the Froebelian kindergarten and the "present day reconstructed kindergarten." She states, "Little remains of the teachings and practice of Froebel and those pioneers who introduced the kindergarten into this country." Further she points out that many changes had taken place between 1900 and 1925, "substituting as far as possible the method of experimentation and proof, for tradition, authority, and opinion."

Perhaps a statement by a kindergarten teacher of that era best describes the contributions of both the progressive and the conservative points of view. Webster (1938, p. 36) states:

"The change from the Froebelian and formal teacher-directed type of kindergartens to the informal type with more childlike opportunities for growth commenced about 1900. The influence of Miss Patty Hill, Dr. William Kilpatrick and other exponents of John Dewey's philosophy strongly affected kindergarten practices ... Gradually the teacher-centered kindergartens became child-centered. Large blocks replaced the tiny gift blocks. Toys, large crayons, paint brushes, hammers, and saws took the place of sewing cards, paper folding, and weaving mats. Creative expression replaced dictation. But the great Froebelian principles of experience, activity, learning by doing, interdependence, and the brotherhood of man still stand as the great foundation stones of kindergarten education."

1903 THE TALE OF PETER RABBIT. Beatrix Potter carried the tradition of the literary fairy tale into the twentieth century with her book, *The Tale of Peter Rabbit*. In many ways, Potter's illustrations have the accuracy of a naturalist — but amid the realism, is the fanciful addition of articles of clothing on the animals who are the central characters in her story. Many of her stories center around a domestic theme in which small animals find themselves in "human-like" or "childlike" situations. Potter once said, "One never gives up a real interest in children or a firm belief in fairies." Potter was not sure that her books would be accepted by the public. After receiving several rejections from publishers, she had 500 copies of *The Tale of Peter Rabbit*, privately printed in 1902. The following year, 1903, it was accepted for publication by Warne and Company.

1904 THE NATIONAL CHILD LABOR COMMITTEE was organized to investigate child labor problems, to report the facts and promote protective legislation. Its specific objectives were to remove children under fourteen from industry, to limit the hours of employment for children under sixteen to eight hours a day and to abolish night work for children under sixteen.

1906 FEDERAL CHILD LABOR LEGISLATION was first proposed in 1906 but failed to pass. In 1907, Congress did authorize a study of the conditions of women and child wage earners. The results of this study were published between 1910 and 1912 and comprised nineteen volumes.

1906 JOSEPHINE S. YATES was a pervading influence during the formative years of the Black kindergarten movement. A college teacher and educational leader, she documented much of the pioneer kindergarten work in her regular column in the *Colored American Magazine*. Her article, *Education and Genetic Psychology* which appeared in 1906, expressed the belief that Froebel's greatest contribution was his emphasis on the value of play and the significance of the Froebelian gifts. In those early years the concept of play as a constructive element in the curriculum was under great attack in some of the Black kindergartens. Yates did much to point out the value of play in the curriculum. Yates' clear writing style was useful in translating the complex Froebelian philosophy into understandable terminology.

Maria Montessori

1907 MARIA MONTESSORI (1870 - 1952).* Maria Montessori
was the first woman in Italy to be granted a medical degree. Through
empirical research, Dr. Montessori scientifically developed an educational method fully grounded in the knowledge and understanding
of human nature, physical anatomy, and a strong religious background. Her influence in the field of early childhood development has
been global in scope and is becoming increasingly more relevant in
today's educational circles. She believed in the universality of
children and their needs. A basic cornerstone of her work was that
individuals must develop all aspects of themselves. Dr. Montessori
spent a long productive lifetime observing children. Based on her
discoveries, she created learning environments and materials.
Continued observations of children at work and experimentations
with materials and environments led to further refinements and
discoveries. Her intent was to design and implement a universal
educational process. In her lifetime, she proved that her method was
appropriate for all types of children all over the world.

Montessori opened the first *Casa dei Bambini* (Children's House)
in a tenement district in Rome in 1907. Special teaching materials
were used to allow children the freedom to develop an inner understanding, awareness, and confidence through concrete experiences
and manipulations. The joy of learning, the discovery process, peace,
harmony, and cooperation are basic concepts inherent in authentic
Montessori programs.

Much of Montessori's work is inclusive of Itard, Rousseau,
Pestalozzi, Froebel, Freud, and has been substantiated, in part, by
Jean Piaget, Jerome Bruner, and Urie Bronfenbrenner. Each of
these individuals have been, or are, interested in the optimal
development of the whole person. However, Montessori credited
Seguin and Itard as having the strongest influences on her work.
They, as well as Montessori, shared in the belief that mental
deficiency was an educational problem rather than a medical one.
Montessori's synthesis of their works resulted in the development of
an educational system appropriate for all children.

- - - - - - - - - - -

* The author is indebted to Sheryl M. Sweet, National Educational
Director, Montessori Unlimited, for this section on Maria Montessori
and for the entry concerning the Association for the Accreditation of
Montessori Teacher Education. *See 1988, AAMTE.*

The Montessori concept is both a philosophy of child growth and a rationale for guiding such growth. Montessori believed that education begins at birth and that the first six years of life are the most important years. During these early years, she believed that children pass through "sensitive periods" which are times when children are particularly ready for the acquisition of certain knowledge and skills. The Montessori program is perceptual and brings the child's senses directly into contact with meaningful materials. Dr. Montessori stated that her objective in education was "to develop a child to the fullest possible realization of his potential by liberating the 'inner force' within him ... to create a ray of light and move on."

Dr. Montessori meticulously trained adults to become astute observers, facilitators, and communicators of the environment. From these groups emerged those who would train other adults in her method and philosophy.

The Montessori classroom director fastidiously prepares and maintains the environment. She observes the children, notes readiness for new materials, and demonstrates proper use of the materials to individual children. Generally, the director is careful not to create in the children a dependence upon her for either physical help or approval.

At the *Casa dei Bambini,* Montessori emphasized the importance of cooperation between school and home. A Children's House was furnished and viewed by Montessori as an extension of the home. The curriculum areas emphasized in the school were: practical life exercises, sensorial exercises, language, mathematics, and cultural exercises.

Evans (1971, p. 264) describes the Montessori method in this manner: "The Montessori method is a provocative combination of philosophy, psychological concepts, and pedagogical techniques. It is fueled, in principle, by love for the child and respect for his natural capabilities. It is the child in whom Montessori placed her hopes for a world based upon fundamental values such as cooperation, self-control, order, responsibility, patience, and the common good."

Montessori came to the United States in 1912 and gave several lectures on her method. An American Montessori Association was formed with Mrs. Alexander Graham Bell as president. She returned

108

to the U.S. again in 1915 to set up a Montessori exhibit at the San Francisco World's Fair.

In 1914, William Heard Kilpatrick published a book, *The Montessori System Examined*, in which he was extremely critical of the Montessori techniques and materials. This criticism, coupled with the criticisms of other educators, was instrumental in keeping the Montessori method from becoming popular for many years.

In the late 1950s, Nancy Rambusch became interested in the Montessori method and established the Whitby School in Greenwich, Connecticut. Largely through the efforts of Ms. Rambusch, many persons once again became aware of this philosophy of early childhood education. The number of Montessori organizations and teacher preparation centers has increased considerably since that time. Today there are between twenty and thirty Montessori organizations in the United States. Each of these organizations sanctions Montessori teacher preparation centers. There are between 500 and 1,000 of these centers. Nearly 3,000 schools in the United States claim to follow the Montessori method. In addition, there are a number of established Montessori programs, as well as pilot Montessori programs in public schools around the country. *See 1988, AATME.* Dr. Montessori's vision of peace through education continues to live in people all over the world who have experienced the Montessori method of education.

1908 HEALTH STUDIES IN ENGLAND revealed that 80% of British infants were well at birth but only 20% of children entering public schools were healthy. The British government moved to establish health clinics whereby children could receive appropriate medical treatment.

In 1908, the first London School Clinic for children under five, was opened by Margaret and Rachel McMillan. However, unlike regular day care centers of that period, the McMillans were interested in the total child, i.e., "the physical, emotional and educational development of young children" Maclure (1970, p. 106).

A former associate, Stevinson (1923), points out that while the McMillans were educators, first and foremost, they did not propose to train the minds of the children until they had healed their bodies. In addition to receiving medical care, the McMillans believed the children needed sunlight and plenty of space to grow and develop. They felt the children would be better educated if they were in healthy surroundings. These concerns ultimately led to the establishment of nursery schools in England.

1909 LAGGARDS IN OUR SCHOOLS. Many states adopted compulsory attendance in schools and attention was focused on "drop-outs." Ayre's, *Laggards in Our Schools,* caused a great deal of public concern about schools and a search for ways to make better assessments of children. In 1910, Goddard translated the Binet-SimonTest and adapted it for American children. The rapid spread of the Binet and other I.Q. testing can initially be traced to this concern for a more accurate assessment of children.

1909 WHITE HOUSE CONFERENCE. In 1909 a number of concerned persons asked President Theodore Roosevelt to hold a conference on problems related to child care and development. As a result of this conference, Congress created the Children's Bureau in 1912. In 1919, President Woodrow Wilson called a second conference to discuss child welfare standards. Subsequent White House Conferences have dealt with various areas of concern to children and families. 1930: Physical growth, child health and protection. 1940: Children in a democracy. 1950: Personality development. By 1960, the conference had enlarged greatly and considered general problems of education, health, and other related concerns. Young people were first invited to participate in the 1960 conference. In 1965, President Lyndon Johnson called a special conference on education. President Richard Nixon divided the conference into two sections in 1970. 1970: Children; 1971: Youth.

1910 FIRST MONTESSORI SCHOOL in the United States was established at Tarrytown, New York by Anne George. The school did not actually begin operation until 1911, In 1913, the National Montessori Education Association was established.

1910 U.S. CENSUS ON CHILD WORKERS IN THE LABOR FORCE. The 1910 Census showed an increase of over 200,000 child workers (aged 10 to 15) since 1900. The total number of child laborers in America in 1910 was estimated at nearly two million. The census reported that one child in six was a laborer. This report, coupled with the outcry of many American citizens, was responsible for the Uniform Child Labor Act to be written and recommended by the American Bar Association in 1911. This recommendation had four major points: (a) A minimum age of fourteen years for employment in manufacturing. (b) A minimum age of sixteen for employment in mining. (c) Documentary proof of age. (d) A maximum workload of eight hours per day. Congress did study this recommendation but failed to enact it into law.

In spite of the public concern a number of states still permitted young children to work. In some states work permits were issued which would allow children under ten to work full time if the adult wage earner was disabled. The work permit presented below is from the State of Georgia and was used in the early 1900s.

CHILD LABOR IN FACTORIES REGULATED

No. 309

Personally appeared *Sarah Hull* who after being duly sworn deposes and says that *she* is *a Widow* and the head of a family having *7* minor children living with and dependent upon her. That *she is* unable to maintain and support said family without the aid of *her son, Thomas*, who is *10* years of age and who has attended school 12 weeks in the previous year, 6 weeks of which were consecutive and can read and write his or her name and simple sentences. That *she* desires to avail *herself* of the privilege allowed fathers and widows dependent upon the aid of their minor children and to get them employed in the factories and workshops of this State as per Bill No. 390, passed by the General Assembly of 1906, page 98. This certificate is good for one year from date.

Sworn and subscribed to before me this *4 June* 19 *09*

Sarah Hull

Robert Purvis

Ordinary, Hall County Georgia

Figure 3. Work permit for child labor.

1911 MARGARET AND RACHEL MCMILLAN established an open air nursery school in the garden of Evelyn House, Deptford. The house was provided rent free by Mr. and Mrs. John Evelyn. Margaret McMillan is credited with coining the term, "nursery school." She established a daily health inspection for children and emphasized play, nurture, and work with the parents. In 1914, the school moved to new quarters and soon numbered thirty children. The children ranged in age from three months to five years.

In 1917, Rachel McMillan died but her sister continued the work they had begun. That same year the nursery school facility was enlarged and renamed the Rachel McMillan Nursery School. Word of this new school spread and parents flocked to enroll their preschoolers. Stevinson (1923, p. 58) states: "In the summer of 1921 the nursery school was full to overflowing. There was an average attendance of 135 children and almost daily we were obliged to turn away mothers who were seeking admittance for their children." A second addition was added to the school and on November 22, 1921, Queen Mary formally opened the new facility. An interesting aside: Abigail Eliot was a teacher in the McMillan nursery during this period and vividly recounts activities in the center plus the Queen's inaugural visit. *See Eliot, 1979.*

1912 THE CHILDREN'S BUREAU. The creation of the Children's Bureau was the first recognition by the Federal government of its responsibility to promote the health and welfare of the children of the entire nation. In 1903, Lillian Wald, director of the Henry Street Settlement House in New York, proposed the idea to President Theodore Roosevelt. However, no action was taken until the first White House Conference in 1909. At the time the conference convened a large number of ministers, educators, women's clubs, and church groups were lobbying for a governmental agency which would concern itself with children.

The Children's Bureau Act of 1912 gave the Bureau broad powers. It authorized research and the power to investigate child health, delinquency, dependency, and child labor (Lathrop, 1912). While the annual budget was only $25,000, the Bureau gave national prominence and leadership to the cause of children. The first bureau chief was Julia Lathrop.

112

Today the Children's Bureau is located in the Administration for Children, Youth and Families (ACYF) and is a division of the Department of Health and Human Services.

1913 WILLIAM HEARD KILPATRICK was Professor of Education at Columbia University and board member of *Childhood Education* for forty years. Kilpatrick is best known in kindergarten circles for two things: his reaction to the Montessori movement and his idea of the "Project Method." In his book, *The Montessori System Examined* (1914) and a speech at IKU (1913), Kilpatrick severely attacked the Montessori method. His major criticisms were that the method was based on faulty psychological theory and the sensory motor materials used in the classroom. Kilpatrick almost single-handedly stopped the Montessori movement in this country. Following World War II, Nancy Rambusch was instrumental in bringing the Montessori movement, in revised form, back to the United States.

1914 UNIT BLOCKS. Froebel had designed a series of blocks as part of his curriculum. Gifts #3, 4, 5, and 6 are specifically referred to as the "building gifts." Many teachers felt that these blocks were too small for young hands. In 1914, Caroline Pratt designed a series of special wooden blocks based on a specific unit. The remaining blocks in the set were fractions and multiples based on this standard unit (Cartwright, 1988). These blocks, popularly known as kindergarten blocks, became staple items in kindergarten and nursery programs. *See the Cartwright reference for extensive bibliography.*

1915 THE FIRST COOPERATIVE NURSERY SCHOOL was established by a group of faculty wives at the University of Chicago. There was also a cooperative nursery at Smith College in 1925. There is a description of both these coops in the 1929 NSSE Yearbook on pages 29-31. The cooperative movement grew slowly from 1925 to the end of World War II. In 1946, many veterans attended colleges and a number of cooperatives were established on college and university campuses. From 1946-1960, the movement enjoyed rapid expansion numbering over 1,000 cooperative nurseries at the height of its popularity.

In 1960, the American Council of Cooperative Preschools was formed. In 1964, the organization changed its name to Parent Cooperative Preschools International (PCPI). Dr. Katherine Whiteside Taylor, author of *Parent Cooperative Nursery Schools*, furnished much of the impetus to post World War II cooperatives and established the first cooperative newsletter in the United States.

1916 FEDERAL CHILD LABOR LAW. Also called the Keating-Owen Bill. This law prohibited the shipment in interstate commerce of goods produced in mines, quarries, factories, manufacturing establishments, mills and canneries where children were employed in violation of hour and wage standards. Children working in factories had to be fourteen years of age or older and youngsters working in mines had to be at least sixteen. The work period was set at eight hours per day and 48 hours per week maximum. The law was to be administered by the Children's Bureau. However, in 1918, the law was declared unconstitutional and it was not until 1938 that the Fair Labor Standards Act was passed which set guidelines and standards for the employment of young people. *See 1887, Child Labor.*

1916 LEWIS TERMAN AND MAUDE MERRILL of Stanford University revised the Binet-Simon Test using children in the United States as test subjects. This test, the Stanford-Binet, was revised in 1937, 1960, and again in 1985.

1918 THE PROJECT METHOD. William Heard Kilpatrick felt this method would bring together Dewey's concepts on education and Thorndike's laws of learning. The project method involved motor, aesthetic, and intellectual activity and emphasized becoming involved in "real life" experiences rather than mere preparation for life. A project was defined as "a whole-hearted purposeful act carried on amid social surroundings." The project method (study unit) was used extensively by kindergarten teachers for many years and can still be seen, in modified form, in some kindergartens today.

1918 LAURA SPELMAN ROCKEFELLER MEMORIAL FOUNDATION was established to encourage, foster, and assist projects for the improvement of the welfare of young children. Funds from this foundation were used to establish a number of research centers for the study of young children. *See 1924, Lawrence Frank.*

1919 THE CITY AND COUNTY SCHOOL was opened in New York by Harriet Johnson for the Bureau of Educational Experiments (later the Bank Street College of Education). Harriet Johnson was a nurse, former teacher and staff worker at the Henry Street Settlement House. In the introduction to Johnson's book (1928, p. 3), Ellis states: "From the beginning, the Experiment was guided less by the past history of educational procedures than by certain fundamental facts and principles ...it is the idea of the director (Ms. Johnson) that the facts of growth and development are the best guide to the knowledge of what is significant in behavior."

In describing the Bureau of Educational Experiments, Mitchell (1953, p. 24) said, "Two different kinds of work with children were just beginning: research organizations studying child development and experimental schools. The essential untried feature of the Bureau plan was to combine these two kinds of thinking and work within one organization in a functional relationship. To this end, our first staff was composed of a group of specialists — doctors, psychologists, social workers, teachers, all of whom had worked directly with children ... the Bureau started its own Nursery School — the first, as far as I know, organized on this research-educational basis."

1920   CHILDREN'S BOOK EDITORS. In the early 1920s, publishing houses began to recognize the need to have an editorial section specifically oriented to the needs of children. Alice Dalgliesh, a children's author in her own right, was the first children's book editor in the United States. The publishing house was Scribner's.

1921 THE HERE AND NOW STORIES. Dewey, Hill and Temple emphasized the importance of interaction with the immediate environment. In 1921, Lucy Sprague Mitchell noted that there were no stories for children under six which dealt with the modern world. Preschoolers had *Peter Rabbit*, the *Mother Goose Rhymes*, the *Three Little Pigs*, and *The Gingerbread Man*. Mitchell wrote a number of realistic stories, using children's activities, and style of language. Arbuthnot points out that Mitchell's success led to the "purr, purr, pat, pat school of writing." Later writers of "here and now" realism moved to realistic stories with laughter plus good literary expression and plot. Examples of later realistic stories include: Clark, *The Poppy Seed Cakes*; Lenski, *The Little Farm*; and Flack, *Wait for William*.

1921   THE COLUMBIA UNIVERSITY NURSERY SCHOOL was started by Patty Smith Hill and The Iowa Child Welfare Research Station Preschool Laboratory was established by Bird T. Baldwin.

1921   ABIGAIL ELIOT worked in London at the Evelyn House Nursery School under the direction of Margaret McMillan. During this same period, in the summer of 1921, Edna Nobel White, Director of the Merrill Palmer School in Detroit, visited the McMillan center to observe their nursery school program. Margaret McMillan was primarily interested in establishing an educational setting for children. In contrast, Dr. Eliot, a social worker by training, was extremely interested in working jointly with children and their parents. Dr. White, a home economist, was also very interested in parents and the training of mothers. Thus, these two persons were probably responsible for one of the most dramatic innovations in American education. With this great interest in home and family, the American nursery school movement worked in partnership with the home from its inception. In contrast to most public schools of the day, the nursery school opened its doors to parents and invited them to participate in the total program. Unlike day care programs, the nursery school was viewed as an educational experience for the child and his family. Emphasis was also placed on the child enjoying the "here and now" and the uniqueness of being his age. Unlike kindergarten, and the first grade, little thought was given to "readiness" but rather to the satisfaction of exploration at two or three or four years of age. In *Children in the Nursery School,* Johnson wrote that the nursery school was not a new way to help school programs handle children *en masse.* As mentioned earlier, Johnson's nursery was governed less by a past history of educational procedures than knowledge of growth and development.

Despite the fact that a cooperative nursery school was established in Chicago in 1916, Abigail Eliot is generally credited with bringing the nursery school movement to the United States. However, credit for the "first" nursery school in the United States can still

116

be a matter of debate. For example, Hewes (1976a, p. 303) states, "Harriet Johnson of the Bureau of Educational Experiments believed her nursery school for children aged fourteen months to three years was the 'first genuine nursery school in the United States'." *See 1919, City & County School.*

Eliot organized the Ruggles Street Nursery (Boston) on January 2, 1922. Since Eliot had been trained by McMillan, the Ruggles Street center probably operated in a manner more consistent with the overall philosophy and practice of the McMillan program. Table IV, p. 119, offers a comparison between the McMillan type program and day care programs of the 1920s.

Edna Noble White established a nursery school program at the Merrill Palmer School of Motherhood and Home Training in Detroit, Michigan, on January 20, 1922. Later the name was changed to the Merrill Palmer Institute. The first nursery school teachers at Merrill Palmer were English. White had hired them from the McMillan center when she was in England in the summer of 1921. Eliot and White, along with Patty Smith Hill, Harriet Johnson, Bird Baldwin, and others would become the leaders of the nursery school movement in the early 1920s. *See 1925, Committee on Nursery Schools.* Eliot presents a lively account of this period in Hymes, *Living History* series.

1921 FRANZ CIZEK. In 1921, Francesca Wilson wrote a small pamphlet entitled, *The Child as Artist*, describing the work of Franz Cizek in Vienna. As early as 1895, Cizek advocated allowing the child freedom to express himself in art. Wilson (1967, p. 4) quotes Cizek as stating:

"Children have their own laws in art, which they must obey. If they feel a head is large, they should draw it large; if they like long bodies; they should draw them long. What right have grown-ups to interfere? People should draw as they feel ...I take off the lid, and other art masters clap the lid on." Cizek has been called, "the discoverer of child art."

The Merrill Palmer Institute about 1924.

TABLE IV

COMPARISON BETWEEN NURSERY SCHOOL
AND DAY CARE— CA. 1920

DAY CARE	NURSERY SCHOOL
Drab appearance	Attractive & colorful
Children inactive; quiet; No organized program	Planned program; children play
Poor equipment	Well designed; child-oriented equipment
Large group size	Small group size
Staff untrained	Staff trained to work with children
Parents HAD to send children	Parents WANTED to send children
Emphasize care	Emphasize educational experience
Service for parents	Service for parents and children; Training for teacher trainees; Research program
Parents passive; no participation	Parents active partners in education process

1921   A. S. NEILL established a "free school" in Leiston, England. Strongly influenced by Freud, Neill felt that if the emotions were free the intellect would look after itself. He stated, "Most schools ignore the fact that we should look at children as free beings who have the consciousness to choose what they want." *See 1960, Summerhill and the Free School Movement.*

1922 NEWBERY MEDAL. In 1922, the John Newbery Medal for the "most distinguished contribution to children's literature" was established. The idea was originated by Frederick Melcher, Editor-in-Chief of *Publisher's Weekly*. The first recipient was Henrick W. van Loon for his book, *The Story of Mankind*.

1922 HABIT CLINICS. The effects of the psychoanalytic movement on the nursery school can be seen in the establishment of habit clinics. Douglas Thom, a psychiatrist, established the first habit clinic in Boston in 1922. The purpose of these clinics was to prevent maladjustments in young children.

In the same year Wilfred Lay published, *The Unconscious Mind: The relation of Psychoanalysis to Education*. In his book Lay (1922, p. 26) states: "The period of the child's life before it is old enough even to go to kindergarten is, in all ways, the most important in its life in the dominating effect it has on the major traits of character of later years."

1923 ARNOLD GESELL (1880-1961) Arnold Gesell was a major catalyst in the early childhood education movement. Gesell had studied with G. Stanley Hall at Clark University. Later he established the Clinic of Child Development at Yale University. Gesell encouraged Abigail Eliot to go to England to study with the McMillan sisters and influenced Edna Noble White in her decision to open a nursery school facility at the Merrill Palmer School of Motherhood and Home Training.

In the early 1930s, Gesell began to record controlled observations in a natural setting. Moving picture photography had recently been developed and Gesell utilized this technique as a means of recording the behavior of young children. Gesell devised a dome-shaped room, painted white to reflect lights, and used one-way mirrors.

For years Gesell and his associates collected normative data on young children. Gesell did not feel that "norms" were rigid, but rather indices of types of behavior likely to occur at a particular age. Late in his career, in a keynote address to the NANE association at their annual conference in Boston, Gesell warned that the "ages and stages" concept had been interpreted too literally. Gesell's warning

120

is still appropriate today. Unfortunately, the lay public, and some professionals, have placed too much emphasis on the ages and stages idea without regard to the concept of individual difference and variation.

Gesell saw the nursery school as a vital part of the total educational system. He said (1924, p. 19): "The educational ladder of the American public school system is a tall one and a stout one, but it does not reach the ground ... the significance of the nursery school lies in the fact that it represents a deliberate attempt to furnish a more solid support for the educational ladder."

In his book, *The Preschool Child*, Gesell (1923, p. 14) emphasized the importance of the early years: (the preschool period) " ...is biologically the most important period in the development of an individual for the simple but sufficient reason that it comes first in a dynamic sequence; it inevitably influences all subsequent development."

Note the similarity to a statement made by Elkind nearly fifty years later. In 1970, Elkind (p. 137) said:

"The preschool period is important, even critical, but not because growth is most rapid at that time ... it is important for a simple reason, namely, mental growth is cumulative and depends upon what has gone before."

1923 THE MULTI-DISCIPLINARY FLAVOR OF THE NURSERY SCHOOL MOVEMENT. In 1922 and 1923 a number of nursery schools had been established in the United States. In Cambridge, Massachusetts, there was a cooperative nursery school. Barbara Greenwood established a laboratory nursery school at UCLA.

The nursery school movement took a multi-disciplinary flavor as persons from home economics, nursing, medicine, social work, psychology and education all participated in the movement. In contrast, the early kindergarten movement had been almost exclusively an educational movement and influenced by leaders in the educational field. Table V contrasts the professional orientation of these leaders.

TABLE V

PROFESSIONAL BACKGROUND OF
EARLY ECE LEADERS

KINDERGARTEN	NURSERY SCHOOL
Pestalozzi (Educ.)	McMillan (Nursing)
Froebel (Educ.)	Eliot (Social Work)
Schurz (Educ.)	Montessori (Medicine)
Harris (Educ.)	White (Home Economics)
Peabody (Educ.)	Baldwin (Psychology)
Blow (Educ.)	Johnson (Nursing)
Hall (Psychology)	Gesell (Medicine)
Dewey (Educ.)	Hill (Education)
Hill (Educ.)	Thom (Psychiatry)

1924 LAWRENCE FRANK AND THE CHILD DEVELOPMENT MOVEMENT. G. Stanley Hall and John Dewey were early disciples for the new psychology and child study movement. In addition, the establishment of research centers like the Bureau of Educational Experiments and the Iowa Child Welfare Research Station helped lay the foundation for research studies in child behavior. As Senn (1975, p. 11) points out: "The 1920s provided an auspicious climate for the start of the child development movement. It was a period in which faith in science as a solution to problems waxed high and in which an aura of business optimism generated funds for research. With rapid strides being made in medicine, biology, chemistry, psychology, and nutrition, there was high hope that scientists could point the way to improved care of the nation's children ... child rearing was seen as a rational process of applying definite methods to produce certain results."

In 1924, the National Research Council changed the name of its committee on children from "Committee on Child Psychology" to "Committee on Child Development." According to the Council the name was changed in order to "recognize a broader approach to the study of children."

The catalyst for this new movement was Lawrence Frank. Frank is credited with the idea of an interdisciplinary approach to the study of children. He believed that the findings and interpretations of various disciplines — anthropology, biology, education, medicine, and psychology should be combined to provide insights into an understanding of the whole child. Frank worked with the Rockefeller Foundation and proposed the idea that funds be given to establish research centers throughout the United States. In 1924, through Frank's efforts, Columbia University received the first grant of $500,000 to set up an institute of child study. In 1925, a second research center was established at the University of Minnesota (Zwicke, 1985). Prior to 1930, other institutes had been established including centers at Yale, Western Reserve, and Berkeley. In addition, Frank helped fund nursery schools and child development programs in schools of home economics. In Senn (1975, p. 21), Lois Meek Stolz mentions these programs: "Larry and I had some differences of opinion about how nursery schools should be developed. He felt that they should be part of home economics because they were a supplement to the family. I felt that they were educational and should be tied in with the whole public school system ... Larry was interested in preschool children, because of his interest in family life. At that time the family was the only educational and socialization source for young children."

In an unpublished document, Frank cited his own contributions to the field. Writing in the third person he said, "In 1923, he foresaw the need for systematic and intensive study of child growth and development and envisioned a nationwide plan for such research and for parent education ... his knowledge of the research needs in the field of human development, particularly of the development of the young child, was accompanied by a vision of programs in home and school, and agencies of child care, in which the needs of the whole child would be central." For a detailed account of the early days of the child development movement, the reader is referred to Anderson (1956), Frank (1962), Sears (1975), and Senn (1975).

1924 CHILD LABOR AMENDMENT TO THE U. S. CONSTI-
TUTION. Since the earlier child labor laws had been declared
unconstitutional, Congress enacted a joint resolution to be submitted
to the states for ratification. This constitutional amendment did not
set up standards, but proposed to give Congress power to limit,
regulate, and prohibit the labor of persons under eighteen years of
age. This proposed amendment was never ratified by enough states
to become law.

Even though earlier laws had been declared unconstitutional,
they were having an indirect effect on the number of children in the
labor force. In addition, the political power of trade unions was a
factor in helping reduce the numbers of children in the labor force.
For example, in 1910, over 12% of all 10-13 year old children were
in the work force. The 1920 census showed a decrease in percentage
to 4.4%.

The census also indicated an increase in the numbers of
children attending high school. The 1920 attendance figure was
200,000 high school students. However, work remained a more
significant factor for the high school aged youngster. In 1920, there
were nearly two million 16-17 year olds in the work force.

1924 CHILDHOOD EDUCATION. IKU established a professional
journal, *Childhood Education.* Mae Murray was the first editor.
Consulting editors included: Gesell, Kilpatrick, Wheelock,
Vandewalker, and Baldwin. The current editor is Lucy Prete Martin.

Note to history buffs: The early volumes (1924-1929) of *Childhood Education* recount the beginnings of the nursery school
movement in this country. Almost every issue has an article on the
philosophy of nursery school education and/or a detailed description of early nursery schools. For example: In volume I, there is a
description of UCLA's nursery, the Iowa preschool laboratory, the
Ruggles Street and Merrill Palmer nurseries plus a description of a
nursery school in China. In volume II, Boyce (pp. 427-28) presents
a detailed account of the historic nursery school conference held in
Washington, D.C., on February 26, 1926, which ultimately led to the
establishment of NAEYC.

1924 PUBLIC SCHOOL NURSERY, Highland Park, Michigan. This nursery school was actually operated in the Highland Park High School as a part of their Family Life program. The Merrill Palmer School helped to establish this program (Woolley, 1925).

Abbot (1924, p. 113) reports day nurseries in operation in Junior High Schools in Oakland, California. She states: " ... these schools are under the supervision of the public school system and in these nurseries students learn the care of young children." Abbot (*loc. cit.*) also reports, "In New York City, girls in eighth grade home economics classes have practical experience in child care with the children of the kindergarten."

1924-1930 NURSERY SCHOOLS ESTABLISHED IN HOME ECONOMICS DEPARTMENTS. Lawrence Frank believed that nursery schools should be an integral part of home economics. *See 1924, Lawrence Frank and the Child Development Movement.* As a result, he funneled large financial contributions from the Rockefeller Foundation to a number of departments of home economics. These included Iowa State, Ohio State, Cornell, Georgia, Bennett College, Spelman College, Atlanta University, and Michigan State.

In addition, nursery schools were established in departments of home economics at Purdue, Kansas, Nebraska, Oklahoma State, Cincinnati, and Oregon State.

Since most colleges of education did not view the nursery school as an integral part of public school education, home economics departments dominated the nursery teacher training area for years. Departments of home economics saw the nursery school as a place to train future mothers and to enhance the study of family life. As a result, the type of training given to nursery school teachers was often different from elementary education trainees.

Colleges of education discussed educational foundations and curriculum methods; home economics training programs emphasized child development, child psychology, psychological learning theories, Freudian and neo-Freudian theory, and family life.

An interesting comparison of the differences in approach can be seen by comparing the "qualifications for teachers" as viewed by Gardner (1964, pp. 338-339) and Leeper *et al.*, (1968, pp. 103-105).

125

In home economics departments little emphasis was placed of "lesson plans." The term "group" was used instead of "class" and great emphasis was placed on the role of the family in the education of the child. The public school wanted to improve society; the home economics nursery school wanted to improve the family.

1925 BALDWIN AND STECHER, THE PSYCHOLOGY OF THE PRESCHOOL CHILD. One of the first books in the United States on preschool children. This book is significant for three reasons: (1) A comprehensive chapter on the historical background of experimental studies on young children, (2) Six chapters are devoted to mental development, and (3) An extensive explanation of the Iowa Preschool Laboratories, outlining the daily program and educational activities. The appendix lists *all* the phonograph records and children's books available at that time. There are a total of 47 entries.

1925 PUBLIC SCHOOL NURSERY. FRANKLIN NURSERY CHICAGO. The first public school nursery established as part of the public school system. Christine Heinig was the first teacher. *See 1924, Highland Park.*

1925 RESEARCH NURSERY SCHOOLS. In the laboratory nursery schools there were usually three major functions: teaching, research, and service. In some laboratory settings (Ruggles Street, Merrill Palmer, Georgia, Iowa State), the teaching function was emphasized more than research or service. However, some of the early laboratory nursery schools were more involved in research efforts than in teacher training. Some of these early research centers were: Iowa, Fels Institute at Yellow Springs, Ohio, and Minnesota.

Much basic research came from these centers: Growth curves (Meredith at Iowa), norms (Gesell at Yale), intelligence tests (Kuhlmann at Minnesota; Stutsman at Merrill Palmer, Terman & Merrill at Stanford), the I.Q. studies (Wellman & Skeels at Iowa; Goodenough at Minnesota), language studies (Day at Georgia; McCarthy at Minnesota), frustration tolerance (Keister at Iowa) are but examples of the numerous studies which came from these early centers. The famous study which gave teachers the familiar terms parallel play,

126

solitary play, and cooperative play was conducted by Parten and Newhall at Minnesota.

Many research studies during this period utilized the longitudinal approach and the retrospective interview. Two books will provide the reader with major studies during this early period: Carmichael (1946) and Barker, Kounin and Wright (1943). Baldwin and Stecher (1921) present a classic description of an early child development laboratory. An article by Senn (1975) entitled, *Insights on the Child Development Movement*, discusses a number of major researchers and their influence on the field during this period.

1925 NATIONAL COMMITTEE ON NURSERY SCHOOLS. In New York City, Patty Smith Hill called a group of 25 persons interested in nursery education together in 1925 to discuss common concerns. The group established a National Committee on Nursery Schools. Patty Hill was designated as temporary chairperson. In 1926, Lois Hayden Meek (Lois Meek Stolz) was named permanent chairperson and Rose Alschuler as secretary. The initial committee included Bird Baldwin, Edna Dean Baker, Mary Dabney Davis, Abigail Eliot, Lucy Gage, Arnold Gesell, Harriet Johnson, Alice Temple, Lee Vincent, and Edna Noble White. The committee held its first conference in Washington, D. C., on February 26, 1926 (Boyce, 1926). A second conference was held in New York in 1927. At this conference there were nearly 300 attendees from 24 states and the District of Columbia. In 1929, a conference was held in Chicago. The group decided to establish a more formal organizational structure and voted to change its name to the National Association for Nursery Education (NANE).

From its inception NANE was multi-disciplinary in nature and included nursery school teachers, home economists, psychologists, pediatricians, nurses, and social workers. In an interview with Senn (1975, p. 20), George Stoddard remembered that in the 1920s, NANE became one of the bonds that pulled ECE professionals together. He said, "it gave us all a sense of not only of working in Iowa, or in New York, or in New Haven, or Chicago, or Stanford, or Minneapolis, but a sense of being together in a real educational movement."

In 1956, NANE established affiliate groups (NAEYC, 1986). In 1964, the name was changed to National Association for the Education of Young Children (NAEYC). Hewes (1976b) presents a detailed

Patty Smith Hill

account of the early developments of the Committee on Nursery Schools and the later organizational changes from NANE to NAEYC.

1926 CHILDREN: THE MAGAZINE FOR PARENTS. In 1926, a number of professionals in the early childhood field felt that there needed to be a magazine targeted specifically for parents. In the first issue of *Children*, the editor, George Hecht, commented that parents were "floundering" and needed help in order to effectively rear their children. The magazine had a large advisory board composed of many experts of the day including: John Anderson, Bird Baldwin, Arnold Gesell, Patty Smith Hill, Lois Meek, and Helen Woolley. In 1928, the name of the magazine was changed to *Parents' Magazine*.

1926 JEAN PIAGET (1896-1980) brought a unique theoretical background to the field of child psychology and development. Piaget's early interests were in the biological sciences, and he published a number of zoological studies before the age of sixteen. He later studied Biological Sciences at the University of Neuchatel, earning his Ph.D., with a thesis dealing with the distribution of mollusks in the Alps. He earned a second doctorate in logic and philosophy soon afterward. Piaget's diverse interests led him to post-doctoral work under Binet in Paris. While contributing to the standardization on intelligence test items, Piaget's fascination with children's thought processes led him to begin formulation of a theory of cognitive development. Later, his own children became the subjects of his careful observations and recordings.

Piaget considered intellectual development a continuous process. However, he found it useful to specify four main periods of intellectual growth:

    I. Sensory Motor (0-2 years)
   II. Preoperational (2-7 years)
  III. Concrete Operations (7-11 years)
  IV. Formal Operations (11 and up)

Piaget makes three main points about the qualitative stages of intellectual growth: they form an invariant sequence, they are hierarchy related, and they show integration within each step.

Piaget published The *Language and Thought of the Child* in 1926. While widely recognized in Europe, his influence in the United States remained relatively unnoticed until the early 1950s. Since then, his theories have had great influence, especially in the movement of the early 1960s toward cognitive stimulation in young children.

1926 BERTRAND RUSSELL published the book, *On Education*, which decried classical British education and the simple memorization of facts. He urged teachers to concentrate on personality development. Russell felt children should work at their own pace; that punishment should be minimized; that children often learn best when taught by other children, and that the young children were highly motivated to work and discover. He believed that children should be provided a climate of learning which made discovery possible and allowed them to experience the joy of success.

1927 FIRST BLACK NURSERY SCHOOL. Dorothy Howard, an educator in Washington D.C., established the first Black nursery school. In describing this center, Kittrell said: "The school was located on 'S' Street, N.W ...Ms. Howard operated this school for more than fifty years."

1928 JOHN B. WATSON did extensive research in the area of children's fears. However, his famous (or infamous) book, *Psychological Care of Infant and Child*, is seldom mentioned in current references. From 1920 to 1940, Watson's theories of conditioning and behavior shaping had a strong effect on child rearing. Many persons were raised on Watson's scheduled feeding. Watson also told parents that they could make of their children whatever they wished. Watson said that he could take any four children and make "One a lawyer, one a doctor, one an Indian chief and one a thief." In his book, Watson (1928, p. 136) advised parents: "There is a sensible way of treating children. Treat them as adults ... never hug and kiss them, never let them sit in your lap. If you must, kiss them on the forehead when they say, 'goodnight'. Shake hands with them in the morning." Spock's philosophy on child rearing and child care was in direct opposition to Watson. Spock's permissive philosophy would replace Watson's approach in the 1940s.

1929 THE NURSERY YEARS. An outstanding book by Susan Isaacs discusses the "mind of the child from birth to six years." The book differs greatly from Watson's behavior shaping and habit training. Isaacs emphasized the child's point of view and discussed play as a medium for learning. According to Isaacs (1929, p. 10): "Play is indeed the child's work, and the means whereby he grows and develops ... through play he adds to his knowledge of the world." Isaacs' philosophy was a major influence in the establishment of the British Infant School. *See 1967, The Open Classroom.*

1929 EARLY BLACK LABORATORY NURSERY SCHOOLS. Two Black laboratory nursery schools were opened within a few months of each other in 1929 and 1930. These laboratory schools were located at Hampton Institute and Spelman College.

Phyllis Jones Tilly was the first director of the nursery school in the School of Home Economics at Hampton and opened that program in 1929. In 1930, Spelman College established a laboratory nursery school under the direction of Pearlie Reed. These nursery schools closely followed the philosophical ideas of other contemporary laboratory schools emphasizing child development principles and the importance of the whole child.

Under Reed's capable direction the Spelman Nursery School became an important early training center in early childhood. Many future leaders in the field including Flemmie Kittrell, Dorothy Neal, Evangeline Ward, and Ida Jones Curry all trained and worked under Reed.

In 1931, Kittrell opened a laboratory nursery school at Bennett College. Three years later, with a grant from the Rockefeller Foundation, this program was enlarged to admit graduate students in early childhood education.

Ida Jones Curry was Reed's first student in the Spelman program. In 1932, Curry left Spelman to assume the directorship of the program at Hampton Institute. Curry travelled extensively in Europe studying early childhood programs and spent a summer with Margaret McMillan in England. Evangeline Ward, past president of NAEYC, was one of Curry's students.

1929 THE GARDEN APARTMENTS NURSERY SCHOOL AND KINDERGARTEN was established in Chicago under the direction of Oneida Cockrell. This early program served as a model for programs operated in urban apartment complexes.

1929 NATIONAL ASSOCIATION FOR NURSERY EDUCATION. At the Chicago meeting of the National Committee on Nursery Schools it was decided to organize the group into a more formal structure. At that meeting the conferees voted to establish the National Association for Nursery Education. The first president was Lois Meek Stolz. In 1964, NANE changed its name to become NAEYC. Hewes (1976b) presents an in-depth account of the history of the National Committee on Nursery Schools and the subsequent development of NANE and NAEYC.

1930 ASSOCIATION FOR CHILDHOOD EDUCATION. In 1930, IKU enlarged its membership to include primary teachers and changed its name to the Association for Childhood Education (ACE). Later the group became an international organization admitting members from Canada and over eighty other countries. Upon adding the international members ACE became ACEI. The first paid executive secretary of ACEI was Mary Leeper.

1930 TWO MAJOR JOURNALS ESTABLISHED. *Child Development* was established in the Spring of 1930. Buford Johnson was the first editor. A second major journal, *The American Journal of Orthopsychiatry*, was also begun that same year. Lawson Lowrey, the editor of *Orthopsychiatry* said he knew many persons who could write books on diagnostics and testing, but knew of no one (in 1930) who could write a book on therapy or treatement of young children.

1930 U.S. CENSUS. The U.S. census in 1930 showed a dramatic drop in ten to fifteen year old children in the work force. While the number was still large by today's standards (over 660,000 children), it represented a great reduction from earlier years. In addition there was a large drop in the number of sixteen and seventeen year olds in the work force. The census also showed a 100% increase in attendance in high schools, from 200,000 in 1920 to 400,000 in 1930.

132

1931   REPORT OF THE PRIMARY SCHOOL published in Great Britain by the Board of Education and harbinger of the British Infant School. Part of the report stated: "The curriculum of the primary school is to be thought of in terms of activity and experience, rather than of knowledge to be acquired and facts to be stored." Later the report said, "The essential point is that the curriculum should not be loaded with inert ideas and crude blocks of fact ... it must be vivid, realistic, a stream in motion, not a stagnant pool."

1932   THE PROJECT METHOD. *See Kilpatrick, 1918.* This method had reached its height in the kindergarten by 1932. One of the most elaborate treatises showing practical implementation of the project method was the book, *Curriculum Records of the Children's School*, published by the staff of the National College of Education. Study units for the kindergarten included: traveling by train, traveling on an ocean liner and traveling in the air. An interesting look at kindergarten philosophy can be seen in the following statement: "Health and happiness are considered the first aims in all work with kindergarten and primary children. Other important objectives of the kindergarten have been, to help children understand their own immediate environment, and to provide the opportunity for social living ... in the worthy modern home and community."

In 1933, Arbuthnot questioned whether or not the large study unit would secure "all the necessary skills and learnings." She warned the teacher to put units in proper perspective stating (1933, p. 185), "The activity (study unit) is not an end in itself but a joyous means to a less obvious end, namely the accumulation of a steadily growing body of concepts and information."

Weber (1969) cites the late 1930s as the time period when many educators began to feel study units were too closely integrated for kindergarten children. As Weber points out, the nomenclature changed and gave rise to the term "interest centers," but the experiences remained substantially the same. The salient feature in the interest center concept was the flexibility and autonomy offered the children.

1932   THE WELLMAN-GOODENOUGH CONTROVERSY. In 1921, the preschool laboratories of the Iowa Child Welfare Research

Station began giving I.Q. tests to their children each Fall and Spring. In the late 1920s, Beth Wellman noticed an average gain of about seven points in the Fall to Spring testing. In 1932, she published an article, *The Effect of Preschool Attendance Upon the I.Q.* Since it was felt that I.Q. could not change, the article created quite a stir in psychological circles. One of Wellman's biggest critics was Florence Goodenough at Minnesota. This controversy lasted through the 1930s and 1940s. Wellman's position is stated in a chapter, *The Effects of Preschool Attendance Upon Intellectual Development*, in Barker, Kounin and Wright (1943). Goodenough's position is stated in a chapter, *The Measurement of Mental Growth in Childhood*, in Carmichael (1946).

By the early 1950s, this argument died a quiet death as everyone agreed that both the biological forces and the environmental forces contributed to the intellectual development of the child.

1933   THE GREAT DEPRESSION. The National Industrial Recovery Act was passed to meet the national emergency of unemployment and industrial disorganization. It incorporated child labor provisions into the industrial codes under the National Recovery Administration (NRA). Between 1933 and 1935, when the codes were declared unconstitutional, child labor provisions were written into over 500 industrial codes. These codes practically eliminated the employment of children under sixteen in industry and trade. In 1936, Congress passed the Walsh-Healey Public Contracts Act, effectively curtailing the employment of children on federal contract work.

At the height of the depression there were nearly 10,000 bank closings and the unemployment rate had reached 13,282,000. Public school kindergartens were among the casualties of the Great Depression. Throughout the country many school districts closed kindergarten programs due to a lack of funds. Most of these programs were not reinstated until the post-World War II years.

1933   WPA NURSERIES. These emergency nurseries were established during the Great Depression under the Federal Emergency Relief Administration. Two million dollars was allocated "for the relief of unemployed teachers."

One form of this relief was the establishment of nursery schools for children 2-6 years of age. Nearly 2,000 schools were in operation by 1935 and over 74,000 children were enrolled. According to Hewes (1976b), employment was provided for 6,770 adults including teachers, clerks, and maintenance workers.

In addition to providing work for many unemployed workers, the Federal Administration stated that these nursery schools were: "designed to promote the physical and mental well-being of children of unemployed parents."

A national committee was created to advise on policy and programs. This group included: Edna Noble White Chairperson, Abigail Eliot, Lois Meek Stolz, Mary Dabne Davis, and George Stoddard. Hewes (1976b) and Heinig (1979) describe the beginnings of the WPA program, the role of these nursery school leaders plus the involvement of NANE in this effort. The WPA nurseries remained in operation until the beginning of World War II.

FLEMMIE PANSY KITTRELL (1904-). Flemmie Kittrell is an outstanding leader in the early childhood movement. She was the first Black woman in the United States to receive a Ph.D. She was also one of the early Black leaders in the nursery school movement. Before her retirement in 1972, Kittrell worked in a number of major colleges and universities throughout the country. She began the early childhood program at Bennett College in 1931 and served as Dean at that institution until 1940. From 1940 to 1944 she served as professor of home economics at Hampton Institute and as director of their early childhood education program. In 1944, she went to Howard University and directed the home economics program and their child development laboratory school until her retirement.

An observer for the United Nations and UNICEF, Kittrell has worked for many years for children throughout the world. She is also a Fullbright Scholar and recipient of Cornell's Outstanding Alumni Award. Kittrell has also been an active member of the American Home Economics Association and ACEI.

1934 THE SOCIETY FOR RESEARCH IN CHILD DEVELOP-MENT was established as a multidisciplinary association to provide meetings and conferences for those persons engaged in child research and to provide a vehicle for the publication of research findings in the area of child development. Buford Johnson made the journal, *Child Development*, available to SRCD as its research publication. In addition, SRCD began publication of the *Child Development Abstracts*, in 1934.

1938   FAIR LABOR STANDARDS ACT. This law, passed in 1938, was a milestone in the history of labor legislation. For all practical purposes, this act eliminated child labor in all industries which shipped goods in interstate commerce. It set a sixteen year minimum age for most jobs and gave the Department of Labor the power to declare certain jobs hazardous and require an eighteen year minimum for those positions. The Supreme Court (U.S. vs. Darby) held that the Fair Labor Standards Act was constitutional.

1939   CALDECOTT MEDAL. Frederick Melcher, Editor of *Publisher's Weekly* suggested the establishment of the Randolph Caldecott Medal for distinguished children's book illustration. The first recipient was Dorothy Lathrop for her illustrations in *Animals of the Bible*.

1942   SIMON AND SCHUSTER established the Little Golden Books and inaugurated the idea of mass marketing of children's books. By 1943, during the years of World War II and despite severe paper shortages, nearly five million copies of Golden Books had been printed.

1942 LANHAM ACT. THE WAR NURSERIES. Nearly one-third of America's women worked in defense plants and factories producing materials for World War II. Obviously facilities were needed to care for the children of working mothers. In 1940, the Lanham Act was passed to provide funds to help war-impacted communities. At its peak about 2,000 Lanham Act nurseries were in daily operation from 6 AM to 6 PM. There were programs in forty-one states and most of the programs were operated by the public schools. In all, about 600,000 children attended these schools. The Lanham centers stopped operation in 1946.

136

The most famous war nurseries were the Kaiser Child Care Service Centers in Portland, Oregon, which were established by the Kaiser Shipbuilding Company. These centers consisted of two units which operated twenty-four hours per day, 364 days a year. During their peak period of operation the two facilities served 1,005 children. The centers were in operation from 1943-1945. However, during that period they served 3,811 children and provided 249,268 child care days of service. Lois Meek Stolz served as consultant to the center and James L. Hymes, Jr. was the Manager of the Child Service Department for the two shipyards. An article by Zinsser (1988) and a recording by Stolz and Hymes, *Living History Interviews* (1972), describes the Kaiser Child Service Centers in detail. In addition, the Stolz and Hymes cassette tape provides the listener with a thorough discussion of the emergency and war nursery programs.

1943 JAMES L. HYMES, JR. helped to establish the Kaiser Child Care Service Centers. In the early beginnings of kindergarten, there were several men in the early childhood field. However, only a few men remained interested in the nursery and kindergarten field in the first part of the twentieth century. Hymes was a notable exception and has had a tremendous influence on the early childhood education field. Hymes received his M.A. and Ed.D. at Teachers College, Columbia in child development and parent education. During the Great Depression, Hymes served as a supervisor in the WPA nursery program and was professor of early childhood education at the State University of New York at New Paltz. During World War II, he served as Manager of the Child Service Department for the Kaiser Shipbuilding Company. *See 1942, Lanham Act, The War Nurseries.* Following World War II, Hymes taught at several colleges and universities including Peabody and the University of Maryland. A prolific writer, one of his most significant contributions is his *Living History* series in which he chronicles recent events in the field of early childhood education.

Dr. Hymes is past President of NAEYC, past Vice President of ACEI, and one of the founders of SACUS. He also served on the original planning committee of Project Head Start.

1943 COMPREHENSIVE DAY CARE. New York City established comprehensive day care centers in 1943. Unlike many day care

Shipyard workers at a shift change.

Kaiser Child Service Center at Oregonship.

centers of that period, these centers moved far beyond actual "care" for children. Cornelia Goldsmith was director of this program which was designed to care for the child's health and social-emotional needs. This program, like other nursery programs, emphasized the value of educational experiences for children under six. Dr. Goldsmith describes this program in Hymes, *Living History* series. In 1964, Goldsmith was appointed as the first full-time executive secretary for NAEYC.

1945 NANE BULLETIN. This professional publication for early childhood educators was established in 1945 by NAEYC (then NANE) and originally called the *NANE Bulletin*. The early issues of the *Bulletin* were mimeographed. Millie Almy, Marjorie Craig, Janet Learned, and Theodora Reeve were members of the first Bulletin committee from 1945-1948. In 1956, the name of the publication was changed to *The Journal of Nursery Education*. Docia Zavikowski was the editor during this period. In 1964, the name of the journal was again changed to its present name, *Young Children*. An article in *Young Children* (November 1986) recalls the evolution from a mimeographed newsletter to a professional journal and contains interesting information about the editors and articles from 1945 to 1986. The current editor is Polly Greenberg.

1946 TELEVISION. Without doubt the most influential invention in the electronic age, television is certainly the most beguiling. A fabulous sound and light "dog and pony show with all the bells and whistles," it draws one like the Pied Piper of old. Infants as young as six months are fascinated by its magic, and small children sit in front of it for hours. A powerful part of everyday life, it determines how people spend their time, how they think, how they talk, how they act, and how they learn. Probably no other invention in the history of mankind has so influenced opinions and shaped behavior. More Americans have television than refrigerators or indoor plumbing.

The first commercial television program was broadcast in New York City in 1936 and featured a popular cartoon character of that era, Felix the Cat. However, commercial television did not really get underway until after World War II. In 1946, there were 10,000 sets in the United States. The figure soared to six million sets in 1950. Today there are over 238 million sets — or about one set for each person in the United States. Ninety-seven percent of all homes have a television set and over eighty percent of the American homes have color television. It is estimated that children spend one-third of their waking hours viewing TV programs. It is estimated that by the time a child graduates from high school he will have spent over 16,000 hours viewing TV. It is also estimated that on any given night over 40 million children are watching TV during the prime time evening hours.

Hymes stated (1977, p. 57): "We do not have school for all three, four-and five-year-olds — but nearly all of them have television. TV is, in a real sense, the one school, the big school for the young child."

In 1952, Dr. Frances Horowitz, past President of NANE and Professor of Education at Roosevelt College, began a program for children and parents called *Ding Dong, School*. This popular show continued until 1963.

Unfortunately not all programs were as appropriate for viewers. In 1950, Newton Minnow referred to television as "the vast wasteland." In that same year, Wayne Coy, Chairperson of the FCC noted: "Our files protesting crime programs are bulging. The situation is gradually worsening ... propriety has been sacrificed for profits."

The first academic study on the effects of television on young children was authored by Schramm, Lyle, and Parker in 1961. The U.S. Senate has held four separate hearings related to TV violence — 1954, 1961, 1964, and 1969. The 1964 report concluded, "The excessive amount of televised crime, violence, and brutality can and does contribute to the development of attitudes in many young people that pave the way for delinquent behavior."

In 1969, Congress asked the Surgeon General to organize a Committee on Television and Social Behavior. In 1972, the committee, under the direction of George Comstock and Eli Rubinstein, responded with a five volume report, the most extensive analysis of television's effect on children to date.

In 1974, the Federal Communications Commission stated, "Children are a unique audience whose special needs and interests every commercial broadcaster has an obligation to serve." As a result, the FCC adopted a series of policies and guidelines designed to increase the amount of educational and informational television programs for preschool and school-aged children, to decrease the amount of advertising on children's programs, and to eliminate certain selling practices. Unfortunately in 1979, an investigative committee of the FCC found these policies and guidelines were never implemented. In their report the investigators stated (FCC, 1979, p. 4): "There have been insignificant changes in children's programming since 1974, (and) ... there has been no broadcaster compliance in the area of educational and instructional programming for children." In short, commercial broadcasters totally ignored the FCC policies regulating children's television.

In the late 1970s, television took a dramatic turn in day time serials (soap operas) and in some prime time evening shows. Mild profanity (like "damn," "hell," and "bastard") began creeping into program dialogue. In addition, some highly suggestive scenes expressed a new freedom in sex. Television critics dubbed this approach "soft core pornography."

In the early 1980s, private television cable companies were licensed which allowed nationwide coverage. These companies were not subject to the same rules and regulations as the three major television networks As a result, cable stations began showing extremes in violence, heavy sexual content, and strong vulgar language. In the late 1980s, in order to counteract the competition, networks gradually increased their own version of sex and violence.

1946 UNICEF. The United Nations International Children's Emergency Fund was established in 1946 to provide food, clothing, and medicine to children who were victims of World War II. Today the official name of this organization is the United Nations Children's Fund. It helps children in more than 100 countries in areas of health, hunger, and education. In 1965, UNICEF received the Nobel Peace Prize for its work in aiding needy children throughout the world.

1946-1964 RESEARCH IN EARLY CHILDHOOD. Over this period research moved more and more into a laboratory context. During the first few years, research centered on social-emotional development of the preschool aged child. The work by Dollard and Miller in 1950 represented an attempt to integrate psychoanalytic thought and learning theory. Some studies were begun on the application of learning theory to behavior modification. Near the end of this period two major foci emerged: the study of infants and cognition. Hoffman and Hoffman (1964) and Carmichael (1970) provide the reader with an overview of studies made during this period. The chapter by Swift (in Hoffman & Hoffman) and the article by Sears and Dowley (1963) will give the reader an overview of the effects of the nursery school experience on the child and the role of the teacher in early childhood education.

Kindergartens were indirectly effected by the general concern over the problem of reading with elementary school children (Flesch, 1955). A major question was raised during this period: "Can children under five years of age learn to read?" While this question was resolved (the child under five can be taught to read), the question arose: "Should the kindergarten curriculum teach reading?" Another question posed was: "What are the consequences of early reading?" Mindless and Keliher (1969) present research related to these questions.

In the late 1950s and early 1960s, researchers began working on enrichment programs for young children. Some of these workers and their programs included: Susan Gray at Peabody (Gray & Klaus, 1968); Morton and Cynthia Deutsch at the Institute for Developmental Studies in New York City (Deutsch, 1966); David Weikart at the Perry Preschool Project in Michigan (Weikart, 1978); Annamarie Roeper and Irving Sigel at the Merrill-Palmer Institute and the City and Country School in Detroit (Roeper &Sigel, 1969).

1948 OMEP. Following World War II, the *Organization pour L'Education Pre-Scholaire* (World Organization for Early Childhood Education) was founded. OMEP aims to promote the study of education of children from birth to eight years of age. OMEP has consultative status with UNICEF and UNESCO and over forty countries are members of OMEP.

Shortly after the second World War, Lady Allen Hurtwood was lecturing in Scandinavia on young children. She met Ms. Ella Esp and the two women began discussions on the value of an international organization for young children. A group was formed and met in Paris in 1948. Two outstanding educators, Madame Herbinere-Lebert of France and Ms. Jens Signgaard helped the organization in its early formative days. In the United States, the U.S. National Committee for Early Childhood, is a member organization to OMEP. Dr. Bess Goodykoontz, a staff member of the U.S. Office of Education, was the first chairperson of the U.S. Committee.

1949 THE STORY OF A SCHOOL. In 1940, Arthur Stone was appointed Headmaster of Steward Street Primary School in Birmingham, England. Influenced by Cizek and Dewey, Stone felt children should be free to develop and changed his rather dreary school to match his philosophy. Glegg, visiting the school in the 1940s, offers these impressions: "They were so short of space in this lamentable inadequate building that there were children in the cloakrooms painting on sheets of paper spread on the floor. There were children play acting in the hall, having dressed themselves up in all kinds of odd garment and pieces of cloth ... but the thing that struck me about this school was the fact that the children were utterly engrossed and absorbed in what they were doing."

Stone outlined his philosophy in a pamphlet entitled, *The Story of a School*, which was published by the British Ministry of Education in 1949.

1948 THE NASHVILLE COUNCIL FOR THE EDUCATION OF CHILDREN UNDER SIX. On March 27, 1948, a group of 27 individuals met in Nashville, Tennessee at the invitation of Polly McVickar, then director of Vanderbilt Cooperative Nursery School. This small group was the forerunner of the Southern Association for Children Under Six. The council agreed to the following goals:

"To promote an understanding of sound standards for nursery and kindergarten education by acquainting the public with the values of good education for children under six.

To coordinate all individuals and organizations engaged in the various services for young children in the community.

To promote and support nursery school and kindergarten legislation as well as all other measures dealing with the welfare of young children.

To extend and widen information on the educational needs of children under six, through meetings to include discussions, educational films, demonstrations, talks, and reports."

Invitations for membership were sent to all persons in the community who were interested in these goals. One thing that was unusual for that period of time in the South was the fact that the Nashville Council was open to all persons, "regardless of race or religious belief." The Nashville Council was one of the first organizations in the South to work for a positive change in race relations.

In 1950, the Nashville Council held its first conference and invited interested parties from the southern part of the U.S. to join in their efforts on behalf of children. One hundred and thirty-four persons from nine southern states attended the conference. In 1951, a second conference was held with 140 persons in attendance. The keynote speaker for both meetings was Jimmy Hymes. *Note*: Most of the material on the Nashville Council and the later material on SACUS comes from unpublished notes by Dr. Alma David (*See David nd*).

1952 SACUS THE SOUTHERN REGIONAL ASSOCIATION ON CHILDREN UNDER SIX was formally organized in March 1952, in Louisville Kentucky as a logical outgrowth of the Nashville Council. The first officers were: Gean Morgan, Chairperson, Ralph Witherspoon, Vice-Chairperson for Programs, Opal Wofford, Vice-Chairperson for Public Relations. In 1954, the word "regional" was deleted and the official name became the Southern Association on Children Under Six (SACUS).

In 1971, SACUS opened a business office in South Carolina. Helen Harley served as the first business manager. In 1973, SACUS began publication of its journal, *Dimensions*. The original editor was Joan First. In 1990, SACUS had over 16,000 members. The current business offices of SACUS are in Little Rock, Arkansas. For detailed highlights concerning the development of SACUS, see David (nd), and Osborn (1989).

1952 THE NEW MATH. Following World War II, a number of educators began working to change the teaching of mathematics.

This group felt that children should know the "why" of mathematics as well as the "how." According to Johnson and Rahtz (1966, p. 3): "What is valuable about the new mathematics is not that it is new but rather that it offers an opportunity to learn mathematics in a more meaningful way that had been heretofore possible." In 1952 at the University of Illinois, Beberman began working on the logical structure of mathematics and creative ways of teaching. Other projects quickly followed at the University of Maryland, Minnesota, and Syracuse. At Stanford, Suppes designed a program for the elementary grades. Suppes found first graders could perform geometric constructions usually taught in tenth grade geometry. As a result of Sputnik, large federal grants were made for the improvement of math in the curriculum.

1953 THE DEPARTMENT OF HEALTH, EDUCATION, AND WELFARE (HEW) was established to replace the old Federal Security Agency. Also in 1953, Dr. Jonas Salk developed the first effective vaccine for preventing poliomyelitis.

1954 THE U.S. SUPREME COURT (Brown vs. Board of Education). Surprising as it may seem, there is no reference to education and/or schools in the United States Constitution. Apparently our founding fathers meant for schools to be regulated at the local level. Nevertheless, one of the most powerful influences in the field of education over the past four decades have been the decisions reached by the Supreme Court. During this period, the courts have applied the concept of constitutional rights to nearly every aspect of education.

In 1954, the Supreme Court felt that local doctrines of "separate but equal" violated the 14th Amendment of the Constitution. In Brown vs. Board of Education (1954), the court ordered school districts to integrate their programs and "proceed with the integration of schools with all deliberate speed." In 1960 the court added, "the vigilant protection of constitutional freedoms is nowhere more vital than in the community of American Schools" (Shelton vs. Tucker, 1960).

1956 LE LECHE LEAGUE was established by a group of women to provide mothers with information on breast feeding.

Research showed that this method contributed to the child's well-being and the mother-child relationship. The league also provides information on child birth, child care, and related subjects (*Le leche* is Spanish for the milk).

1957 THE NATIONAL COMMITTEE FOR THE DAY CARE OF CHILDREN was established during a meeting of the National Conference on Social Work in Philadelphia. Sadie Ginsberg and Elinor Guggenheim were the founders of this group. It is concerned with the betterment of children in day care and has worked to get the federal government to assume responsibility for child care which had lapsed with the ending of the Lanham Act. Originally the committee was composed of professionals. In 1968, they broadened their scope and changed their name to the Day Care and Child Development Council of America.

1957 SPUTNIK. Russia launched the first manned spacecraft. Following this event there was great competition between Russia and the United States to establish "first achievements" in space. During this period, several surveys were conducted which suggested that Russia led the United States in technological and scientific study. Many persons in the United States, fearful that America would "lose the race in space" began pressuring the schools to improve courses in the sciences and technological areas. As a result, many schools began to accelerate programs in science and mathematics.

In 1958, Congress passed the National Defense Education Act (NDEA). The overall concern prevalent in the United States at that time can be seen in the wording of the first section of the NDEA Bill (HR 13274). It read: "It is no exaggeration to say that America's progress in many fields of endeavor in the years ahead; in fact, the very survival of our free country — may depend in a large part upon the education we provide our young children now."

There was no doubt — from the nursery to the university, a number of critics questioned the entire educational system. Perhaps the foremost critic was Admiral Hyman Rickover, father of the nuclear submarine. In his book, *Education and Freedom* (1959), Rickover emphasized the return to "basic education" as the best way to restore the United States to its position of educational prominence.

1960. SHELTON VS. TUCKER. In a case involving teachers in Arkansas, the Supreme Court applied the constitutional principle of free speech to the field of education. An Arkansas statute had required teacher applicants to reveal any organization to which they held membership. Some teachers refused to do so, citing the fourteenth amendment and their "right to personal association and academic freedom." The Supreme Court agreed and held that teachers had "a right to free association, a right closely allied to freedom of speech and a right which, like free speech, lies at the foundation of a free society." The court added, "the vigilant protection of constitutional freedoms is nowhere more vital than in the community of American Schools."

1960 SUMMERHILL AND THE FREE SCHOOL MOVEMENT. The free school or "natural" school movement can be traced to the philosophical writing of Rousseau and Freud. The most famous exponent of the point of view is A. S. Neill. His book, *Summerhill*, describes forty years of experimenting with the free school concept in Leiston, England. At Summerhill, children attend classes only if they wish. Paradoxically, however, the classes are rather formal. Neill is most interested in the child as he is — "The end product will take care of itself. If the child has the love and freedom to function as a human being ... he will have the chance to live a happy life." Snitzer (1968, p. 6) quotes Neill, "Freud discovered that the unconscious is the important thing ... There are schools based on the intellect alone. I started a school where emotions would come first."

Holt, Kozol, Goodman, and others have described the stress on grades, school discipline, and the authoritarian structure of the contemporary school. A number of communities have organized free schools to offer alternatives to the regular classroom. Frost (1968) has several chapters on the free school movement in *Early Childhood Education Rediscovered.*

1963 BUREAU OF EDUCATION FOR HANDICAPPED CHILDREN. President Kennedy has a sister who was handicapped and he actively lobbied to establish a bureau which would be concerned with the education of the handicapped. Later this bureau became the Office of Special Education and Rehabilitative Services.

1963 COLORADO: CHILD ABUSE LAW. Child abuse is not a new phenomenon. What is new is the attempt to recognize and deal with the problem more effectively. Today all states have laws against cruel and unusual punishment of children. However, prior to 1963, cases often went unreported and estimates on the extent of child abuse were largely unknown. Physicians were often reticent to report cases of abuse because of the danger of lawsuits. Colorado, recognizing the problem, passed the first law in 1963, which made it mandatory for health care professionals to report any suspected case of child abuse to welfare authorities for civil or criminal action.

By 1964, all states had laws which required physicians to report suspected child abuse. In 1975, the Department of Health, Education and Welfare required state agencies administering social services to "provide for the reporting of known and suspected instances of child abuse and neglect." These regulations were extended to include not only parents but persons who may care for young children.

By 1985, each individual state had some legal sanctions which protected children from abuse and neglect. In 1989, twenty states had laws which required *all citizens*, regardless of professional status, to report any case of suspected abuse. Most states require that teachers and caregivers *must immediately* report any suspected case of child abuse.

Please note the term, "immediately." The courts have generally held that while caregivers may report a case of abuse to a supervisor (director, principal, etc.) — it is still the responsibility of the caregiver to personally determine that the proper authorities have been notified. In other words, just notifying your supervisor is not sufficient ... if the supervisor fails to report the incident to the proper agency or authority.

In *Slaughter of the Innocents*, Bakan (1971, p. 7) graphically describes the problem of child abuse as follows: "Children have been brought to hospitals with skulls fractured and bodies covered with lacerations ... Children have been beaten, starved, drowned, held in ice water baths ... and burned with hot irons and steam pipes. They have been systematically exposed to electric shock; forced to swallow pepper, soil, feces, urine, and alcohol ... had their limbs held in open fire; placed on roadways where automobiles would run over them ... bitten, knifed, and had their eyes gouged out."

148

Estimates on the extent of child abuse range from 50,000 to 500,000. Most authorities in the field feel that there are still many cases of abuse which go unreported. In 1970, Gallup conducted an extensive national survey and reported that an average of 9. 3 children per 100,000 suffered from physical abuse.

1964   GRIFFIN VS. THE SCHOOL BOARD.   In 1955 the Supreme Court said (Brown vs. Board of Education) that school districts should, "proceed with the integration of schools with all deliberate speed." However, progress was very slow in the years following the Brown decision. Finally in 1964 (Griffin vs. The School Board), the Supreme Court declared that "the time for 'deliberate speed' has run out and that schools can no longer justify denying children their constitutional rights." As a result of this decision, a number of procedures were set up to insure integration. *See 1971, Swann vs. Charlotte-Mecklenburg Board of Education.*

1964   NAEYC.   In 1964, the National Association for Nursery Education (NANE) changed its name to the National Association for the Education of Young Children. The Association felt that this name more accurately described the group and its mission. Witherspoon (1976) describes the period from 1958-1968 as a period of transition for NANE. It was during this period that NANE was reorganized into NAEYC. Witherspoon refers to this period as the "tempestuous years." In 1964, NAEYC also changed the name of its journal from, *The Journal of Nursery Education* to *Young Children. See NANE Bulletin, 1945.* In the period following this organizational change, NAEYC experienced phenomenal growth in membership. In 1990, NAEYC had 73,000 members. The reader is referred to Hewes (1976b) for a more detailed description of the history of NAEYC.

1964 EVENTS LEADING TO HEAD START. By the Fall of 1964, the wheels were in motion for Project Head Start. No single person or event caused Head Start but rather a series of events which culminated in the creation of the program. In many ways, all the events described in this book contributed to bringing the early childhood field to this moment in time. However, several things seem particularly significant:

Freud prepared the way by citing the importance of the early years; Eliot in bringing the nursery school to this country and making it an effective educational experience; Piaget in his studies on intelligence; Wellman in pointing out that I.Q. was not fixed; the WPA and War Nurseries in showing that the nursery school experience could be profitable for all children; the professional organizations, NAEYC and ACEI, in keeping the idea of preschool education before the profession and the public.

The Civil Rights movement led by Dr. Martin Luther King, Jr. and the 1954 Supreme Court decision helped America to focus on the needs of all minority groups. Books like Galbraith's *The Affluent Society* and Herrington's, *The Other America* provided the general public with a intensive view of the effects of poverty. Bloom's, *Stability and Change in Human Characteristics* dramatically illustrated the importance of the early years of life and the relative difficulty of effecting changes in later life.

The Moynihan Report. This report was actually titled *The Negro Family: The Case for National Action.* The report surveyed social implications of family instability and concluded that basic difficulties incurred by the American Negro had one common source: the weakness of the family structure which served to perpetuate the cycle of poverty and deprivation.

In the late 1950s and early 1960s, researchers were working with enrichment programs for young children. Some of these workers and their programs (cited earlier) included: Susan Gray at Peabody; Morton and Cynthia Deutsch at the Institute for Developmental Studies; David Weikart at the Perry Preschool Project in Michigan; Annamarie Roeper and Irving Sigel at the City and Country School and the Merrill-Palmer Institute in Michigan. The Ford Foundation also sponsored experiments in early school admissions for poor children.

In 1961, the U.S. Office of Education brought together supervisors of elementary education from 64 major American cities to discuss the problems of urban elementary education. Describing these meetings in *American Education*, Mackintosh said, "It was a litany of failure loss and anxiety ... a number of supervisors noted that often much damage was done before the children started to school ... special tutoring, home study centers, field trips ... have all been tried, but the lag is so great."

In a special message to Congress (January 12, 1965), President Lyndon Johnson discussed his recommendations for education. Included in this message was a special reference to preschool programs. He said, "Education must begin with the very young. The child from the urban or rural slum frequently misses his chance even before he begins school ... Today almost half of our school districts conduct no kindergarten classes. Public nursery schools are found in only about 100 of our 26,000 school districts. We must expand our preschool program in order to reach disadvantaged children early. Action on a wide front will begin this summer with a special 'Head Start' program for children who are scheduled to begin school next fall."

By the time President Johnson launched the Great Society and established the Office of Economic Opportunity, the nation was ready. As one early childhood educator said, "The iron is hot," and another replied, "The field of early childhood education will never be the same." The programs for preschool children had moved to the national level and began to offer programs for all the nation's children.

1964 MATERNAL AND CHILD HEALTH. Congress passed the Maternal, Child Health, and Mental Retardation Act to provide funds to deal with premature birth, infant mortality, retardation, and neurological disease. Another law, The Mental Retardation and Community Health Centers Act improved service, teaching, and research in the area of the mentally retarded.

1965 THE ELEMENTARY AND SECONDARY EDUCATION ACT. Public Law 89-10 was an act "To strengthen and improve educational quality and educational opportunities in the Nation's elementary and secondary schools." The bill was approved by the House in March of 1965 and adopted by the Senate one month later. This bill was the largest appropriation ever made by the federal government to education. The law authorized $1,300,000,000.00 in federal funds "to be channelled into the nation's classrooms." This law, ESEA, and the Office of Economic Opportunity Act (which included the Head Start program) caused the 89th Congress to be named "the Education Congress."

There were five titles to ESEA: (1) To strengthen elementary and secondary school programs for educationally deprived children in low-income areas. (2) To provide additional school library resources, textbooks, and other instructional materials. (3) To finance supplementary educational centers and services. (4) To broaden areas of cooperative research. (5) To strengthen state departments of education.

1965 PROJECT HEAD START. In the fall of 1964, the Office of Economic Opportunity considered establishing a "Kiddie Korps" to help the children of poverty. Fortunately the name was changed to Project Head Start. According to Greenburg (1990, p. 41): "Head Start had been 'invented' ... as a 'military strategy' in the War on Poverty." Its purpose was to provide a comprehensive health, nutritional and educational experience for young children. It was hoped that providing an enriched summer program for lower class children would give them a "head start" into life and ultimately reverse the poverty cycle. Sargent Shriver, Director of OEO, established a planning committee to frame the broad outlines of Head Start. The committee included: Robert Cooke (Chairperson), George Brain, Urie Bronfenbrenner, James L. Hymes, Jr., John H. Niemeyer, D. Keith Osborn, Jacqueline Wexler, and Edward Zigler. The executive secretary of the committee was Jule Sugarman. Greenburg (1990) details many of the significant events and little known facts which created the concept of Head Start and which led up to the establishment of the Head Start planning committee.

In February, 1965, the planning committee submitted a report to Mr. Shriver. In the report the committee said, "The early years of childhood are the most critical point in the poverty cycle ... Special programs can be devised for four and five year olds which will improve the child's opportunities and achievements." The committee also emphasized the importance of the family in the education of the child (See Osborn reference 1966, for a full committee report). That month President Johnson formally announced Project Head Start. Julius Richmond, Dean of the New York Upstate Medical School, was named the Project Director. Jule Sugarman, an official in the Community Action Program of OEO, was named Assistant Director, and D. Keith Osborn, Chairman of Community Services of the Merrill-Palmer Institute, was named Educational Director.

In its first summer there were 652,000 children in 2,500 centers employing 41,000 teachers and using over 250,000 other workers including volunteers. In August 1965, President Johnson announced that Project Head Start would continue on a year-round basis as a permanent program. The ripple effect of Head Start on subsequent nursery, kindergarten, and other programs is discussed in the *Living History* series, edited by James Hymes. A comprehensive history of Project Head Start has been written by Zigler and Valentine (1979).

In 1989, there were approximately 450,000 children enrolled in Project Head Start. Of this group 10% were five years old; 62%, four; 25%, three; 3% under three years of age. In the twenty-five years from 1965 to 1990, Head Start had served almost 11 million children.

1965 CONTRIBUTIONS OF HEAD START. Head Start made many contributions to the early childhood movement. Perhaps foremost was the awakening of the general public to the importance of the early years. Head Start also laid a foundation for further research in early childhood—in terms of preschool curriculum, learning materials, evaluation, the role of the teacher, and the role of the family. By utilizing the concept of the Child Development Center, Head Start emphasized the contributions of various disciplines to childhood — particularly, child development, education, medicine, social work, and nutrition. Head Start's medical, dental, and psychological program aided in early identification of physical and psychological problems. Head Start made extensive use of volunteers, utilizing over 100,000 persons in the Summer of 1965. Volunteers ranged from Ms. Lyndon Johnson and her daughter to congressional wives, church groups, students, and parents of children attending the program.

Recognizing that only a few persons were actually qualified (in terms of expertise of early childhood plus knowledge of the needs of poor children and their families), Head Start established a massive training program. In its first year, Head Start contracted with the National Universities Extension Association (NUEA) to provide a six day orientation for 40,000 teachers. In 1966, in order to continue training, the project established regional training officers in each state. In 1967, Head Start began in-service programs to upgrade paraprofessionals.

153

One of the most significant contributions occurred in the changes which took place in families and communities. Parent Advisory Boards were established and many of these groups took executive responsibilities; making decisions on curriculum and hiring personnel. The true flavor of parental and community involvement is seen in Greenberg's insightful, *The Devil Has Slippery Shoes.*

Head Start was not without problems. Early research reports showed significant gains, particularly in I.Q. scores and language development. However, some follow-up studies (Wolff & Stein, 1966) often showed that these initial gains "washed away." In answer to some of these criticisms, Project Follow Through was established in the hope that further enrichment (following the child's departure from Head Start) would provide a sustained pattern of gain. Gordon Klopf, Bank Street College, served as Chairperson of the Planning Committee for Follow Through. Committee members included three persons from the old Head Start Planning Committee: Edward Zigler, Urie Bronfenbrenner, and D. Keith Osborn. Robert Egbert served as the first director of Follow Through. Established in 1968 (under the OEO Act) Follow Through subsidized nineteen program models each utilizing various curriculum alternatives. Klein (1969) discusses these "planned variations" in detail.

1965-1970 ENRICHMENT VS. INSTRUCTION. In the years following Head Start, a controversy arose which Elkind labelled enrichment vs. instruction. Some educators and psychologists attacked the "child development type" of nursery school program which emphasized the Freudian slanted social-emotional approach and utilized play, movement, the dramatic and creative arts as a major part of the curriculum. These critics suggested a structured, systematic program which emphasized cognitive skills. Some programs like Bereiter-Englemann, placed heavy emphasis on language and a "no nonsense" approach to early childhood education. By the early 1970s some changes had begun to take place — with both sides recognizing some values relative to each point of view. The cognitive group began to recognize the value of play and manipulation of materials. The child development group began to introduce cognitive concepts in the curriculum in a more systematic fashion. The reader is referred to several articles which give the flavor of this controversy: Fowler (1962); Elkind (1969, 1970); Biber (1968, 1971); Bereiter (1972); and Zigler (1970).

154

1965-1980 INNOVATIVE PROGRAMS IN EARLY CHILDHOOD. Lavatelli, in her introduction to Evans' book, stated that the sixties might be called the "Decade of Early Childhood Education." Fallon (1973) stated, "Early childhood education in the United States appears destined for as much development as any other single level of education during the decade of the seventies."

Following Head Start's initial program during the summer of 1965, millions of dollars were made available for programs in early childhood education. The Office of Economic Opportunity provided over 20 million dollars for program research under Title II of the OEO Act. In addition, the Elementary and Secondary Education Act (ESEA) provided large sums of money, particularly under Titles I and II for research, demonstration, and innovative programs. Project Follow Through received thirty million dollars initially to provide innovative programs to continue progress made by Head Start children.

As a result a proliferation of programs ensued. For example, Klein (1969) distinguishes twelve planned variations; Fallon (1973) forty innovative programs. In an extensive analysis, Parker (1972) cites fourteen different programs in terms of their curriculum goals and objectives. The reader is referred to these references for a discussion of program variations. In addition, Evans (1971) and Weber (1970) are recommended for their treatment of the various philosophies influencing early childhood education programs.

While it is difficult to compare this wide variety of program models, a few generalizations can be drawn: (a) Most models believe that children should not be left to "unfold" like the old Froebelian philosophy. (b) Children under six can profit from an enriched, systemic curriculum. (c) Most programs believe in the importance of the family becoming involved in the total educational process — many programs send teachers into the home to work directly with the parents Example: Gordon and Weikart. (d) Models emphasize the importance of ego development, or enhancement of self image. (e) Most programs have provisions for individualized instruction. (f) Programs usually emphasize skills which are deemed necessary to insure success in later school performance.

While all programs emphasize the importance of the early years of life, some programs emphasize education prior to two years of age and often make use of home instruction. Programs differ in other ways: (a) Structure: Some programs use high structure (Becker-Englemann), some a moderate amount (New Nursery School; Montessori, Ypsilanti); other models have very little structure (British Infant School). (b) Reinforcement: Some programs utilize token reinforcement; most rely on social reinforcement and all models strive ultimately for intrinsic reinforcement. (c) Curriculum: Some programs emphasize cognitive aspects of curriculum; others social-emotional, creative areas. While all programs recognize the importance of language, there is variation on how much emphasis is placed in this area. (d) Teacher role: Some programs emphasize an active, direct role for the teacher; others assign the teacher the role of "stage setter;" others a passive, non-directive role. (e) Activities: In some models, children have a wide variety of activities available; in others, there is little or no choice in activity selection.

In studying the various innovative models available in early childhood education, there are some reservations which the student should recognize: (a) Model programs are usually well-funded. Because of the experimental nature of many models, they are often expensive, costing several thousand dollars per child, per year. Duplication of a program and expensive educational material, is usually too costly for the average school system. (b) Child to teacher ratio in a model program is usually 3:1 to 4:1. (c) Model programs have an intensive in-service program complete with on-going evaluation available to the teacher. (d) There may be a "halo" effect. A new model often motivates teachers to "do their best." As a result of the high motivation, rather than the model, per se, children may show improvement. (e) Some models have experienced difficulty in "traveling," i.e., a model may work well in the research setting, but may not yield the same results when tried in another section of the country. (f) Generally children in a program will show improvement in areas which have been emphasized by the model. Thus: Children in a program which emphasizes language — generally improve in language; children in a program which stresses creativity and problem solving became more skilled in these areas.

Perhaps a final generalization is the most valuable to remember: *To date, no single program has been found to be the best program for all children — boys and girls; low-income and middle class.* As Hodges (1985) so aptly stated, "It would seem that any well designed, well implemented program carefully delivered with care and with careful supervision of teachers and with support of supervisors pack the 'same wallop' irrespective of model ... you get what you teach for — and teachers do make the difference."

In his review of program models and teaching practices Powell (1986, p. 65) states: "Taken together or separately these studies do not provide a solid empirical base for advocating one program or teaching method over another." However, in his review of a wide variety of studies Powell does raise some probing questions in terms of different types of programs. He states (p. 66): "The studies do raise crucial questions about the effects of didactic versus nondidactic approaches, and the experiences of boys versus girls in early childhood programs."

Unfortunately there is still no definitive answer for the elusive "best program." There are major research limitations in curriculum comparison studies. In the final analysis it would seem that all models can "point with pride" at their successes and "view with alarm" some of their shortcomings. *Note*: Not everyone would agree with this statement. *See the section entitled, Child Development vs. Academic Curriculum.*

1965 LEARNING CENTERS. In the 1960s and 1970s the idea of a "learning center" gained in popularity. According to Norton (1966, p. 7): "There has been a shift in emphasis from teaching to learning. There is now a greater responsibility placed on the student for self-direction, self-learning, and self-evaluation."

The learning center serves as an area for experimenting with new materials, allows for pupil self-selection, provides economy of teacher time, and encourages the use of all types of instructional materials. Norton has an extensive bibliography listing descriptions of learning centers throughout the country and commercial sources of supply.

1966 THE PLOWDEN REPORT and THE BRITISH INFANT SCHOOL. The British Central Advisory Council published a massive 1,200 page report entitled, *Children in Their Primary Schools*. The president of the Advisory Council was Lady Bridget Plowden and the report is popularly known by her name.

The Plowden Report clearly shows the influence of Froebel, Dewey, Russell, Issacs, Piaget, and Stone in outlining ideas for British Infant Schools. The report states that the child is an active agent in his own learning. The role of the school is to support the child's individual development.

The report also cites the importance of the undifferentiated day. "The strongest influence making for the free day has been the conviction of some teachers ... that it is through play that young children ... may plan when to do work assigned to them and also have time in which to follow personal or group interests of their own choice."

Early roots of the British Infant School can be seen in Rousseau and Dewey. *See Bertrand Russell (1926); Report of the Primary School (1931);* and *The Story of a School (1949).*

Lillian Weber and Barbara Day have studied in England and intensively examined British Infant Schools. Their books: Weber, *The English Infant School and Informal Education,* and Day, *Open Learning in Early Childhood,* present the reader with a comprehensive discussion of these programs.

1967 BEHAVIORAL OBJECTIVES. Since Rousseau, if not before, the field of education has a way of jumping on band wagons and "going with the flow." In 1967, USOE requested proposals from Colleges of Education which called for educational specifications for a comprehensive teacher education program for elementary teachers. New terms began creeping into educational jargon. Many of these terms were taken over from the U.S. Department of Defense and were terms which had heretofore been used exclusively by industry. Terms like accountability, mastery learning, performance criteria, flow charts, behavioral objectives and competency based education (CBE), and competency based teacher education (CBTE). By 1975, sixteen states had mandated CBE and CBTE programs for Colleges of Education.

CBE is an educational system where expected pupil outcomes are specified; learning activities focus on the attainment of these outcomes; and both pupils and teachers are assessed to determine whether or not the expected outcomes have been achieved.

158

In the 1970s, CBE programs were designed for elementary and secondary schools. Vance (1973) has written an interesting book using this approach. Chapters 1, 2, and 3 will be particularly helpful to the student interested in CBE. Robison and Schwartz (1972) as well as Butler, et al., (1975) have texts which deal extensively with the subject.

1966 NATIONAL ORGANIZATION FOR WOMEN was founded by Betty Friedan. NOW has over 100,000 members in the U. S. and has worked toward the elimination of sexual discrimination in all areas of society. NOW believes that women should be equal partners in society and share equally in the responsibilities of family life.

NOW, along with the general changes in attitudes about the roles of men and women in society, has caused teachers in the field of early childhood education to re-evaluate the teaching of sex roles to young children.

1967 ERIC/EECE. The Office of Educational Research and Improvement, ERIC (the Educational Resources Information Center) is the largest educational database in the world. Included in the ERIC system are 16 clearinghouses, each responsible for collecting and disseminating information on a specific area in education. The ERIC Clearinghouse on Elementary and Early Childhood Education (ERIC/EECE) deals specifically with information relating to the education and development of children from birth through age twelve.

Each month, abstracts and bibliographic information for more than 1,200 documents and 1,500 journal articles on all phases of education are entered into the ERIC database and listed in two publications: RIE, *Resources in Education*, and CIJE, *Current Index to Journals in Education.* ERIC/EECE was established at the University of Illinois in 1967. Dr. Lilian G. Katz is director of the elementary and early childhood center.

1968 ELEMENTARY AND SECONDARY EDUCATION ACT is amended by Congress to authorize regional centers for the education of handicapped children and special centers for deaf and blind children.

1969 OFFICE OF CHILD DEVELOPMENT. In 1969, President Richard Nixon transferred Project Head Start from the Office of Economic Opportunity to the Department of Health, Education and Welfare and created the Office of Child Development (OCD). This office was established to administer Head Start and the Children's Bureau. Jules Sugarman served as Acting Director until the President appointed Edward Zigler as first director of OCD. In 1977, under the Carter administration, this office was "reorganized" out of existence and the Administration for Children, Youth, and Families was established. Blandina Cardenas was named Commissioner of ACYF.

1969 INTERNATIONAL JOURNAL OF EARLY CHILDHOOD was first published in 1969. This journal is operated under the sponsorship of the World Organization for Early Childhood Education. *See OMEP 1948.* Each article in the journal is written in two to three languages. The first editor was Ann Mullins from London, England.

1969 THE OPEN CLASSROOM. During the 1960s a number of educators visited the British Infant Schools and brought the concept of the open classroom to the United States. However, as Devaney (1974, p. 3) points out, "... some American teachers worked this way for years without thinking they were borrowing from the British." Certainly the concept of the open classroom has many roots — Rousseau emphasized the importance of "natural education." Cizek and Dewey mention the value of allowing children to work according to their own interests. Child development and humanistic psychology have influenced this movement as have writers like Kohl, Holt, and Moustakas.

Day (1980, p. 6) defines the open classroom as a humanistic approach that centers on developing responsibility for discovery learning in children. "The teacher no longer teaches just by telling but instead facilitates or guides learning by providing an interesting and meaningful environment. Classroom organization is more informal and the curriculum emphasis is focused on integrating various subject areas to take advantage of the children's interests."

Weber (1971, p. 11) defines informal education in this manner, "Informal as I understand it, refers to the setting, the arrangements,

160

the teacher-child, and child-child relationships that maintain, restimulate, if necessary, and extend what is considered to be the most intense form of learning, the already existing child's way of learning through play and through the experiences he seeks out for himself."

A number of publications have been issued since 1969 which discuss the open classroom concept. The reader is referred to Day (1980), Kohl (1969), and Silberman (1975).

1969 TINKER vs. DES MOINES. In this historic case the Supreme Court stated that the rights established in the Shelton decision *See 1960, Shelton vs. Tucker*, extended to students. In its decision the court stated, "First amendment rights, applied in light of the special characteristics of the school environment, are available to teachers and students. It can hardly be argued that either students or teachers shed their constitutional rights to freedom of speech or expression at the schoolhouse gate."

The decision by the court was far from unanimous. In a strongly worded dissent, Justice Black stated that the court had begun "a new revolutionary era of permissiveness in this country fostered by the judiciary by taking on authority to itself rather than to the State's elected officials charged with running the schools, the decision as to which school disciplinary regulations are reasonable."

1969 THE RIGHT TO READ PROJECT. Educators had become increasingly alarmed that children were unable to read effectively. On September 23, 1969, James Allen, Commissioner of Education, spoke before the National Association of State Boards of Education and launched the Right to Read program.

Allen cited the following statistics: (a) One out of every four students nationwide has a significant reading deficiency. (b) In large city school systems, up to half of the students read below expectations. (c) There are more than three million illiterates in the adult population and (d) About half of the unemployed youth (16-21 years) are functionally illiterate.

In launching the program Allen said, "Therefore, as U.S. Commissioner of Education, I am herewith proclaiming my belief

161

that we should immediately set for ourselves the goal of assuring that by the end of the 1970s the right to read shall be a reality for all — that no one shall be leaving our schools without the skill and the desire necessary to read the full limits of his capability. This is education's 'moon' — the target for the decade ahead."

In 1973, the International Reading Association (IRA) began publishing a series of special reports entitled, *The Right to Read Effort.* These reports are designed to disseminate information on teaching practices which can be adapted to schools and communities.

1969 SESAME STREET In 1969, the Ford Foundation, Carnegie Corporation, and the Department of Health, Education and Welfare (HEW), subsidized the Children's Television Workshop (CTW) under the direction of Joan Ganz Cooney. CTW produces *Sesame Street.* In 1989, after twenty years of continuous operation, *Sesame Street* has an estimated audience of 14 million viewers in the United States and 80 foreign countries.

1969 CHILD PROTECTION AND TOY SAFETY ACT. This act enabled the federal government to recall or prohibit the sale of toys which were shown to be harmful. These toys can include items which contain poisonous substances, have loose parts which a young child can swallow, have sharp points or sharp edges, and catch fire easily.

1971 THE YEAR IN REVIEW. Dr. James L. Hymes, Jr., issued his first annual report on significant events in early childhood. Since its inception, this publication has been one of the best sources for a year by year summary of highlights in the ECE field. It is certainly "must reading" for anyone writing a history book (like this one) — and should be required reading for serious students in early childhood education. The yearly reports were published by Hacienda Press from 1971 to 1987. *See references for complete listing.* Since 1988, *The Year in Review* has been published by NAEYC.

1971 SWANN VS. CHARLOTTE-MECKLENBURG BOARD OF EDUCATION. On April 20, 1971, the U.S. Supreme Court ordered bussing to achieve racial balance in schools. In its ruling the court stated that if a legally enforceable freedom to transfer students was ineffective in achieving the redistribution of races, then the races must be specifically reassigned and bussed to a school in order to achieve that goal.

1971 THE WEEK OF THE YOUNG CHILD. In the early 1970s, a few affiliate groups in NAEYC sponsored a "day" or a "week" to honor young children. This practice became so popular that, in 1971, NAEYC sponsored a "Week of the Young Child." Since that time this event has attained national prominence. Every year thousands of communities across the country join in the celebration and emphasize the need for better educational programs and quality child care. The "Week of the Young Child" usually occurs in the first or second week of April. In 1976, during the U.S. bicentennial year, NAEYC sponsored a "Year of the Young Child."

1972   TITLE IX of the Education Amendments of 1972, prohibited discrimination on the basis of sex by schools receiving Federal funds. In 1974, government rules and regulations specifically prohibited discrimination in admissions, athletics, and course offerings.

1972 THE CHILD DEVELOPMENT ASSOCIATE CONSORTIUM was established through the Office of Child Development. In November 1971, Dr. Edward Zigler, Director of OCD, announced the plans for the CDA at the NAEYC Convention in Minneapolis. In his statement, Zigler said,

"The need for child care workers in this country over the next decade will be so great that ... we must develop a middle level profession in this country, a middle level professional group to care for our nation's children. The need for the Child Development Associate, an individual who has not had as much scholastic training as those with college degrees, but nevertheless has the competencies to care independently for children, is really central to a major issue in child care. Are we going to provide the children of this nation with developmental child care or are we going to merely provide them with babysitting?"

In his remarks, Zigler particularly acknowledged the role of NAEYC in helping to create the concept of the CDA. Dr. Milton Akers, Executive Secretary of NAEYC, and Dr. Marilyn Smith, Associate Executive Secretary, played active roles in creation of the consortium. Dr. Raymond Williams was the first Executive Director of CDA. The first credential was issued on July 24, 1975.

1972 PROJECT HEAD START established a requirement that ten percent of its enrollment should be reserved for children with handicaps. Because of Project Head Start's national scope, this policy was a contributing factor in helping set the stage for mainstreaming and for PL 94-142. *See 1976, PL 94-142 and 1976, Mainstreaming.*

1972 DAY CARE. The Council of Jewish Women, under the editorship of Mary Keyserling published a revealing study entitled, *Windows on Day Care.* Based on a study of 431 day care centers, Keyserling painted a picture of mothers striving hopelessly to obtain even minimal care for their children.

For years day care has been an unfulfilled promise. Robert Owen established the first Day Care Center in New Harmony, Indiana, in 1822. In 1854, the Nursery and Child's Hospital in New York City established a center for employed mothers of the hospital. Similar nurseries opened in other cities and by 1897, it was estimated that there were 175 day nurseries in the United States (Bremmer, Volume III, p. 677). Early day care was primarily custodial and offered little to children except minimal care.

The 1960 White House Conference stated that the most pressing need was for adequate day care. Past experience leaves little doubt that there will be increasing numbers of women in the work force. In 1940, there were 13,000,000 working women; in 1958, 22 million. During this period the proportion of working women doubled from 16% to 32%.

The Keyserling group recommended federal appropriations of two billion dollars for comprehensive day care. In 1971, Congress passed a day care bill but it was vetoed by President Nixon. In his veto statement the President said, "One of our needs is day care to enable mothers ... to take full time jobs." However, his veto also stated that the intent of the bill was overshadowed by " ... fiscal irresponsibility, administrative unworkability, and family-weakening implications of the system it envisions."

In 1972, the Senate overwhelmingly passed a 2.9 billion dollar child development bill. However, the bill never reached the House.

In 1970, there were over four million working mothers with children under six years of age. In 1980, seven and one half million preschoolers had working mothers. In 1990, the figure had risen dramatically and it was estimated that there were over ten million preschoolers with working mothers.

It is estimated that there are only licensed facilities for 1.7 million children in the United States. An alarming statistic revealed that 1.5 million preschoolers are left alone at least part of every day. The one hundred and first congress finally passed a major child care bill which was signed into law by President Bush on November 5, 1990. *See PL 101-508*. This bill was a significant step for the welfare of children but as Edelman (1990, p. 1) remarked, " ... there are still many battles to be fought to improve the lot of children in the United States."

1973 MULTICULTURAL EDUCATION. In 1973, the Commission on Multicultural Education issued a report which stated that multicultural education should be more than a curriculum — rather it should reflect a whole attitude toward society. According to Parker, Multicultural Education should: (a) Recognize and accept the cultural differences and cultural diversity in the U.S. as a valuable resource. (b) Support a healthy interaction among cultural groups. (c) Support the individual's right to his uniqueness and freedom of choice. Both ACEI and NAEYC have emphasized the importance of a multicultural approach in working with young children.

1973 DIMENSIONS. Published by the Southern Association for Children Under Six, the journal, *Dimensions* first appeared in 1973. Joan First was the original editor.

1974 CHILDREN'S TELEVISION REPORT. The Federal Communications Commission (FCC) adopted a policy statement setting forth voluntary programming and advertising guidelines for children's television. The policy required stations to schedule more meaningful programming for both preschoolers and school aged children. It also required more children's programming to be spread throughout the week. The report did not define "more meaningful" but left the interpretation to the broadcasting industry.

This policy, while laudable in intent, had little effect on the broadcast industry. In 1990, sixteen years later, the FCC was still trying to encourage commercial television to act responsibly in terms of children's TV. At a senate committee meeting, Senator Daniel Inouye called commercial television's programming for children, "rubbish."

1974 THE SUPREME COURT in two similar cases — Goss vs. Lopez and Wood vs. Strickland, ruled that students had the right to fair and responsible treatment in disciplinary actions and that educators were liable in money damages if students' constitutional rights were violated.

1974 PUBLIC LAW 93-247. The nation was becoming more and more aware of the problem of child abuse. In 1974, it was estimated that there were over 300,000 incidents of possible child abuse and maltreatment. In addition, there were over 2,000 child deaths in circumstances where abuse or maltreatment was suspected. In response to public outcry, Congress passed PL 93-247. This law, known as the Child Abuse Prevention and Treatment Act, established the National Center on Child Abuse and Neglect. The first director was Douglas J. Besharov.

The act defines child abuse as: (a) Nonaccidental injury or pattern of injuries without reasonable explanations, such as burns, bites, or beating. (b) Neglect with regard to food, clothing, shelter, or medical care. (c) Sexual molestation of a child for the gratification of an adult, such as rape, incest, fondling of the genitals, or exhibitionism, and (d) Aggressive or excessive emotional deprivation or abuse, or verbal assault to force the child to meet unreasonable demands.

166

In 1975, the Department of Health, Education and Welfare required state agencies administering social services to "provide for the reporting of known and suspected instances of child abuse and neglect." These regulations were extended to include not only parents but persons who may care for young children. By 1985, each individual state had some law protecting children from abuse and neglect. In 1989, twenty states had laws which required *all citizens*, regardless of professional status, to report any case of suspected abuse. Most states require that teachers and caregivers *immediately* report any suspected case of child abuse.

1975 THE EVOLUTION OF CHILDHOOD. In his book, *The History of Childhood*, DeMause devises a psychogenic theory of history. The theory postulates (p. 3) " ... the central force for change in history is neither technology nor economics, but the psychogenic changes in personality occurring because of successive generations of parent-child interactions." Several hypotheses are advanced: (a) Evolution of parent-child relations is an independent source of historical change. (b) The history of childhood is a series of closer approaches between adult and child, with each closing of psychic distances creating fresh anxieties. As the adults work to reduce this anxiety, new child rearing practices are created. (c) The further one goes back in history, the less effective parents are in meeting children's needs.

While psychogenic evolution proceeds at different rates in terms of families or societies, DeMause presents six modes of parent-child relationships over the years.

(1) Infanticide Mode (Antiquity to 4th Century A.D.) As illustrated in this text, children were often seen as the unhappy result of sexual relations and the practice of infanticide was quite common in Greek and Roman times.

(2) Abandonment Mode (4th Century to 13th Century) The rise of Christianity created problems for parents of unwanted children. Christianity claimed that children had souls and infanticide was murder. Parents resorted to the practice of abandoning their children or leaving them with wet nurses.

(3) Ambivalent Mode (14th Century to 17th Century) As the child became a part of the family's emotional life, parents began to

"mold" the lives of their children. The child was seen as clay to be bent or beaten into shape.

(4) Intrusive Mode (18th Century) The intrusive child, according to DeMause (p. 52) was "nursed by the mother ... toilet trained early, prayed with, but not played with, hit, but not regularly whipped."

(5) Socialization Mode (19th to Mid-20th Century) During this period parents were more concerned with training a child, than with conquering his will. Parents attempted to teach the child and to socialize him. DeMause states (p. 52): "The socializing mode is still thought of by most people as the only model within which discussion of child care can proceed and it has been the source of all twentieth century psychological models, from Freud's channeling of impulses to Skinner's behaviorism."

(6) Helping Mode (Mid-20th Century) This mode holds that the child knows his own needs at each stage of his development — even better than his parents. The role of the parents is to empathize with the child, helping him fulfill his own needs. Child rearing is quite permissive — children are seldom struck or scolded and parents often apologize for their actions. The helping mode involves vast amounts of time and energy, active involvement with the child — tolerating his regressions and often being a servant to the child.

This text is somewhat at variance with DeMause on the Infanticide mode. Our position is that there was a long period *prior* to the Infanticide mode. We believe that the prehistoric child (from 2 million BC to the advent of cities — about 3000 BC), was generally desired, nurtured, and cared for. Further, because of the simplicity of life in the hunting and gathering era, the child became almost entirely self-sufficient — perhaps as early as four or five years.

In addition, it is the author's hypothesis that during the 1800s and early 1900s, in sparsely populated regions in the U.S., (e.g., rural areas and along the American Western frontier) — that child rearing practices were more in concert with the Intrusive mode. While the writings of the late 1800s are increasingly child oriented, the writer does not believe this information was readily available to the farmer and the pioneer.

1976 MAINSTREAMING. In 1976, the Council for Exceptional Children defined the concept of "mainstreaming" as follows:

"Mainstreaming is a belief which involves an educational placement procedure and process for exceptional children, based on the conviction that each such child should be educated in the least restrictive environment in which his educational and related needs can be satisfactorily provided. This concept recognizes that exceptional children have a wide range of special educational needs, varying greatly in intensity and duration; that there is a recognized continuum of educational settings which may, at a given time, be appropriate for an individual child's needs; that to the maximum extent appropriate, exceptional children should be educated with non-exceptional children; and that special classes, separate schooling, or other removal of an exceptional child from education with non-exceptional children should occur only when the intensity of the child's special education and related needs is such that they cannot be satisfied in an environment including non-exceptional children, even with the provision of supplementary aids and services."

In mainstreaming it is important for the teacher to encourage interactions between handicapped and nonhandicapped children. The program should be designed to enable the handicapped child to take full advantage of the program. Another plus to mainstreaming is that nonhandicapped youngsters have the opportunity to learn to accept differences in people.

1976 PUBLIC LAW 94-142. This law provided for free and adequate public school education for the nation's eight million handicapped children. This law required that these standards be met by September 1978. The rights included: (a) Access to a free public education in the least restrictive setting. (b) Due process in all matters regarding identification, evaluation, and placement of the handicapped child. (c) Assurances that testing materials and procedures did not discriminate racially or culturally.

1977 PUBLIC LAW 95-49 authorized 1.1 billion dollars for educational programs for handicapped persons. It was estimated that the funds would serve eight million children including deaf, blind, retarded, speech-impaired, emotionally disturbed, and other health impaired children.

1978 PUBLIC LAW 95-225 prohibited the use of minors engaged in sexually explicit conduct for the purpose of promoting any film or printed matter. The committee investigating sexual abuse of minors reported that the sexual exploitation of children for profit had become a multi-million dollar business.

1979 CHILDREN'S TELEVISION TASK FORCE established by the FCC concluded that broadcasters had failed to meet their obligations to improve programming for children. *See 1974, Children's Television Report.* The report did state that the television industry had complied in general with the suggested advertising policies of the FCC. The task force recommended that the FCC institute regulatory action to mandate minimum children's programming requirements. The FCC did not implement this recommendation.

1979 INTERNATIONAL YEAR OF THE CHILD. In 1959 the United Nations passed a *Declaration of the Rights of the Child.* Twenty years later, in recognition of this event, the UN declared 1979 as the International Year of the Child. In April 1978, President Jimmy Carter created a National Commission to lead the effort in the United States. Ms. Jean Young, wife of Ambassador Andrew Young, was named Chairperson of that committee. To celebrate the year, ACEI and NAEYC jointly published eight position papers concerning the welfare of children. With the acclaim given the child through IYC, children received attention and support for their uniqueness and special qualities including their sex roles, legal rights and intellectual freedom.

1979 NAEYC ISSUES SURVEY. In 1979 the NAEYC Governing Board identified six issues — areas of significance to persons working and caring for young children. These issues were: Children's Television Advertising, Child Safety, Care of Infants and Toddlers, Family Support Systems, Child Health and Nutrition, and Multicultural Early Childhood Education. In the March 1980 issue of *Young Children,* background papers are presented which amplify these large issues.

1980 THE DEPARTMENT OF EDUCATION was established by Congress as a separate cabinet level department of the federal government. The department became operational on May 7, 1980. President Jimmy Carter appointed Shirley Hufstedler, a federal judge, the first Secretary of the department.

With the establishment of the Department of Education, the old Department of Health, Education and Welfare (HEW) was changed to the Department of Health and Human Services. President Carter appointed Patricia Harris as the first Secretary of HHS.

1980 INCREASE IN DRUG USE. A 1980 report prepared by the National Institute on Drug Abuse (HEW) pointed out that drug use was increasing at an alarming rate among children.

The report showed that 10.3% of high school seniors in the United States smoked marijuana daily — compared to 5% in 1975 and less than 1% in 1970.

Sixty percent (60%) of all high school seniors had experimented with marijuana at least once — compared to 47% in 1975 and less than 8% in 1970.

Another alarming finding was that marijuana was being used by younger children. In the 12-17 age range about one-fifth (21%) of the children had used pot. Some reports show a one-third increase each year in usage by this age group. Some studies report an increasing number of children used drugs (primarily marijuana and glue sniffing) in the first, second, and third grade.

In 1985, a new drug, crack cocaine, begin to make an appearance in the public schools. From 1985 to 1990, the use of crack cocaine by high school students has increased over 200%. In 1987, a Gallup poll conducted for *Phi Delta Kappa* indicated that the general public rated drug abuse as the number one problem facing the public schools. *See 1990, Major Problems Confronting Public Schools.*

1981 PARENTS AS TEACHERS. This innovative program was established in four Missouri school districts as a home-school partnership designed to give children a good start in life and to assist parents in their role as the child's first teacher. PAT is designed to maximize children's overall development during the first three years of life. In 1985, the Missouri Department of Education provided funds for statewide programs. Other states became interested in this program and by 1990, there were 133 PAT sites in 33 states (Hausman, 1989; PAT, 1990). Mildred Winter was the first National Director of the program.

1983 CONSORTIUM FOR LONGITUDINAL STUDIES. In an analysis of fourteen early intervention studies which included a wide variety of curriculum models, this consortium of outstanding researchers found no significant differences between programs in terms of curriculum variation. Royce, Darlington, and Murray (1983, p. 442) state: "We found no significant differences in later school outcomes related to curricula. All the curricula were successful in reducing school failure ... it may be that finer-grained outcome measures or measures of social learning would find differential effects, but the present indicators did not. It appears that a variety of curricula are equally effective in preparing children for school and that any of the tested curricula is better than no preschool program at all."

1984 THE PERRY PRESCHOOL PROJECT. In 1984, the High/Scope Foundation published results of a 22 year longitudinal study based on children who attended the Perry Preschool in Ypsilanti, Michigan. The initial investigator for this study was Dr. David Weikart. The study was designed to answer the question, (Berrueta-Clement, *et al.*, *1984*, p. *xiii*): "Can high quality early childhood education help to improve the lives of low income children and their families and the quality of life of the community as a whole?"

The study included 123 children. The experimental group was composed of fifty-eight, 3-4 year old children who attended the Perry Preschool for 5 mornings per week for 2.5 hrs/day. The control group did not have a preschool experience. When these children were 19 years of age, the researchers compared the two groups. Table VI shows the results.

172

TABLE VI
COMPARISON OF EXPERIMENTAL & CONTROL GROUPS
HIGH/SCOPE PROJECT

Category	Experimental	Control
Juvenile Crime	31%	51%
Employed	50%	32%
Completed High School	67%	49%
Attended College/Univ	38%	21%
On Welfare	18%	32%

The investigators from High/Scope concluded that the research evidence was "so clear and conclusive and the economic benefits so clear-cut" that public investment in preschool education for disadvantaged children would be advantageous.

In a Ford Foundation report Weikart emphasized that his research findings were not an endorsement of *all* preschool programs. He stated (1989, p. 18), "there is no intrinsic value in a young child leaving home for a few hours a day ... a preschool classroom is just another place for a child to be, unless the quality of the program is carefully defined and maintained." Weikart felt that only programs of "high quality" could benefit youngsters both immediately and over a long period of time.

What does Dr.Weikart mean by high quality? He states (1989, p.18): "The concept is dynamic. It is not a matter of teacher education degrees or even of resources; rather it consists in steadily focusing on the most efficient use of staff skills within a curriculum. The results depend upon the process by which the curriculum is implemented. Thus, programs can be successful in many different settings and with a variety of curricula: home delivered, family-based approaches ... the key remains excellent supervision preferably within a child development curriculum model." Later in this same report Weikart states that a clearly articulated, validated curriculum features child-initiated activities and accepts children at their own developmental level. The program should provide opportunity for problem solving, working effectively with peers and adults and having the opportunity to explore a variety of materials and interests.

173

The reader is referred to the complete study which details the preschool's effects on school success and on socioeconomic success as well as the preschool's effects on social responsibility. *See Berrueta-Clement, et al.; (1984); Schweinhart, et al., (1986); Weikart, (1989).*

1984 DEVELOPMENTALLY APPROPRIATE EDUCATIONAL EXPERIENCES. The author of this text has not been able to determine who initially coined the term, "developmentally appropriate," to describe educational experiences and curriculum practices. Certainly the idea of this concept has been known and discussed for many years. Rousseau, Pestalozzi, and Froebel recognized individual patterns of growth in children. In the late 1800s, teachers like Hill and Bryan would be concerned that the kindergarten curriculum should remain age appropriate to the five year old. In the 1940s, 50s, and 60s, many persons in early childhood would voice concern over pushing children and pressures exerted on youngsters. Harbingers of the concept of "developmentally appropriate" can be seen in journal articles in the 1960s. For example: Bain (1960), *With Life So Long, Why Shorten Childhood?*; Keliher (1961), *Do We Push Children?*; and Butler (1962), *Hurry! Hurry! Hurry! Why?* These articles were twenty years before Elkind (1982), *The Hurried Child.*

In the 1980s both SACUS and NAEYC developed position papers which discussed the needs of children and appropriate learning environments to meet the needs of children. In their position paper, SACUS, (Swick, Brown, & Graves, 1984) described appropriate educational experiences for kindergarten and stated, "Recent trends to incorporate developmentally inappropriate teaching strategies such as workbooks, ditto sheets, and formal reading groups as well as academic skill-oriented curriculum content in kindergarten, raise serious concerns."

In 1986, NAEYC developed a position statement which was similar, but broader in scope. The original NAEYC statement was developed by a commission created for the purpose of developing a position paper on four and five year olds. Bernard Spodek served as Chairperson of the Commission. However, as the Commission developed their statement they believed that "a broader developmental perspective was needed," and decided to enlarge the original work. These original position statements were printed in *Young Children*, September 1986. An expanded version is available in the booklet form (Bredekamp, 1986).

174

NAEYC believes that developmental appropriateness has two dimensions: age appropriateness and individual appropriateness." The position paper defines these concepts as follows: (Bredekamp, 1986, p. 2).

"*Age appropriateness.* Human development research indicates that there are universal, predictable sequences of growth and change that occur in children during the first nine years of life. These predictable changes occur in all domains of development — physical, emotional, social, and cognitive. Knowledge of typical development of children within the age span served by the program provides a framework from which teachers prepare the learning environment and plan appropriate experiences.

Individual appropriateness. Each child is a unique person with an individual pattern and timing of growth, as well as individual personality, learning style, and family background. Both the curriculum and adults' interactions with children should be responsive to individual differences. Learning in young children is the result of interaction between the child's thoughts and experiences with materials, ideas, and people. These experiences should match the child's developing abilities, while also challenging the child's interest and understanding."

These two position statements by SACUS and NAEYC are milestones in articulating appropriate experiences and practices in early childhood programs. The booklet, *Developmentally Appropriate Practice,* will serve as an excellent guide for both professionals and the laity. The state of Virginia has an excellent pamphlet entitled, *Developmental Kindergarten,* which provides a definition and an operational description of their state program (Virginia, Department of Education, 1989).

CHILD DEVELOPMENT VS. ACADEMIC CURRICULUM. *See 1965, Enrichment vs. Instruction.* The controversy of the 1960s, continued to make its presence known in the 1980s. In an extensive research review, Powell (1986) reports studies by Miller and her colleagues (1975) and (1983) comparing the results of didactic and nondidactic programs.

Reports from High/Scope (Berrueta-Clement, *et al.,* 1984; Schweinhart, *et al.,* 1986) traced the effects of three preschool curriculum models on children through age 19. In an interview (Brandt, 1986), Schweinhart stated that researchers at High/Scope had *originally* believed diverse preschool programs could yield positive results with children in spite of their philosophical diversity. For instance in a 1978 study, Weikart had reported (p. 40) "The startling conclusion was reached that, insofar as we could measure intellectual and scholastic performance, all three preschool curriculum models appeared to achieve the same positive results."

However, subsequent studies in 1984 and 1986 (cited above) caused the High/Scope researchers to alter their point of view. In analyzing data from three different programs: (a) a Distar type model, (b) a Piagetian model, and (c) a traditional preschool model, the researchers concluded that *child initiation* models (b) & (c) yielded more positive results in the long run. The reasons for this conclusion? Schweinhart, *et al.*, (1986a, p. 41) reported that the study: "found significant differences at age 15 in social-behavior outcomes among the groups experiencing the various preschool curriculum approaches. The group that received a preschool program using the teacher-directed Distar model, when compared to groups receiving preschool programs that encouraged children to initiate their own activities ... evidence substantially higher rates of self-reported juvenile delinquency and associated problems." The authors added, "The curriculum study's most recent data suggest that there are important social consequences to preschool curriculum choices."

As one would expect, proponents from the "academic camp" vigorously responded to these charges (Gersten 1986; Gersten & White 1986; Bereiter 1986a, 1986b). In their response Gersten and White (p. 19) stated: "Cleverly hidden among the platitudes, voluminous census data and brief but emotional history of the preschool movement ... a disturbing theme is introduced: that direct teaching of academic material to disadvantaged preschoolers tends to socially damage these children and lead to juvenile delinquency." Bereiter and Gersten also criticized the size of the High/Scope sample (18 students per approach) and the methodology employed.

What is the answer? Most researchers and teachers would agree that high quality programs are needed. However, there is still disagreement on the definition of quality. Mitchell (1989, p. 669) provides one of the most complete definitions of quality. "Quality in an early childhood program consists of five essential elements: small group size; favorable staff/child ratios; well-trained staff; a thorough understanding of theories of child development and of principles of early childhood education, coupled with direct experience working with young children; curriculum - a clearly communicated philosophy of education that is based on theories of child development and that is supported by training and good supervision; and strong parent participation - frequent communication between parents and teachers, a variety of ways for parents to participate directly in the education of their children, direct parental influence on the governance of the program, and attention to the needs of parents."

We encourage readers to examine the research studies and critical responses cited in this section and form their own opinion. The research review by Powell, cited above, raises some probing questions concerning the programs and the limitations of the research studies. However, Powell does state (1986, pp. 65-66): "The findings of the studies reviewed here challenge the idea that any theoretically coherent, well-implemented preschool program can have positive effects on children ... now there is persuasive evidence to the contrary."

Perhaps the last word, at least for the present, goes to Schweinhart and Weikart (1986, p. 22): "While Gersten and White make token criticisms of our whole article, likening it to a Fourth of July speech, it is clear that the principal object of our critics' scorn in this 49-paragraph article is a 5-paragraph description of our curriculum study, which we summarized as part of our discussion of the child development curriculum. Bereiter fears that this small study might undo the well-documented case for the educational benefits of direct instruction. By itself it obviously will not, but we hope that it does encourage further early childhood curriculum research and widespread thought about the potential consequences of early childhood curriculum choices."

1985 THE NATIONAL ACADEMY OF EARLY CHILDHOOD PROGRAMS. In one of its most ambitious initiatives, the National Association for the Education of Young Children established the National Academy of Early Childhood Programs. The Academy administers the only professionally sponsored national, voluntary accreditation system for early childhood centers and schools. According to Dr. Marilyn Smith, Executive Director of NAEYC (Quoted from the *Guide to Accreditation*, 1989), "The goal of the accreditation system is to improve the quality of care and education provided for young children in group programs ... All children in group programs must not only be safe and protected but must have the opportunity to experience an environment that enhances children's development." Further she adds, "What does accreditation mean for the field of early childhood education? Accreditation assists families in making decisions about their children's care and education. Accreditation offers agencies, employers, and other program supporters a system for identifying high quality programs ... (and) provides program directors and teachers with guidelines for professional practice."

By 1990, the Academy had accredited over 1,000 programs in fifty states and over 3,600 more programs were in the process of submitting credentials for accreditation. Bundy (1988) presents an interesting account of the process involved when a center decides to apply for accreditation.

1986 EARLY CHILDHOOD RESEARCH QUARTERLY. NAEYC, in association with ERIC/ECE and Ablex Publishing Company, sponsor the *Early Childhood Research Quarterly*. Lilian Katz was the first editor.

1986 RESEARCH IN CHILDHOOD EDUCATION. A second professional research journal also previewed this year. The journal, *Research in Childhood Education*, is published two times a year and is sponsored by ACEI. Robert Cryan was the first editor.

1987 PUBLIC LAW 99-457. This law is similar to PL 94-142 and extends services to children three to five years of age. In addition, the law provides fifty million dollars as a supplemental grant to states to serve handicapped and developmentally delayed children from birth to two years of age. In 1987, only 19 states had some services for children in this age group.

1988 EVEN START was established this year by the U.S. Department of Education. Even Start is a combined child care and parent education/literacy program whose goal is to include parents

178

as "full" partners in the education of their children. The Department of Education provides funds to state and local education agencies.

1988   THE ASSOCIATION FOR THE ACCREDITATION OF MONTESSORI TEACHER EDUCATION.* Montessorians are a diverse group of people. This diversity is recognized in the various Montessori organizations and teacher education courses, each of which emphasizes different aspects of the method. Goodman (1990, p. 8) writes: "Montessori education has become like a multi-faceted jewel, each brilliant reflective surface representing a distinct part of a beautiful whole."

In recognition of and respect for this diversity and a desire for unity among Montessorians, a group of men and women, representing between twenty and thirty training programs met together in February of 1988 in Berkeley, California. The purpose of the meeting was to form a recognized accrediting organization. This organization would establish "essential standards to ensure the quality of courses preparing Montessori teachers; the evaluation and accreditation of Montessori teacher education courses through a process of external peer review; and the encouragement of continued self-improvement of Montessori teacher education courses" (Goodman, *op. cit.*, p. 9). According to Goodman, *loc. cit.*, "an Ad Hoc Committee was formed in the hopes that by working together in the formation of an accrediting agency, the uniqueness of each individual teacher education course could be expressed within a defined Montessori framework." The Association for the Accreditation of Montessori Teacher Education (AAMTE) is a non profit organization incorporated in the State of California. Progress is being made in the refinement of the By-Laws and the accreditation document for final approval and ratification.

- - - - - - - - - - - -

*The author is indebted to Sheryl M. Sweet, for this report on the organization of AAMTE. *Note*: In a private communication with the author, Sweet (1990), observed: "The establishment of AAMTE, with recognition by the United States Department of Education, will remove Montessori education from the classification of 'other' early childhood approaches and bring the method the distinction it deserves in the field of early childhood education. In this final decade of the Century of the Child, Montessori education will have emerged as a recognizable force in the early childhood educational practices."

1988 STATE CERTIFICATION OF ECE TEACHERS. In 1988, McCarthy conducted a survey of all fifty states and the District of Columbia to determine the current standards for teacher certification. McCarthy points out (1988, p. 2): "The certification processes which states use to prepare teachers of young children can best be summed up with one word: *variety.*" Thirty-four states and the District of Columbia have certification specifically identified as "early childhood education" or having some type of certification similar in nature. Generally, patterns of certification, "lie on a continuum from working with children from birth through age 4 to working with children from ages 5 to 9." McCarthy's pamphlet supplies a detailed analysis of the various types and patterns of certification as well as tabular information which lists states who mandate competency assessments.

1989 CDA CONFERENCE. In the summer of 1989, CDA held its first conference in Washington D.C., with 600 persons in attendance. Since its inception in 1975, CDA has awarded over 30,000 credentials, including a number with a bilingual specialization. The CDA credential is now an accepted credential. Forty-eight states and the District of Columbia have incorporated the CDA credential into their regulations for child care staff (Head Start, 1990; Phillips, 1990).

1989 HISTORY OF ECE IN DETROIT. Several years ago Hymes (1972,1977, 1978, 1979) rendered the field of early childhood a great service by conducting a series of "Living History" interviews. Using this oral history technique, Ethel Baker, Sally Brown, Ester Callard, Charlene Firestone, Mary Frew, and Emma Shiefman gathered data on early childhood education and day care in metropolitan Detroit. The result of their efforts is a lively book entitled, *Serving Children Then and Now* (Langlois, 1989). The book traces early kindergartens, the establishment of the Merrill-Palmer School, early day care centers, and Project Head Start in the Detroit area.

Suggestion to other communities: The oral history technique can be an invaluable tool in weaving the history of ECE in your community and/or your state. The Detroit committee recognized that if they did not quickly gather this information, much of it would be lost forever.

1989 ECE CODE OF ETHICS In 1984, the NAEYC Governing Board established an Ethics Commission to explore appropriate principles of ethical action and to identify ethical dilemmas which confront professionals in the early childhood field. Stephanie Feeney was chairperson of the commission. Two surveys were conducted and workshops were held between 1984 and 1988. A working code of ethics was presented at the NAEYC conference in 1988. There are four sections in the code which include responsibilities to: children, colleagues, employees, and the community (Feeney & Kipnis, 1989).

1989 THE YEAR IN REVIEW. Hymes discusses highlights and key events relating to young children in the United States in 1989. A major portion of the review discusses child care in detail and points out the need for federal support. The review also discusses corporate day care and day care in the public school.

For many parents of preschool children the number one problem is the lack of quality child care. Recent statistics indicate that nine million preschoolers spend part of their day in some type of child care. Twenty-eight percent of parents surveyed were dissatisfied with the type of care their children were receiving. In one study by the Census Bureau (1987), mothers with children under one year of age stated that their biggest problem was finding good day care for their infant children. One alarming statistic reveals that 1.5 million preschoolers are left alone at least part of every day.

While the need for good quality child care is ever-present, Hymes points out (1989, p. 4): "National policy on child care has not been seriously discussed since 1971." *Note*: Finally in 1990, Congress and the President responded to parents and the advocates of children and passed a child care bill (see the next entry, PL 101-508). Three professional organizations have excellent position papers and information related to quality day care: (ACEI, Gotts, 1988), (NAEYC, Caldwell & Hilliard, 1985, Phillips, 1987, Howes, 1988), and (SACUS, Dickerson, Ross, & Crum, 1986),

1990 PUBLIC LAW 101-508. FEDERAL CHILD CARE BILL. On November 4, 1990, President Bush signed into law the federal child care bill. According to many child care advocates this legislation was, "one of the most important pieces of family legislation in our nation's history." According to Edelman, (1990, p. 1): "The enactment of federal child care legislation is not only a critical step forward for children and families, but also a milestone in the evolution of a permanent and powerful children's movement ... The bill provides 2.5 billion dollars of new federal child care block grant funds and provisions to protect children in child care. It also provides 1.5 billion dollars over the next five years to help low income families at risk of welfare dependence purchase child care; and 18.2 billion in tax relief for low-income working families."

1990 THE STATUS OF KINDERGARTENS TODAY. In 1950 only about half of the nation's children could avail themselves of kindergarten. Robinson (1987) states that in 1974, half of the states provided kindergarten to 90% of the population. By 1990, kindergarten was available to almost all children in the United States. Robinson notes (1987, p. 23): "The opportunity to attend kindergarten in the United States has changed from a privilege to a right." A major problem continues to exist, however. As ACEI pointed out in their position paper on kindergarten, (1987, p. 235):

"Froebel understood that, like growing plants, children need careful nurturing." (Since Froebel's time) ... "the kindergarten has become an integral part of the education system, but the proponents have had a difficult time maintaining that nurturing focus. There is still a year of school called kindergarten ... (but there is) ... a mismatch between the curriculum and the 5-year-old child."

1990 MAJOR PROBLEMS CONFRONTING THE PUBLIC SCHOOLS IN THE 1990s. Each year since 1969, *Phi Delta Kappa* has authorized the Gallup organization to conduct a national poll on the attitude of the public toward public education. In 17 polls, from 1969-1987, the pubic rated discipline as the number one problem in the schools. However, since 1987, the public has rated drugs as the major problem facing our educational institutions. *Note*: During the last three years, the public has continued to view discipline as a major problem and it was ranked number two in the Gallup poll.

In surveys conducted by other organizations, teachers were asked the same question, "What is the number one problems in your school?" Teachers, in both public and private schools, rated drugs and discipline as the two major problems facing education.

182

In the most recent *Phi Delta Kappa* survey, the public mentioned other major problems. These included: lack of financial support, poor curriculum standards, overcrowding in the schools, difficulty in obtaining and keeping good teachers, integration and busing, and low teacher pay (Elam & Gallup, 1990).

In a 1989 Harris poll, high school students and teachers rated the "top seven" school problems. They listed: drug and alcohol abuse, pregnancy, rape, suicide, robbery, assault, and arson. Also high on their list was: extortion, vandalism, and gang warfare.

It is interesting to contrast these problems with a 1940 report from the police department in Fullerton, California. The police reported that the top seven problems in the Fullerton public schools were: talking, chewing gum, smoking, making noise, running in the halls, getting out of line, and wearing improper clothing.

1990 POSSIBLE CHANGES IN THE PUBLIC SCHOOLS. The most recent Gallup poll (Elam & Gallup, 1990), suggests that the public may be ready for some major changes in their public school system. The poll shows that the public, by a 2:1 margin, favors allowing parents to choose which public schools their children will attend. Arkansas, Iowa, and Minnesota have already enacted laws which permit parental choice and several other states are considering legislation in this area.

Other major proposals include: (a) A nationwide curriculum with national standards and standardized tests. (b) Eighty-three percent believe that more should be done to improve the quality of schools in poorer states and communities and are *willing to pay more taxes to make this improvement.* (c) A large percentage of the public (75% to 18%) favors reducing class size in the elementary grades to 15 pupils per class.(d) Most parents (71% to 21%) endorse after school and summer programs for working parents.

1990 TRENDS IN PREGNANCY AND CHILD BIRTH. Surveys indicate that more women are utilizing prenatal training and prepared child birth techniques as opposed to drug intervention methods. LaMaze is one method of prepared child birth training. Recently there has also been a rise in home birth as a method of delivery.

Unfortunately there are other trends connected with pregnancy and child birth. In the decade of the 1980s, there were over 1 million teenage pregnancies each year. As a rule of thumb the figure of one million pregnancies results in approximately 570,600 live births; 378,500 abortions, and 152,000 miscarriages or stillbirths. It is estimated that 40% of today's 14 year old girls will have been pregnant at least once before the age of 20 (Wallis & Booth, 1985).

In addition to these statistics, in 1990:

50,000 babies are born each year to mothers who have abused alcohol. Fetal Alcohol Syndrome (FAS) is a growing problem which can cause serious physical and mental deficiencies. It is estimated that 20% of all cases of mental retardation are the result of FAS.

3,000 infants were born infected with AIDS.

The rise in the incidence of crack related infant problems has reached epidemic proportions. It is estimated that there are 400,000 "crack babies" in the United States.

1990 CHANGES IN THE NURSERY SCHOOL AND CHILD DEVELOPMENT MOVEMENT. During the first seventy years of the nursery school movement many changes in approach and emphasis have taken place. Nursery school practices and child development research often went hand in hand. The following foci seem most evident during this period:

1. In the 1920s and 1930s major attention was given to physical development and intellectual testing. Child development centers and laboratories reflected this emphasis. Research focused on IQ tests and testing and on developmental norms. The reader is referred to the following texts which reflect the "spirit" of these two decades: Baldwin (1925), Gesell (1928, 1936), Updegraff (1938), and NSSE (1929).

2. In the late 1920s and 1930s, the theories of John Watson also exerted an influence — particularly on parents and child rearing. In assessing Watson's contribution to child rearing Kessen said, "As far as he touched the raising of a child in America, I think it was a total disaster."

3. From the 1940s to the 1960s scant attention was devoted to intellectual growth and more attention is given to physical and social-emotional development. The rising influence of Freud and psychoanalytic theory is particularly noticeable during this period. Texts like Read (1950), and Erikson (1950) reflect this emphasis. The theme for the 1950 White House Conference, *Personality in the Making*, clearly reflects this trend. Erikson's, *Childhood and Society*, was used as the basic reference for the conferees and the sense of trust, autonomy, and initiative formed a philosophical backdrop for the nursery school teacher. Osborn (1960) and others took the Erikson frame of reference and illustrated its practical application in the nursery school. Child development research was dominated by psychoanalytic thought. Referring to this period, Almy states (1968, p. ix): "Psychoanalytic theories dominated child development research and permeated the child-rearing advice of many experts. Too often, the free expression of impulse rather than its eventual mastery and direction was made to seem to be the primary goal for the nursery years."

4. In the 1960s and 1970s, early childhood educators continued to devote attention to social-emotional development but intellectual development began to receive increasing attention from both the researcher and the practitioner.

The beginning of the swing away from the great emphasis on social-emotional development is reflected by Ward as early as 1957. She states (p. 7): "Believing that a very weak point in early childhood education, especially in nursery education, has been the failure of teachers to give adequate attention to ways of developing and guiding the effective thinking of the young child, I have endeavored to challenge fellow teachers to think and experiment in this field." Certainly the flight of Sputnik also caused educators to reflect and reexamine the total educational experience. Writers like Wann, Dorn, and Liddle (1962), Flavel (1963), Almy (1966), and Sigel (1968) had begun to reawaken early childhood educators and researchers to Piaget and cognitive development.

Books like Kamii and DeVries (1978), Weikart (1978), Osborn and Osborn (1985), DeVries and Kohlberg (1987) have presented implications of Piagetian theory for the early childhood educator.

5. Early childhood educators and child development researchers also became involved in another movement during the 1960s and

1970s. The civil rights movement and the war on poverty caused ECE professionals to rethink their priorities and to look for solutions to the social needs of children and families. Researchers are asked to examine diverse school learning conditions for children from a variety of cultural milieus. References which reflect some of the "flavor" of this development include, Greenberg (1967), Miller and Dyer (1975), Schweinhart (1986), and Powell (1986).

Where will the next emphasis be placed? At different periods it seems that child development researchers and early childhood educators "choose" a prophet for the time. Through the years we have gone from Rousseau to Froebel to Hall to Dewey to Gesell to Watson to Freud to Piaget. In an interview with Senn, Sears (1975, p. 42) said, "There does seem to be a kind of tendency in most of us (persons in the ECE and Child Development field) to pick on the works of a great man, and use them as the stepping stone ... and maybe in the early stages as a kind of Bible, for moving forward in a particular scientific field ... Nonetheless, this kind of interest, this enthusiasm for a particular approach, does lead people to study and do research, and ultimately they broaden the problems beyond the special language of the great man and we have a particular area of science moving forward vigorously and expanding."

1990 THE CURRENT STATUS OF THE YOUNG CHILD AND THE FAMILY. In the earlier editions, a number of statistics were presented on the status of the young child and the family. A number of pertinent statistics can be found throughout the text. For the interested reader, a few more salient statistics are presented below which provide insight into the status of American children and their families. At the end of this section, the reader is referred to several sources which will provide additional information on children and families.

•• As late as 1965, only 47% of all American children attended kindergarten. In 1990, 94% of all five year olds attend some kind of kindergarten.

•• 60 percent of mothers of children under six are in the work force. Approximately 25% of these mothers are also heads of household. The forecast is that this figure will increase to 80% within the next five years.

186

•• Sixty-five percent of all mothers with school aged children work outside the home.

•• It is estimated that last year working parents spent over sixteen billion dollars on day care. Hofferth (1989) puts the child care proportion of the family budget at 26% for poor families and 10% for middle income families.

•• Four out of ten children born in the 1990s will spend part of their growing years in a single parent home.

•• There are more than 900,000 fathers in the United States who head single-parent households and who are raising children on their own

•• Twenty-four percent of U.S. infants are born to unmarried women. This figure compares to four percent in 1950.

•• One in five American children lives at the poverty level.

•• Each year 700,000 children are victims of child abuse and neglect.

•• Twelve million children have no regular source of medical care.

•• Four million young women 15-19 are sexually active. Three in ten sexually active teenage females become pregnant. Fifty percent of all out-of-wedlock births are to teenagers.

•• One in every five births in the U.S. is to a teenager. It is estimated that 40% of today's 14 year old girls will have been pregnant at least once before the age of 20.

•• Twenty-five percent of all students are dropouts. In the 10 states with the highest dropout rate the average percentage is 37%. It is estimated that 14 million students are functionally illiterate, even though they graduate from high school.

•• Sixty percent of prison inmates are high school dropouts.

•• By the time they graduate from high school, 75% of all students will have used alcohol.

•• Forty thousand teenagers are injured every year in auto accidents. Eight thousand are killed in alcohol related accidents.

•• Between 4 and 5 million youngsters between the ages of 11 to 17 are smoking pot on a reasonably regular basis.

•• Twenty percent of all current teenagers will spend some time in an alcohol or drug rehabilitation center before they reach 35 years of age.

•• Ninety percent of all persons in the U.S. either has a family member or close personal acquaintance who has a serious alcohol or drug problem.

In their *1990 Report Card*, the Children's Defense Fund lists provides some interesting statistics and tables concerning the U.S. child and family in 1990. A number of the tables offer state by state comparisons on areas ranging from prenatal care, infant mortality, and the status of quality child care. The following statistics are taken from this source:

•• In the year 2000, there will be 4.1 million fewer young adults (18-24) entering the work force than there were in 1985, a decline of 14%.

•• In the year 2000, nearly one-third of the young adults will be from minority groups, compared to less than 25% in 1985.

•• Since 1973, young men's marriage rates have declined by one-third, and the proportion of births that were out of wedlock doubled.

A number of sources were used for the statistics presented above. Several major agencies provide helpful information concerning children and their families. These agencies include UNICEF, U.S. Department of Health and Human Services, Vital Statistics of the United States, U.S. Department of Commerce, Bureau of the Census, Federal Register, National Center for Disease Control, and Children's Defense Fund.

188

1991 TWENTY YEARS IN REVIEW. In 1991, NAEYC plans to publish a book which will contain all twenty of the *Years in Review* written by Hymes.

IN CONCLUSION. This text has attempted to bring together a series of events which have effected young children. Some of these events are encouraging; some give cause for alarm.

We can see wide movement in history's view of its children. From a nonentity (which permitted infanticide and "potting") to a miniature adult (which permitted slavery and sweatshops) to mainstreaming — which attempts to provide all children with the opportunity to reach their fullest potential.

Cultures have ignored children, whipped children, spoiled children, pampered, and shaped them. Teachers have provided catechisms, interest centers, M & Ms, and workbooks.

We see from recent events that as teachers of young children, our task is far from complete. We need to move along many fronts if we are to enhance the lives of children.

Over the years parents and teachers of children have emphasized various "parts" of the child — his religious development, his utility as an economic asset, the development of his character, his physical development, his social development, his emotional development and most recently, his cognitive development.

Zigler has pointed out the dangers of emphasizing one facet of growth to the exclusion of total development. Of course the concept of the "Whole Child and His Total Development" has been around for many years. Perhaps as we view the panorama of historical events we can place all areas of development into their proper perspective and learn the true meaning of this concept. It is often used, but more often misunderstood.

PART II
References, by State, to Significant Events in ECE

This section is for ECE "history buffs." Following earlier editions of *Early Childhood Education in Historical Perspective*, a number of persons asked the author for specific early references to ECE activities on a "state by state" basis. In response to this request, the author conducted an extensive state by state search of "old" references. These included books, journals, and magazines from 1867 to 1960.

The US Department of Education was established in 1867. In accordance with a request from Congress, the Commissioner of Education submitted annual reports on the status of education in the United States. This report is a rich resource for tracking early developments in the kindergarten movement. The Commissioner's first report, 1868-1869, does not contain any mention of kindergarten. In 1870 there is a report on the "*Kindergarten Culture*" by Peabody. In 1871, Peabody wrote a report entitled, "*The Objects of the Kindergarten*" (See references in Bibliography). In reports 1870- 1873, there are some general statistics plus references to specific kindergarten programs. These individual references are recorded below. After 1873, there are general kindergarten statistics from all the states and U.S. territories. From 1875 onward, individual states usually submitted a general report on the status of the kindergarten movement in their particular state.

In July 1990, queries were sent to every state Department of Education and the District of Columbia, asking for information concerning the beginnings of kindergarten and other early childhood programs. In October 1990, queries were sent to state NAEYC presidents for their assistance. The material from state early childhood education supervisors and NAEYC state presidents was quite useful and I wish to gratefully acknowledge their assistance and encouragement. Names of persons who were particularly helpful are listed at the end of Part II. However, I should like to point out that there is considerable variation among states in the definition of terms and in the way that legislation was framed in terms of "permissive or mandatory" legislation. In most cases, I have used the terminology designated by the state. In some instances, respondents were unfamiliar with historic events within their state which had an impact on early childhood education and this information was gathered from other sources. Where possible, the "best" date for the first kindergarten and the first nursery school are given.

What started out to be a "small project" became a giant undertaking. Please be advised that this reference source is far from complete — rather it is a starting place for persons interested in researching reference sources in the early childhood field. The author hopes that this compendium will also help interested parties who wish to research ECE activities which have occurred within their own state. In a number of states there are "history committees" connected with state ACEI and NAEYC groups. For inspiration look at the book published by ECE workers in Detroit (see p. 180).

Symbols: To conserve space, reference numbers are used. The first number refers to a specific journal or magazine reference. The second number to the volume and the third number to the page in that volume. If the reference is a book, an initial is used and the numbers refer to the specific pages in the book. One * is used to designate early kindergartens in the state. Two ** designate the first nursery school in the state. If the name of the first teacher is known, that name is placed in parentheses after the city in which the kindergarten was founded.

Key to Notations:
1 *Kindergarten Magazine*
2 *Kindergarten Review*
3. *Childhood Education*

NE (ACEI, 1935) Kgn. movement in New England
MW (ACEI, 1938) Kgn. movement in Midwest & New York
SE (ACEI, 1939)) Kgn. movement in Southeast, DC, NJ, DE, & PA
W (ACEI, 1940) Kgn. movement in West & AK, HI
KC (ACEI, 1937) Kgn. centennial
N NSSE Yearbook, 1929.
V Vandewalker (1908)
P Committee of Nineteen (1924)

Reports from Commissioner of Education
Note: Pages which appear in the preface are in italics.
E0 = 1870
E1= 1871
E2 = 1872
E3 = 1873
E4 = 1874
E5 = 1875

ALABAMA:
* 1896 Tuscumbia (Lindsay); 1898 Florence (Lindsay)
  1898 Florence free kgn. assn.
* ca. 1900 1st public school kgn., Birmingham
* ca. 1900 Black kgn. est. Calhoun, Tuskegee.
  1948 Full statewide funding
General references: V: 80,123. SE:5,6,7. 1:13,55. 1:9,397.
Industrial kgn: 1:15,505. SE:5,6-7

ALASKA:
* 1919 Fairbanks (Creelman & Bixby)
* 1921 1st public school kgn., Juneau
  1977 State funds specifically appropriated for Head Start

General references: 3:1,262-263. W:67

ARIZONA:
* 1881 Tucson (Moorhouse)
* 1895 Prescott (McGill)
  1898 Arizona State Normal School, kgn. courses
  1901 Permissive legislation for public school kgns.
General references: 3:1,146,487. W: 5-7.

ARKANSAS:
* 1892 Hot Springs
* 1895 1st public school kgn., Hot Springs
    1897 Froebel kgn. assn. (Hot Springs)
** ca.1930 U. of Ark. laboratory nursery school
** 1930 Laboratory nursery school in Little Rock high school home economics dept.
    1937 Permissive legislation for public school kgns.
General references: W:7-9.

CALIFORNIA:
* ca.1870 California (Weddigen?)
* 1873 San Francisco (Semler)
* 1875 Sacrament (Hill);Los Angeles (Marwedel,Severance)
* 1876 Sacramento (Hill)
    1876 Pacific normal trng. school, Los Angeles (Marwedel)
* 1878 Kgn. for deaf & dumb, Berkeley (Stewart)
    1880 Golden Gate kgn. assn.
    1880 CA kgn. trng. school (Wiggin)
* 1880 1st public school kgn., San Francisco
    1893 Permissive legislation for public school kgns.
    1913 mandatory kgn.
    1927 U of CA, Child Study Institute
    1946 state aid to kgn.
General references: V: 18,77, 1: 8,237. W:9-29. 1:9,121. 1:10,584. 2: 5,3.
    2:5,234. 2:5,250. 2:6,71. 2:8,772. 3:1,146, 168-175,233-242,483,488
    3:2,53. P:10. KC: 9,10
Associations: V:57,66. 1:17,569. N:35,90 W:12,14, 27-28. E5:25.
    Note: There is an extensive historical review of California Kindergartens in the ACEI 1940 reference.

COLORADO:
* 1876 Denver (Barrett)
* 1881 Denver (Allen & Williams)
    ca.1881 Denver free kgn. assn.
* 1891 1st public school kgn., Montclair (Johnson)
    1892 State normal school, Greeley. kgn. dept.
    1894 Denver normal school, kgn. trng.
General references: 1:5,639. 1:8,29. 1:8,735. 2:9,258,329. W:29-31. KC:9

CONNECTICUT:
* 1875 Bridgeport (Terry); New Haven (Newcomb)
    1882 CT Valley kgn. assn (Brooks)
* ca. 1884, New Britain (in the normal school)
    1884 New Britain Normal School,kgn. trng. program
* 1886 1st Law for public school kgns in US (also IN & VT)
* 1886 1st public school kgn., Hartford
* 1888 1st public school kgn. building constructed in US
    1897 Free kgn. assn. (Bridgeport)
** 1925 Guidance nursery school (Yale Clinic)
General references: N:33,164-172. 1:7,396. 3:1,146,304. 3:2,17-20. NE: 22-28.
    E4:*47*. E5:48.

DELAWARE:
*   ca. 1880, Wilmington (Negandank)
       1890 St. Michael's Day Nursery (Rev. Coleman)
       1893 Delaware kgn. assn.
*   1903 1st Black kgn. Howard School,Wilmington (Brooks)
*   ca. 1922,1st public school kgn.,Wilmington
**   1931 Madame Layton's School (for children under five) (Layton)
       1984 Kgns. mandated by the state
General references: SE:7,8,9,10.
Industrial kgn: SE:8.

DISTRICT OF COLUMBIA:
*   1870 (German Speaking)
       1872 Training school (Marwedel)
*   1883 1st public school kgn.
*   1886 Berean Baptist Church (Taylor)
*   ca.1888 1st Black kgn. in DC (Murray)
       1892 Woman's League (Black kgn. assn.)and Columbian kgn. assn.
       1896 1st Black kgn. trng. program (Murray)
*   1898 1st public school kgn.(8 white; 6 black) funded by Congress
**   1927 1st Black nursery school (Howard)
General references: V:69,70. SE:10,11. 1:12,58. 1:12,452. 1:14,290. 2:9,200.
       2:11,558. N:37,38 3:1,146. E0:359,484. E2:*86* E3:846. E4:*47, 472*.
       E5:484. P:9. KC: 8,9.

FLORIDA:
*   1893 Jacksonville
       1893 Jacksonville free kgn. assn.
       1893 Training school (Warringer)
*   1904, 1st public school kgn.,St. Petersburg.
General references: SE:11,12,13,14,15. 1:5,857. 3:1,146.

GEORGIA:
*   ca. 1880 Atlanta, 1888 Augusta
*   ca. 1890, 1st Black kgn., Atlanta
       1892 State Normal School, kgn. dept.
*   1895 Altanta (Cheyney & Walsh)
       1905 Gate City kgn. association, Atlanta
*   1905 1st public school kgn. Columbus
**   1929 Univ. of Georgia laboratory nursery school (Knapp)
**   1930 Spelman College, Atlanta Univ. laboratory nursery school (Reed)

General references:V:122,123. SE:21. 2:9,461. 2:12,55,241.
       2:13,427,575. 2:14,60. 2:15,505, 570. 3:1,146.
Industrial kgn: SE: 19,21. 1:15,505

HAWAII:
*   1892 In a Chinese mission home (Damon)
*   1893 Queen Emma Hall
       1894 Honolulu kgn. trng. school
       1895 Hilo free kgn. assn.
**   1901 Mary Castle day nursery
**   1927 1st nursery school, Honolulu (Brown & Shinn)
General references: 3:1,21-28,146 3:2,65-68 W:63-67.

IDAHO:
    ca. 1897 Wallace kgn. assn.
*   1897 Wallace
*   1899 1st public school kgn., Boise
    1945 1st child care licensing law
General references: W:31-32.

ILLINOIS:
    1873 Chicago Froebel kgn assn., Chicago
*   1874 Chicago (Putnam)
*   ca 1875 1st public school kgn, Forestville.
    1883 1st kgn. est. by WCTU, Bethel Mission, Chicago
    1889 Permissive legislation for Chgo. to est. kgns.
    1893 Ida B. Wells Club (Black kgn. assn.) Chicago
    1893 Two kgns. at Columbian Exposition
    1895 Permissive legislation for state public school kgns.
**   1915, U. of Chgo., Cooperative Nursery School
**   1925, Franklin Public School Nursery, Chicago (Heinig)
    1970 mandated kgns. for state
    1985 permissive legislation for prekgn. programs
General references: V:73,78,79,90,124. N:29.,157-164,185-193.
    1:5,720,729,734. 1:6,186. 1:9,679. 2:10,568. 2:11,58,485.
    2:15,448. 3:1,147. MW: 18-23. E3:84 E4:47. E5:83. KC:9-12.

INDIANA:
*   ca1822 Infant school, New Harmony (Owen)
*   1875 Indianapolis (Anderson & Chapin)
    1882 Indianapolis free kgn. assn.
    1882 Indiana kgn. trng. school (Blaker)
*   1886 1st Law for public school kgns in US (also CT & VT)
**   1930 Purdue Univ laboratory nursery school
General references: 1:11,305. 1:12,440. 1:16,458. 2:8,546. 2:9,326.
    3:1,147. MW: 53-54. E5:102.

IOWA:
*   1876 Des Moines (Collins)
    1882 Des Moines kgn. assn.
*   1884 1st public kgn., Des Moines
    1885 Kgn. trng. program, Des Moines
    1896 Permissive legislation for public school kgns.
    1917 Iowa Child Welfare Station, State Univ. of Iowa
**   1921 Iowa City laboratory nursery school
**   1924, Nursery school in Home Economics, Iowa State
General references: 1:6,577. 1:9,531. 1:12,328-329. 2:16,126,180-185,
    211-217. 3:1,147,277-279,304,490. MW: 47-53. V:80 N:28-29

KANSAS:
*   1882 Topeka (Davidson)
    1882 Kgn. dept. in Emporia Normal School
    1893 Topeka kgn. assn.
    1907 Permissive legislation for public school kgn.
**   1926 Kansas State, laboratory nursery school
**   1930 U of Kansas, laboratory nursery school
General references: V:71. 2:8,355. 2:10,179. 3:1,147. W:32-34.

194

KENTUCKY:
* 1865 Louisville (German Speaking, Hailmann)
* 1881 Louisville (Adams)
  1886 Free kgn. assn. of Louisville
  1887 Louisville kgn. training school (Bryan)
  1899 Normal school class of Black kgn. teachers (Cowans)
* ca.1900 Black kgn. established. city unknown.
  ca1936 Permissive legislation for public school kgns.
General references: V:79. 1:1,281. 1:2,383. 1:6,827. 2:8,444. 2:8,574. KC:8,
    2:10,176. 3:1,147. MW: 54-59. E3:846. E4:47. E5:140. P:9-10.

LOUISIANA:
* 1876 1st public school kgn.,New Orleans
* ca.1900 Black kgn. established. city unknown.
  1900 Phyllis Wheatly Club, New Orleans
  1900 Permissive legislation for public kgns.
General references: SE:21,22. 1:10,227,352. 2:7,397,445. 2:8,575.

MAINE:
* 1874 Portland (Proctor)
* 1883 1st public school kgn.,Portland
  1890 Bangor kgn. assn.
  1896 Trng. classes for kindergartners (Bangor ?)
  1917 Permissive legislation for public schoolkgns.
  1984 State funds specifically appropriated for Head Start
  1984 Mandated statewide kgns.
General references: 1:5,310. 3:1,147,304. NE:29-32. E4:47. E5:161.

MARYLAND:
* ca. 1880, Baltimore
* 1888 Sparrows Point (Industrial kgn.)
  1893 Froebel club (Baltimore)
  ca. 1900 Training school, Baltimore (Beatty)
* 1901 1st public school kgn.,Baltimore
** 1925 Child research center, Johns Hopkins
  1926 Permissive legislation for public school kgns.
  1967 Statewide aid for kgns.
General references: SE:23,24. 1:7,456. 3:1,147. E3:846. E4:47. E5:189.

MASSACHUSETTS:
* 1860 Boston (Peabody) 1st English speaking kgn in U.S.
  1861 West Newton (German speaking)
  1868 First kgn. training school in U.S., Boston
* 1873 Comm. Educ. shows a public school. kgn., Boston
* 1887 Boston, public school kgn.
  1888 Boston normal school (Fisher)
  1889 Wheelock trng. school, Boston and Eastern kgn. assn.
  1893 Boston Era Club (Black kgn. assn)
** 1922 Boston,1st Nursery school in U.S. (Eliot)
General references: V:13,15,28,57-79. 1:12,454. 2:11,20. 2:12,279,283, 352,474.
    N:27,30,33,147-151,200-211. 3:1,148,452-456. 3:2,475-478. NE:5-22.
    E0:359. E2:86. E3:186,115. E3: 846. E4:47,182. E5:189. P:9. KC: 7-9.
    *Note: There is an extensive review of Massachusetts kgns. in the
    ACEI 1935 reference.*

195

MICHIGAN:
    1830 Infant school, Detroit (Williams)
*   1869 German Speaking kgn., Detroit
    1881 Detroit day nursery and kgn. assn.
    1888 Mich. state normal college (Vandewalker)
    1889 Grand Rapids kgn. assn.
    1892 Permissive legislation for public school kgns.
*   1895 Detroit, public school kgn.
** 1922 1st nursery school, Merrill-Palmer, Detroit (Henson)
** 1924 Nursery school in public school, Highland Park
** 1930 Michigan State University laboratory nursery school
General references: V:79,80,81,90,124. 1:5,264,459,558 1:9,572. 2:11,83.
        2:12,186,218,264. 3:2,72-73. N:28,32,36,193-200. 3:1,148,413-417.
        3:2,123-128. MW:30-37. E2:185 E3:846. E4:47,205. E5:212. KC: 8

MINNESOTA:
*   1868 St. Paul
*   1880 Kgn. in Winona normal school (Eccleston)
    1885 St. Paul kgn. assn.
    1891 Minneapolis kgn. assn.
    1894 Mankato normal school, kgn. dept.
*   ca1895 1st public school kgn., Winona
** ca 1917 pre-kgn. program for 4s, Winona
** 1925 Child Welfare Institute, U. of Minnesota
General references: 1:2,257,416. 1:6,834. 1:10,297. 3:1,148. MW:42-46.
        E5:205. KC: 10

MISSISSIPPI:
    1884 Miss. Industrial Institute, kgn. instruction available
*   ca.1900 Black kgn. established. city unknown.
*   1906 Hernando
*   1911, Miss. State College for Women, 1st college program
    1980 1st integrated state financed public school
    1985 kgns. mandated by state
General references: SE: 25. 3:1,148.

MISSOURI:
*   1873 1st public school kgn. in U.S. Susan Blow, teacher
    1886 WCTU kgn in Kansas City
    1890 Harper Woman's Club (Jeff City)
    1892 Crow kgn. assn. (St. Louis)
    1981 Parents as Teachers Program
General references: 1:1,266. 1:2,57. 1:6,373. 2:8,675. 2:12,441. 3:1,148,150.
        MW: 37-41. E3:225,115. E3:846. E4:47. E5:244. P:9-10. KC:7.

MONTANA:
*   1892 Five kgns. reported, cities unknown.
*   1897 Helena kgn. assn.; Phillipsburg kgn. society
*   1902 1st public school kgn., Helena
General references: 2:8,399. 2:14,665. W:34-35.

NEBRASKA:
* 1892 1st public school kgn., Omaha (Shields & Smith)
* 1893 public school kgn., Lincoln. (Barker)
1893 Froebel kgn. assn., Omaha
** 1930 U of Nebraska laboratory nursery school
1967 Permissive legislation for prekgn. programs
1987 Full statewide funding
General references: 1:6,733. 1:12,453. 2:8,611. W:35-38.

NEVADA:
* 1881 City unknown
* 1890 Carson City (Babcock)
1894 Reno kgn. assn.
* 1895 1st public school kgn., Reno
1947 Permissive legislation for public school kgns.
General references: W:38-39.

NEW HAMPSHIRE:
* 1879 Concord (Proctor)
* 1891 1st public school kgn.,Concord
1896 Trng. school in Concord (Proctor)
** ca. 1927 Nursery school operated by Durham kgn. assn.
** 1928 Nursery school, UNH (Home economics)
General references: 1:12,459. NE:32-35. E5:269.

NEW JERSEY:
* 1861 Hoboken and Newark (German speaking)
1887 NJ tchrs took kgn. course in NY (Kraus-Bolte)
* 1888 1st public school kgn.,Trenton (White)
1898 Trenton normal school, kgn. instruction available
1900 Permissive legislation for public school kgns.
1940 Statewide minimum stds. for kgns.
General references: SE:25-31. 1:8,606. 2:8,292,330. 2:11,187,316.
3:1,148. E2:86. E3:846. E4:47. E5:278. KC:8.

NEW MEXICO:
* 1882 City unknown
* 1898 Santa Fe
* 1902 1st public school kgn., Santa Fe.
1926 Permissive legislation for public school kgns.
General references: W:39-40.

NEW YORK:
1828 Seminary of infant educ., Albany
* 1864 New York City (German speaking)
* 1868 kgn. for feeble minded Syracuse (Seguin)
* 1871 1st public school kgn in Normal College (now
Hunter College.)
1872 Kgn. trng. school (Kraus-Boelte in NYC)
* 1878 Kgn. for deaf mutes, Rochester
* 1880 Kgn. for blind, New Rochelle
1882 Kgn. dept. in Oswego Normal School

NEW YORK (Cont.)
        1887 Albany kgn. assn. 1888 NYC kgn. assn.
        1887 kgn. dept. established at Teachers College (NYC)
*   1887 1st public school kgn.,Rochester (Tooke)
        1893 Permissive legislation for public school kgns.
        1900 Walton Black kgn. NYC (Walton)
        1911 1st Montesorri school in U.S., Tarrytown
**   1919 City & County School (Johnson)
**   1923 Vassar & Smith Colleges laboratory nursery school
        1924 Columbia U., child study institute
        1925 Nursery school in Home Economics, Cornell
        1928 Office of Director of CD and Parent Ed. established
        1942 Free public kgn. part of ele. educ.
        1946 Permissive legislation for free nursery schools
        1966 5 million dollars allocated for prekgn. programs
General references: V:77,79,90,124. N:140-147. 1:5,83,850. 1:11,105,433,574.
        1:12,305. 2:10,462. 2:15,178. 2:17,137,478. N:25,27,29,34,35,
        37,39,172-180,223-228. 3:1,148. MW: 62-78. E2:*86.* E3:846.
        E4:*47*,295. E5:293. P:9. KC:8,9. *Note*: There is an extensive historical
        review of New York Kindergartens in the ACEI 1938 reference.

NORTH CAROLINA:
*   1885, Asheville (Garrison)
        1889 Asheville kgn. assn.
*   ca.1900 Black kgn. established. city unknown.
*   1907 1st public school kgn.,Asheville
        1923 Permissive legislation for public school kgns.
**   ca.1930 NC Woman's College laboratory nursery school
General references: V:91. SE:31,32,33,34,35,36,37. 1:5,234. 3:1,149.

NORTH DAKOTA:
*   ca.1885 Fargo
        1885 Fargo kgn. assn.
*   1915 1st public school kgn., Fargo (Emmons & Alm)
General references: 3:1,149. W:40-41.

OHIO:
*   1858 Columbus (German speaking) Second kgn. in the
        United States (Frankenberg)
        ca. 1870 Training school, Columbus (Ogden)
        1870 Cincinnati kgn. assn.
*   1877 Trinity Church, Toledo. 1st church kgn.
        1892 Permissive legislation for public school kgns.
*   1894 1st public school kgn., Columbus
**   1923 Nursery school at Rainbow Hospital, Cleveland
**   1925 Nursery school in Home Economics, Ohio State
**   1930 Nursery school in Home Economics, U. Cincinnati

General references: V:76,80,81. 1:5,151,456. 1:8,690. 1:11,362. 2:4,261,656.
        2:13,246,381. N:35,151-157. 3:1,149. MW:9-17. E3:846. E4:*47*, 328.
        E5:331. KC:7,9.

OKLAHOMA:
*   1883 Oklahoma Indian Territory, no city.
*   1900 1st public school kgn., Guthrie; Oklahoma City
**   1925 Nursery school at OSU, Stillwater. Home Ec. Dept.
      1970 Statewide funding
General references: 2:17,51. W:42-44.

OREGON:
*   1881 Portland (Dunlop)
      1884 Portland kgn. assn.
      1886 Oregon Froebel Union
      1887 Permissive legislation for public school kgns.
      1917 mandatory-on-petition law.
**   1930 Oregon State University laboratory nursery school
      1988 Oregon prekgn. program
      1989 full statewide funding
General references: 2:11,516. 3:1,148. W:44-45.

PENNSYLVANIA:
      1874 Society of Froebel Kindergartners
*   1875 Scranton (Dickson)
*   1876 Demonstration kgn. at Phila. Centennial Expo.
      1876 Training school in Philadelphia (?) (Burritt)
*   1879,1st public school kgn.,Philadelphia
      1881 Phila kgn. assn; 1892 Pittsburg kgn. assn.
**   ca. 1925 Haverford nursery school.
General references: V:78. SE:37-45. 1:5,717. 1:10,388. 1:15,489.
      2:15,300. 2:14,667. 3:1,148. 3:2,370-373. E3:846.
      E4:47, 360. E5:358. P:10. KC:9.

RHODE ISLAND:
*   1882 1st public school kgn.,Newport
      1885 Providence free kgn. assn.
      1889 Public school kgn.,Pawtucket
General references: 3:1,148. NE:28,29. E3:846.

SOUTH CAROLINA:
*   1873, Charleston (Smith); 1876 Orphan School kgn.
      1876 Charleston Female Seminary, kgn. dept.
      1891 Charleston kgn. assn.
      1906 Kgn. assn. of SC
*   ca. 1900 Black kgn. est. in Anderson, Charleston
      1900 Winthrop College kgn. dept.
      1913 Permissive legislation for public school kgns.
*   1st public school kgns. (ESEA)
      1978 kgns. mandated by state
General references: V:122. SE:45,46,47,48,49. 2:9,253. 2:10,631.
      2:11,57,379.
Industrial kgn: SE: 45,46,47.

SOUTH DAKOTA:
* ca.1880 Souix Falls (Parker)
* 1903 1st public school kgn., Souix City (Beaumont)
General references: 1:14,93. W:45-47.

TENNESSEE:
* ca. 1890 Knoxville
1890 Chattanooga kgn. assn.
ca.1891 Kgn. trng. Summer School of the South, Knoxville
* ca. 1900 1st public school kgn. Knoxville
* ca. 1900 Black kgn. established. city unknown.
1917 Permissive legislation for public school kgns.
** 1930 Univ. of Tenn. nursery school in home economics.
General references: V:80. 1:5,716. 3:1,487. MW: 59-62.

TEXAS:
1891 Galveston kgn. assn.
1892 Fort Worth kgn. assn.
* 1892 Fort Worth
1892 El Paso,Woman's study circle
* ca.1893 1st public school kgn., El Paso (Jones ?)
* ca.1900 Black kgn. established. city unknown.
General references: V:80. 1:5,376. 2:9,72. 2:13,446.
3:1,148. 3:2,115-120. W:48-54.
Associations: W:52-53.

UTAH:
* ca.1875 Salt Lake City (Cobb & Jones)
1893 Salt Lake kgn. assn.
* 1893 1st public school kgn., Salt Lake City (Goodrich)
ca.1935 Statewide kgns.
General references: 1:11,216. 2:11,250. W:54-58.

VERMONT:
* 1886 1st Law for public school kgns in US (also CT & IN)
* 1895 1st public school kgn.,Burlington (Ryan)
* ca. 1895 Private kgn, Bennington
** ca. 1934 Nursery school, Vergennes.
1989 full statewide funding
General references: NE:35,36.

VIRGINIA:
1873 Butler school at Hampton Institute
1893 Kgn. training school, Hampton Institute
* ca. 1899, Richmond (Arents)
1899 Richmond kgn. assn.
* 1901,1st public school kgn., Richmond
** 1929 Hampton Institute laboratory nursery school (Tilly)
1966 Permissive legislation for public school kgns.
1972 Statewide kgns.
General references: V:80. SE:49,50. 2:12,179. 2:15,129. *Note*: VAECE has a
paper entitled, *Highlights of VAECE History*.

200

WASHINGTON:
*   1882 Seattle (Blaine)
*   1882 (German Speaking) (Guttenberg)
*   ca. 1889 Tacoma (Dunlap)
      1892 Spokane kgn. assn.
*   ca. 1894 kgns. in Everette, Spokane, Tacoma, Seattle
*   1897 1st public school kgns.(3), cities unknown
*   ca. 1912 Federal kgn. on Tulalip Indian Reservation
*   ca. 1912 kgn. for the blind
      1899 Washington state normal school
      1918 Laboratory kgn. at Western Washington College
      1936 Permissive legislation for public school kgns.
General references: 1:8,529. 2:10,117. 2:13,247. 3:1,488.
      W:58-62.

WEST VIRGINIA:
*   ca. 1899 Charleston (Adams)
      1899 Permissive legislation for public school kgns.
*   1923 1st public school kgn., Charleston
      1965 Legislature votes to establish Head Start statewide
General references: SE: 50,51,52,53,54. 3:1,148.
Industrial kgn: SE:51.

WISCONSIN:
*   1856 Watertown (German speaking, Schurz)1st Kgn. in
      the United States.
      1880 1st kgn. in U.S. affiliated with a normal
      school, Oshkosh
*   1880 1st public school kgn., Milwaukee
      1880 Froebel kgn. assn., Milwaukee
General references: V:13,14,15,21,57. 1:5,312,717. 1:7,552. 1:14,165.
      1:18,385. 2:13,120. 2:16,387,400. 3:1,148. MW:23-30.
      E3:846. E4:47. E5:454. KC:7.

WYOMING:
*   1885 City unknown
      1895 Permissive legislation for public school kgns.
*   1905 1st public school kgn., Casper.
*   1910 Lauder
General references: W:63.

ACKNOWLEDGMENTS:

In gathering material for Part II, I received assistance from a number of NAEYC state presidents, ECE state specialists, and state librarians. I would like to acknowledge their help and interest plus the following individuals. AL: Jacquelyn Autrey, CA: Gary Strong, CO: Catherine Sonnier, DC: Floretta Mckenzie, Carol Phillips, Dollie Wolverton, DE: Sheryl Parkhurst, Ginny Burns-Ferrara, IA: Carol Phillips, ID: Mary Lou Kinney, IL: Eileen Borgia, Karen Stephens, KS: Ivalee Long, MAEYC President, Audrey Witzman, MD: Frances Witt, ME: Jenifer Van Deusen, MO: Mildred Winter, MT: Cheri Bergeron, MS: Cathy Grace, NE: Harriet Egertson, NH: Helen Schotanus, NJ: Tynette Hills, NV: Patricia Hedgecoth, NY: Mary Bondarin, OH: Mary Rush, OK: Judy Franks, OR: Nancy Conklin, SC: Janet Perry, VA: Jane Goldman, Helen Kelley, VT: Mary Luciano.

REFERENCES

Abbot, J. (1923). A twenty-four hour day for the preschool child. *Childhood Education*, **1**, 111-118.

ACEI. (1935). *The kindergarten movement in New England*. Washington: ACEI.

ACEI. (1937). *The kindergarten centennial: 1837-1937*. Washington: ACEI.

ACEI. (1938). *History of the kindergarten movement in the Midwestern states and New York*. Washington: ACEI.

ACEI. (1939). *History of the kindergarten movement in the Southeastern states and Delaware, District of Columbia, New Jersey and Pennsylvania*. Washington: ACEI.

ACEI. (1940). *History of the kindergarten movement in the Western states, Hawaii and Alaska*. Washington: ACEI

ACEI. (1987). Position paper on the child-centered kindergarten. *Childhood Education*, **63**, 235-242.

Adams, B. (1953). *About books and children*. New York: Holt.

Adamson, J. (1930). *A short history of education*. Cambridge: University Press.

Allen, J. (1969, September 23). *The right to read — Target for the 70s*. Address delivered to the National Association of State Boards of Education, Los Angeles, CA.

Almy, M. (1966). *Young children's thinking*. New York: Teachers' College Press.

Almy, M. (1968). Introduction in S. Isaacs, *The nursery years*. New York: Schocken, 1968.

Alschuler, R. (1942). *Children's centers*. New York: Morrow.

Anderson, J. (1956). Child development: An historical perspective. *Child Development*, **27**, 181-196.

Anderson, R. (1971). *As the twig is bent*. Boston: Houghton Mifflin.

Antler, J. (1987). *Lucy Sprague Mitchell: The making of a modern woman.* New Haven: Yale University Press.

Arbuthnot, M. (1933). The unit of work and subject matter growth. *Childhood Education,* **9**, 182-188.

Arbuthnot, M. (1974). *Children and books.* Chicago: Scott, Foresman and Company.

Ardrey, R. (1970). *The social contract.* New York: Atheneum.

Aries, P. (1962). *Centuries of childhood.* New York: Alfred Knopf.

Attenborough, R. (1977). *Life on earth.* Boston: Little, Brown.

Atwood, N. (1916). *Kindergarten theory and practice.* Boston: Houghton Mifflin

Ayers, L. (1909). *Laggards in our schools.* New York: Survey Associates.

Bain, W. (1961). With life so long, why shorten childhood? *Childhood Education,* **38**,15-16.

Bakan, D. (1971). *Slaughter of the Innocents.* San Francisco: Jossey Bass.

Baker, E. (1937). *The kindergarten centennial: 1837-1937.* Washington: ACEI.

Baldwin, B., & Stecher, L. (1925). *The psychology of the preschool child.* New York: Appleton.

Banks, W. (1972). *The Black church in the U.S.* Chicago: Moody Press.

Barker, R., Kounin, J., & Wright, H. (1943). *Child behavior and development.* New York: McGraw-Hill.

Barnard, H. (Ed.). (1890). *Kindergarten and the child culture papers.* Hartford: Office of American Journal of Education.

Baylor, R. (1965). *Elizabeth Peabody: Kindergarten pioneer.* Philadelphia: University of Pennsylvania Press.

Bereiter, C., & Englemann, S. (1966). *Teaching disadvantaged children in preschool.* Englewood Cliffs: Prentice-Hall.

Bereiter, C. (1986a). Does direct instruction cause delinquency? *Early Childhood Research Quarterly,* **1**, 89-292.

Bereiter, C. (1986b). Response to Schweinhart and Weikart. *Educational Leadership, 43*, 20-21.

Berrueta-Clement, J., Schweinhart, L., Barnett, S., Epstein, A., & Weikart, D. (1984). *Changed Lives: The effects of the Perry Preschool Program.* Ypsilanti, MI: High/Scope Press.

Berson, M. (1959). *Kindergarten: Your child's big step.* New York: Dutton.

Bettmann, O. (1974). *The good old days: They were terrible!* New York: Random House.

Biber, B. (1969). Challenges ahead for early childhood education. *Young Children, 24*, 196-205.

Biber, B. *et al.* (1971). *Promoting cognitive growth: A developmental interaction point of view.* Washington: NAEYC.

Billingsley, A., & Geovannoni. J. (1972). *Children of the storm: American child welfare.* Atlanta: Harcourt, Brace, Jovanovich, Inc.

Blow, S. (1876). Report to the superintendent quoted in Harris' Report. *Twenty-first annual report of the board of directors of the St. Louis public schools for the year ending August 1871.* St. Louis: Board of Education.

Blow, S. (1895). *The mottoes and commentaries of Friedrich Froebel's mother play.* New York: Appleton.

Blow, S. (1908). *Educational issues in the kindergarten.* New York: Appleton.

Boldt, R., & Eichler, W. (1982). *Friedrich Wilhelm August Froebel.* Leipzig: Pahl-Regenstein.

Borstelmann, L. (1983). Children before psychology: Ideas about children from antiquity to the late 1800s. In Paul Mussen (Ed.). *Handbook of child psychology. Volume I.* New York: John Wiley.

Bossard, J., & Boll, E. (1966). *The sociology of child development.* New York: Harper & Row.

Bowman, B. (1989, October). Educating language-minority children: Challenges and opportunities. *Phi Delta Kappan, 71*, 118-120.

Boyce, E. (1926). Nursery school conference. *Childhood Education, 2*, 427-428.

Boyd, W. (1914). *From Locke to Montessori.* London: G. G. Harrap.

Brandt, R. (1986, November). On long term effects of early education: A conversation with Schweinhart. *Educational Leadership, 43,* 15-18.

Braun, S., & Edwards, E. (1972). *History and theory of early childhood education.* Worthington, OH: C. A. Jones.

Brawley, B. (1937). *Negro builders and heroes.* Chapel Hill: The University of North Carolina Press.

Bredekamp, S. (Ed.). (1986). *Developmentally Appropriate Practice.* Washington: NAEYC.

Bredekamp, S. (Ed.). (1989a). *Accreditation criteria & procedures.* Washington: NAEYC. (5th printing)

Bredekamp, S. (Ed.). (1989b). *Guide to Accreditation.* Washington: NAEYC. (4th printing)

Bremner, R. (Ed.). (1971). *Children and youth in America.* Cambridge: Harvard University Press. (Three volumes).

Brim, O. (1965). *Education for child rearing.* New York: The Free Press.

Bronfenbrenner, U. (1979). *Is early intervention effective?* Lexington, MA: Lexington Books.

Brown , M. (Ed.). (1988). *Quality environments: Developmentally appropriate experiences for young children.* Champaign, IL: Stipes Publishing Co.

Buhler, C. (1939). *The first year of life.* New York: John Day.

Bullock, H. A. (1967). *A history of Negro education in the South: From 1619 to the present.* Cambridge: Harvard University Press.

Bundy, B. (1988, September). Achieving accreditation: A journal of one program's experience. *Young Children, 43,* 27-34.

Burke, A. *et al.* (1923). *A conduct curriculum for the kindergarten and first grade.* New York: Scribners.

Butler, A. (1962). Hurry! hurry! hurry! why? *Childhood Education, 39,* 10-11.

Butler, A. (1970). *Current research in early childhood education.* Washington: EKNE.

Butler, A., Gotts, E., & Quisenberry, N. (1975). *Early childhood programs — Developmental objectives and their use.* Columbus: C. E. Merrill.

Cagle, L. (1972). Unpublished memorandum contrasting Dewey and Froebel. Knoxville: University of Tennessee.

Caldwell, B., & Hilliard, A. (1985). *What is quality day care?* Washington: NAEYC.

California Bureau of Elementary Education. (1956). *Teachers guide to education in early childhood.* Sacramento: Education Department.

Camp, J. (1988). The demise of the little ladies under six: Communicating through networking. *Dimensions,* **16,** 2, 23-24.

Carmichael, L. (1946). *Manual of child psychology.* New York: John Wiley & Sons.

Cartwright, S. (1988, July). Play can be the building blocks of learning. *Young Children,* **43,** 44-46.

Clegg, A. (1971). *Revolution in the British Primary Schools.* Washington: NAESP.

Committee of Nineteen. (1913). *The kindergarten.* Boston: Houghton Mifflin.

Committee of Nineteen (1924). *Pioneers of the kindergarten in America.* New York: The Century Co.

Comstock, G., & Rubinstein, E. (1972).*Television and Social Control.* Washington: Superintendent of Documents. (Five volumes).

Consortium for Longitudinal Studies. (1983). *As the twig is bent ... lasting effects of preschool programs.* Hillsdale, NJ: Erlbaum.

Cremin, L. (1970). *American education: The Colonial experience, 1607-1737.* New York: Norton.

Cubberley, E. (1920). *Readings in the history of education.* Boston: Houghton Mifflin.

Cubberley, E. (1922). *A brief history of education.* Boston: Houghton Mifflin.

Cunningham, C. (1976). *God bless the child: A history of the Black preschool.* Unpublished Ed.S. thesis University of Georgia,Athens.

Cunningham, C., & Osborn, D. (1979). A historical examination of Blacks in early childhood education. *Young Children,* **34**, 3, 20-29.

Curtis, F., & Tappan, R. (1916). Tribute to Susan E. Blow. *The Kindergarten and first grade,* **1**, 238-241.

David, A. (nd). Draft: *SACUS History.* Unpublished notes from Dr. Alma David containing a short review of SACUS plus highlights from the Annual Conferences, 1949-1988.

Davis, G. (1976). *Childhood and history in America.* New York: Psychohistory Press.

Davis, M. (1964). How NANE grew. *Young Children,* **20**, 106-109.

Day, B. (1980). *Open learning in early childhood.* New York: Macmillan,

De Mause, L. (1974). *The history of childhood.* New York: The Psychohistory Press.

Dennis, W. (1948). *Readings in the history of psychology.* New York: Appleton-Century-Crofts.

Dennis, W. (1949). Historical beginnings of child psychology. *Psychological Bulletin,* **46**, 224-235.

Department of Labor (1965). *The Negro family: The case for national action.* Department of Labor. Washington: Superintendent of Documents, 1965.

Deutsch, M. (1966). Early social environment: Its influence on school adaptation in, *Preschool education today.* New York: Doubleday.

Devaney, K. (1974). *Developing open education in America.* Washington: NAEYC.

DeVries, R., & Kohlberg, L. (1987). *Programs in early childhood.* New York: Longman.

Dickerson, M., Ross, M., & Crum, R. (1986). *A SACUS position paper on quality day care.* Little Rock: SACUS.

Dollard, J., & Miller, N. (1950). *Personality and psychotherapy.* New York: McGraw-Hill.

Douglass, F. (1845). *Narrative of the life of Frederick Douglass*. Boston: Anti-slavery office.

Douglass, F. (1855). *My bondage and my freedom*. New York: Miller, Orton, & Mulligan.

Downs, R. (1978). *Frederich Froebel*. Boston: Twane Publishers.

Drummond, M. (1924). *The dawn of mind*. London: Edward Arnold Co.

Dunbar, A. (1903). A kindergarten club. *The Southern Workman, 32*, 386-390.

Dworkin, M. (Ed.). (1959). *Dewey on Education*. New York: Teachers' College Press.

Edelman, M. (1990). Letter addressed, "Dear friend of children," dated, October 31, 1990. This letter was sent to individuals who had supported PL 101-508.

Education News Service. (1974). *Report on Preschool Education* (Bi-weekly newsletter). Washington: Education News Service.

Elam, S., & Gallup, A. (1989). The 21st annual Gallup poll of the public's attitudes toward the public schools. *Phi Delta Kappan, 71*, 1, 41-54.

Eliot, A. (1972). Nursery schools fifty years ago. *Young Children, 27*, 4, 208-213.

Elkind, D. (1969). Preschool education: Enrichment or instruction? *Childhood Education, 45*, 321-328.

Elkind, D. (1970). The case for the academic preschool: Fact or fiction. *Young Children, 25*, 132-140.

Elkind, D. (1982). *The hurried child*. New York: Addison-Wesley

Elkind, D. (1988). *Miseducation*. New York: Knopf.

Elkind, D. (1989, October). Developmentally appropriate practice: Philosophical and practical implications. *Phi Delta Kappan, 71*, 113-117.

Elkind, D., & Flavell, J. (Ed.). (1969). *Studies in cognitive development*. New York: Oxford University Press.

Endsley, R., & Osborn, D. K. (1970). Children's reaction to TV violence. *Young Children,* **25,** 4-11.

Erikson, E. (1950). *Childhood and Society.* New York: W.W. Norton.

Evans, E. (1971). *Contemporary influences in early childhood education.* New York: Holt, Rinehart and Winston.

Fallon, B. (1973). *Forty innovative programs in early childhood education.* Belmont, CA: Fearon Publishers.

FCC. (1974). *Children's television report and policy statement.* Washington: Federal Communications Commission.

Featherstone, J. (1971). *Schools where children learn.* New York: Liveright.

Felkin, H., & Felkin, E. (1895). *Herbart's science and practice of education.* Boston: D. C. Heath.

Flesch, R. (1955). *Why Johnny can't read.* New York: Harper Row.

Folmsbee, B. (1942). *A little history of the hornbook.* Boston: The Horn Book, Inc.

Foster, J. (1939). *Nursery school education.* New York: Appleton-Century.

Fowler, W. (1962). Cognitive learning in infancy and early childhood. *Psychological Bulletin,* **59,** 116-152.

Frank, L. (1962). Beginnings of child development and family life education in the 20th century. *Merrill-Palmer Quarterly,* **8,** 207-227.

French, V. (1977). History of the child's influence: Ancient Mediterranean Civilizations. In Bell & Harper, *Child effects on adults.* New York: Wiley.

French, W. (1964). *America's Educational Tradition.* Boston: D. C. Heath.

Froebel, F. (1889). *Autobiography of Friederich Froebel* (trans. by Emilie Michaelis). Syracuse: C. W. Bardeen.

Froebel, F. (1911). *The education of man.* New York: D. Appleton & Co.

Frost, J. (1968). *Early childhood education rediscovered.* New York: Holt, Rinehart & Winston.

Frost, J. (Ed.). (1973). *Revisiting early childhood education.* New York: Holt, Rinehart & Winston.

Frost, J., & Sunderlin, S. (Eds.). (1985). *When children Play.* Wheaton, MD: ACEI.

Frost, J., & Wortham, R. (1988, July). The evolution of the American playground. *Young Children,* **3**, 19-28.

Furth, H. (1970). *Piaget for teachers.* Englewood Cliffs, NJ: Prentice Hall.

Gaines, D. (1974). Story of an English cotton mill lad. *History of Childhood Quarterly,* **2**, 249-264.

Gans, R., Stendler, C., & Almy, M. (1952). *Teaching young children.* Yonkers-on-Hudson, NY: World Book Co.

Gardner, D. (1964). *Development in early childhood.* New York: Harper & Row.

Garrison, C., Sheehy, E., & Dalgliesh, A. (1937). *The Horace Mann Kindergarten.* New York:Teachers' College Press.

Gersten, R. (1986). Consequences of three preschool curriculum models. *Early Childhood Education Quarterly,* **1**, 293-302.

Gersten, R., & White, W. (1986). Castles in the sand: Response to Schweinhart and Weikart. *Educational Leadership,* **43**, 19-21.

Gesell, A. (1924). The significance of the nursery school. *Childhood Education,* **1**, 11-20.

Gesell, A. (1928). *Infancy and human growth.* New York: Macmillan.

Gesell, A. (1936). *The first five years of life.* New York: Macmillan.

Gilder, R. (1903). The kindergarten: An uplifting social influence in the home. *National Education Association Proceedings,* 390-391.

Goffin, S., & Lombardi, J. (1988). *Speaking Out: Early Childhood Advocacy.* Washington: NAEYC.

Goldsmith, C. (1972). *Better day care for the young child through a merged governmental and non governmental effort.* Washington: NAEYC.

Good, H., & Teller, J. (1969). *A history of western education.* New York: Macmillan.

Goodman, E. (1990, Winter). Diamond in the rough. The association for the accreditation of Montessori teacher education (AAMTE). *The National Montessori Reporter,* pp. 8-9.

Gordon, I. (Ed.). (1972). *Early childhood education: Seventy-first NSSE Yearbook.* Chicago: University of Chicago Press.

Gotts, E. (1988). An ACEI position paper on the right to quality child care. *Childhood Education,* **64,** 268-275.

Gray, S., & Klaus, R. (1968). The early training project. *Monographs of the Society for Research in Child Development,* **33.**

Greenberg, P. (1969). *The Devil has slippery shoes.* New York: Macmillan.

Greenberg, P. (1987, July). Lucy Sprague Mitchell: A special book review. *Young Children,* **42,** 70-84.

Greenberg, P. (1990, September). Head Start ... Before the beginning: A participant's view. *Young Children,* **45,** 40-52.

Greenleaf, B. (1978). *Children through the ages.* New York: McGraw-Hill.

Greven, P. (1973). *Child rearing concepts.* Itasca, IL: Peacock Publishers.

Griffin, M. K. (1906). The Hope day nursery. *The Colored American Magazine,* **10,** 397-400.

Hafer, Lilla D. (1938). The growth of kindergarten in New York City. In L. Wheelock (Ed.). *History of the kindergarten movement in the Midwestern states and in New York.* Washington: ACEI.

Hailmann, W. (1873). *Kindergarten culture in the family and kindergarten.* New York: Van Antwerp, Bragg & Co.

Hammond, S. *et al.* (1963). *Good schools for young children.* New York: Macmillan. (See also, Leeper, 1968).

Harrington, M. (1963). *The other America.* New York: Macmillan.

Harris, W. (1872). Report of the Superintendent. *Seventeenth annual report of the board of directors of the St. Louis public schools for the year ending August 1871.* St. Louis: Board of Education.

Harris, W. (1876). Report of the Superintendent. *Twenty-first annual report of the board of directors of the St. Louis public schools for the year ending August 1875.* St. Louis: Board of Education.

Hartup, W., & Smothergill, N. (Eds.). (1967). *The young child.* Washington: NAEYC.

Hausman, B. (1989, Fall/Winter). Parents as teachers: The right fit for Missouri. *Educational Horizons,* **68,** 35-39.

Head Start. (1990). *Head Start: A child development program.* Washington: U.S. Department of Health & Human Services.

Heffernan, H. (1959). *Guiding the young child.* Boston: D. C. Heath.

Heinig, C. (1979). The emergency nursery schools and the wartime child care centers: 1933-1946. In Hymes, J. *Living History Interviews: Book 2, Care of the children of working mothers.* Carmel, CA: Hacienda Press.

Heinz, M. (1959). *Growing and learning in the kindergarten.* Richmond: John Knox Press.

Herford, W. (1904). *The student's Froebel.* Boston: D. C. Heath.

Hess, R., & Baer, R. (1968). *Early education.* Chicago: Aldine Press.

Hess, R., & Croft, D. (1972). *Teachers of young children.* Boston: Houghton Mifflin.

Hewes, D. (1975). *W. N. Hailmann: Defender of Froebel* (Publication #75-15, 939). Ann Arbor: University Microfilms.

Hewes, D. (1976a). Patty Smith Hill: Pioneer for young children. *Young Children,* **31,** 4, 297-306.

Hewes, D. (1976b). NAEYC's first half century: 1926-1976.*Young Children,* **31,** 6, 461-476.

Hewes, D. (1981). Private correspondence, dated, November 18, 1981.

Hill, P. (1907). Some conservative and progressive phases of kindergarten education. *NSSE Yearbook.* Chicago: Univ. of Chicago Press.

Hill, P. (1916a, September). Kindergartens of yesterday and tomorrow. *Kindergarten Primary Magazine,* **21,** 4-6.

Hill, P. (1916b). Personal reminiscences of Miss Blow. *The Kindergarten and first grade*, **1**, 241-242.

Hill, P. (1923). *A conduct curriculum for the kindergarten and first grade.* New York: Charles Scribner's Sons.

Hill, P. (1925). Changes in curricula and method in kindergarten education. *Childhood Education*, **2**, 99-106.

Hill, P. (1927a). Forty years in kindergarten. *The Survey*, **11**, 506-509.

Hill, P. (1927b). The education of the nursery school teacher. *Childhood Education*, **3**, 72-80.

Hill, P. (1941). Kindergarten, in *American Educators Encyclopedia*. Lake Bluff, IL: United Educators.

Hill, P. (1987, July). The function of the kindergarten. *Young Children*, **42**, 20-27.

Hodges, W. (1985). *Future research in early childhood.* Keynote address delivered at the University of Georgia Elementary Education Symposium, April 26, 1985.

Hodges, W. (1987). Upon what can we build our children's educational future. *Dimensions*, **15**, 1, 4-7.

Hofferth, S. (1989). What is the demand for and supply of child care in the United States? *Young Children*, **44**,(5), 28-33.

Hoffman, M., & Hoffman, L. (1964). *Review of child development research.* New York: Russell Sage Foundation. (2 volumes).

Holmes, D. (1934). *The evolution of the Negro college.* New York: AMS Press.

Holt, J. (1964). *How children fail.* New York: Dell Publishing Co.

Horton, L., & Horton, P. (1973). *The learning center.* Minneapolis: T. S. Denison Co.

Howes, C. (1988). *Keeping current in child care research.* Washington: NAEYC.

Hunt, J. (1961). *Intelligence and experience.* New York: Ronald Press.

Hunton, A. (1908). The NACW: Its real significance. *The Colored American Magazine*, **14**, 417-422.

Huus, H. (1960). *The education of children and youth in Norway*. Pittsburgh: University of Pittsburgh Press.

Hymes, J. (Ed.). (1972). *Living history of early childhood education*. Washington: Childhood Resources. (Eight audio cassettes).

Hymes, J. (1972). *The year in review: A look at 1971*. Carmel, CA: Hacienda Press (P.O. Box 222415, 93922). Note: Also available from the Hacienda Press are the reports for 1971-1987.

Hymes, J. (1977). *Living History Interviews: Book 1, Beginnings*. Carmel, CA: Hacienda Press.

Hymes, J. (1978). *Living History Interviews*: Book 2, *Care of the children of working mothers*. Carmel, CA: Hacienda Press.

Hymes, J. (1979). *Living History Interviews*: Book 3. *Ding Dong School*. Carmel, CA: Hacienda Press.

Hymes, J. (1989). *The year in review: A look at 1988*. Washington: NAEYC.

Hymes, J. (1990). *The year in review: A look at 1989*. Washington: NAEYC.

IRA. (1973). *The right to read effort*. Newark, DE: International Reading Association.

Isaacs, S. (1929). *The nursery years*. London: Routledge, 1929. (Paperback available: Schocken Books, 1968).

Isaacs, S. (1930). *Intellectual growth in young children*. London: Routledge. (Paperback available: Schocken Books, 1968).

Jerrolds, B. (1989). *The history of the college of education: The University of Georgia*. Athens: University of Georgia.

Johnanson, D., & Edey, M. (1980). *Lucy: The beginning of humankind*. New York: Simon & Schuster.

Johnson, D., & Rahtz, R. (1966) *The new mathematics in our schools*. New York: Macmillan.

Johnson, F. B. (1966). *The Hampton album.* New York: The Museum of Modern Art.

Johnson, H. (1928). *Children in the nursery school.* New York; John Day.

Johnson, H. (1936). *School begins at two.* New York: New Republic.

Joiner, O. (1979). *A history of public education in Georgia.* Columbia, SC: R. L. Bryan Co.

Jones, E. (1953). *The life and work of Sigmund Freud.* New York: Basic Books, (3 vols.).

Joyner, J. (1985). *Beginnings: Education in colonial south.* Chicago: Wentworth Publishing Corp.

Kagan, S. (1989, October). Early care and education: Reflecting on options and opportunities. *Phi Delta Kappan,* **71,** 104-106.

Kamii, C., & DeVries, R. (1978). *Physical knowledge in preschool education.* Englewood Cliffs: Prentice-Hall.

Katz, L. (Ed.). (1982). *Current topics in early childhood education.* Norwood, NJ: Ablex Publishing Corporation.

Keliher, A. (1960). Do we push children? *Childhood Education,* **37,** 108.

Kellogg, R. (1949). *Nursery school guide.* Boston: Houghton Mifflin.

Kessen, W. (1965). *The child.* New York: John Wiley and Sons.

Keyserling, M. (1972). *Windows on Day Care.* New York: National Council of Jewish Women.

Kilpatrick, W. (1918). The project method. *Teachers College Record,* **19,** 319-335.

King, E. W., & Kerber, A. (1968). *The sociology of early childhood education.* New York: The American Book Co.

Kirkpatrick, E. (1906). The psychologic basis of the kindergarten. *NSSE Yearbook.* Chicago: Univ. of Chicago Press.

Kittrell, F. (1977). Private correspondence, dated, September 6 and October 22, 1977.

Klein, J. (1969). *Head Start planned variation program.* ERIC Clearinghouse on Early Childhood Education. 1969.

Kohl, H. (1969). *The open classroom.* New York: Random House.

Kozol, J. (1972). *Free schools.* Boston: Houghton Mifflin.

Kuo, P. (1915). *The Chinese system of public education.* New York: Teachers' College Press.

Landreth, C. (1942). *Education of the young child* . New York: John Wiley & Sons.

Langer, W. L. (1974). Infanticide: A historical survey. *History of Childhood Quarterly*, **1**, 353-366.

Langlois, J. (1989). *Serving children then and now.* Detroit: Wayne State University.

Laslett, P. *(1965). The world we have lost.* New York: Scribners.

Lathrop, J. (1912). Federal Children's Bureau. *Child Welfare Magazine*, **7**, 117-120.

Lay, W. (1922). *The child's unconscious mind.* New York: Dodd, Mead.

Leakey, R., & Lewin, R. (1977). *Origins.* New York: E. P. Dutton.

Leakey, R., & Lewin, R. (1978). *People of the lake.* New York: Doubleday

Leeper, S., Dales, R., Skipper, D., & Witherspoon, R. (1968). *Good schools for young children* (2nd ed.). New York: Macmillan.

Lerner, G. (Ed.). (1972). *Black women in white America: A documentary history.* New York: Pantheon Books.

Lerner, G. (1974). Early community work of Black club women. *Journal of Negro History*, **59**, 158-167.

Lesser, G. (1974). *Children and television: Lessons learned from Sesame Street.* New York: Random House.

Lewis, C. (1946). *Children of the Cumberland.* New York: Columbia University Press.

Lipsitt, L., & Spiker, C. (Eds.). (1963). *Advances in child development and behavior. Volume I.* New York: Academic Press.

Maclure, S. (1970). *One hundred years of London education: 1870-1970.* London: Allen Lane Press.

Majors, M. (1893). *Noted Negro women.* Chicago: Donohue & Henneberry.

Meredith, D. (1985, June). Mom, dad and the kids, *Psychology Today,* **21**, 62-67.

McClinton, K. (1970). *Antiques of American childhood.* New York: Bramhall House.

McCoy, E. (1981, January). Childhood through the ages. *Parents,* **54**, 60-65.

McLoughlin, J., & Kershman, S. (1979). Mainstreaming in early childhood. *Young Children,* **34**, 4, 54-63.

Mcmillan, M. (1919). *The nursery school.* New York: E. O. Dutton.

Mann, M., & Peabody, E. (1863). *The moral culture of infancy and kindergarten guide.* Boston: Macmillan.

Miller, L., & Bizzell, R. (1983). Long-term effects of four preschool programs. *Child Development,* **54**, 725-741.

Miller, L., & Dyer, J. (1975). Four preschool programs: Their dimensions and effects. *Monographs of SRCD,* **40**, 5-6.

Mindless, M., & Keliher, A. (1969). Research related to the advantages of kindergarten. In Osborn, D. K. (Ed.). *Kindergarten: who? what? where?* Orangeburg, SC: SACUS.

Mitchell, A. (1989, May). Old baggage, new visions: Shaping policy for early childhood programs. *Phi Delta Kappan,* **70**, 664-672.

Mitchell, L. (1953). *Two lives.* New York: Simon & Schuster.

Montessori, M. (1912). *The Montessori method.* New York: F. A. Stokes. (Paperback available: Schocken Books, 1964).

Moore, O. K. (1963). *Autotelic responsive environments and exceptional children.* (Report) Haniden, CT: Responsive Environments Foundation.

Moore, O.K., & Anderson, A. (1968). The responsive environments project. In Hess & Baer (Ed.). *Early education.* Chicago: Aldine.

Murray, A. (1900). A new key to the situation. *The Southern Workman,* **29**, 503-507.

NAEYC. (1986, September). NAEYC position statements on developmentally appropriate practice in early childhood programs. *Young Children*, **41**, 3-29.

NAEYC. (1986, May). NAEYC affiliate groups, then and now. *Young Children*, **41**, 33-34.

NAEYC. (1986, November). NAEYC publications, then and now. *Young Children*, **42**, 42-46.

NAEYC. (1989, September). National Academy: Academy reviews accreditation criteria. *Young Children*, **44**, 67-69.

NAEYC. (1989). *Guide to Accreditation.* Washington: NAEYC.

National College of Education. (1932). *Curriculum records of the children's school.* Evanston: Bureau of Publications.

Neill, A. S. (1960). *Summerhill.* New York: Hart.

NIMH. (1982). *Television and behavior.* Rockville, MD: NIMH.

Nimnicht, G., McAfee, O., & Meier, J. (1968). *The new nursery school.* New York: General Learning Corp.

NSSE. (1907). *Sixth Yearbook: The kindergarten and its relation to elementary education.* Bloomington: Public School Publishing Co

NSSE. (1908). *Seventh Yearbook: The coordination of kindergarten and elementary education.* Bloomington: Public School Publishing Co.

NSSE. (1929). *Twenty-eighth Yearbook: Preschool and parental education.* Bloomington: Public School Publishing Co

NSSE. (1939). *Thirty-eighth yearbook: Child development and the curriculum.* Chicago: University of Chicago Press.

NSSE. (1947). *Forty-sixth yearbook: Early childhood education.* Chicago: University of Chicago Press.

NSSE. (1972). *Seventy-first yearbook: Early childhood education.* Chicago: University of Chicago Press.

Olmstead, F. (1861). *The cotton kingdom.* New York: Mason Brothers.

Osborn, D. K. (Ed.). (1960). *Nursery school portfolio.* Washington: ACEI.

Osborn, D. K. (1966). *Head Start: Past, present and future.* Urbana, Ill: Isabelle Bevier Lecture Series, University of Illinois.

Osborn, D. K. (1969). *Kindergarten: Who? what? where?* Orangeburg, SC: SACUS.

Osborn, D. K., & Osborn, J. D. (1978) Childhood at the turn of the century. *The Family Coordinator,* **27,** 27-32.

Osborn, J., & Osborn, D. K. (1975). *Rural American child rearing practices, 1890-1910.* Unpublished manuscript.

Osborn, J., & Osborn, D. K. (1986). *Cognition in early childhood.* Athens: The Daye Press.

Owen, R. (1920). *The life of Robert Owen by himself.* New York: A. A. Knopf.

Panati, C. (1984). *Browser's book of beginnings.* Boston: Houghton Mifflin.

Papalia, D., & Olds, S. (1990). *A child's world: Infancy through adolescence.* New York: McGraw-Hill.

Parker, J. A. (1979). Multicultural education in preschool classrooms. *Dimensions,* **6,** 13-26.

Parker, R. (1972). *The preschool in action.* Boston: Allyn and Bacon.

PAT. (1990). *Parents as teachers.* A pamphlet published by PAT. Jefferson City, MO: Department of Elementary & Secondary Education.

Peabody, E. (1893). *Lectures in the training schools for kindergartners.* Boston: D. C. Heath.

Pei, M. (1966). *The story of language.* New York: New American Library.

Pestalozzi, J. (1898). *How Gertrude teaches her children.* (Translated by Lucy Holland). Syracuse: C.W. Bardeen.

Pestalozzi, J. (1951). *The education of man.* New York: Philosophical Library.

Phillips, C. (1990). Private correspondence with author, dated August 21, 1990.

Phillips, D. (Ed.). (1987). *Quality in child care: What research tells us.* Washington: NAEYC.

Piaget, J. (1952). *The language and thought of the child.* London: Routledge.

Plowden, B. et al. (1966). *Children and their primary schools.* London: Her Majesty's Stationery Office.

Pollock, L. (1983). *Forgotten Children.* Cambridge, MA: Cambridge University Press.

Polsky, R. (1974). *Getting to Sesame Street.* New York: Praeger Publishers.

Ponnamperuma, C. (1972). *The Origins of life.* New York: E. P. Dutton.

Powell, D. (1986, September). Effects of program models and teaching practices. *Young Children,* **41,** 60-67.

Preyer, W. (1882). *Die seele des kindes.* Leipzig: Grieben.

Quarles, B. (1964). *The Negro in the making of America.* New York: Macmillan.

Quarles, B., & Fishel, L. (1976). *The Black American: A documentary history.* Glenview, IL: Scott, Foresman.

Rambusch, N. (1962). *Learning how to learn.* Baltimore: Helicon Press.

Rasmussen, M. (Ed.). (1966). *Readings from Childhood Education.* Washington: ACEI.

Read, K. (1950). *The nursery school.* Philadelphia: W. B. Saunders.

Read, K. (1971). *The nursery school* (5th ed.). Philadelphia: W. B. Saunders.

Reed, P. (1930). Spelman College Nursery School. *Spelman Messenger,* **46,** 12-14.

Reese. H. (Ed.). (1989). *Advances in child development and behavior. Volume XXII.* New York: Academic Press.

Richie, 0., & Koller, M. (1954). *Sociology of childhood.* New York: Appleton Century Crofts.

Rickover, H. (1959). *Education and freedom.* New York: E. P. Dutton.

Robinson, E. (1966). *Readings about children's literature.* New York: David McKay Co.

Robison, H., & Schwartz, S. (1972) *Learning at an early age.* Englewood Cliffs: Prentice-Hall.

Robison, H., & Spodek, B. (1965). *New directions in the kindergarten.* New York: Teachers' College Press.

Robison, S. (1987). The state of kindergarten offerings in the United States. *Childhood Education,* **64**, 23-28.

Roeper, A., & Sigel, I. (1967). Finding the clue to children's thought processes. In W. Hartup & N. Smothersgill (Eds.), *The young child.* Washington: NAEYC.

Royce, J., Darlington, R., & Murray, H. (1983). Pooled analyses: Findings across studies. In Consortium for Longitudinal Studies, *As the twig is bent: Lasting effects of preschool programs.* Hillsdale, NJ: Erlbaum.

Ryerson, A. (1961). Medical advice on child rearing: 1550-1900. *Harvard Educational Review,* **31**, 302-323.

SACUS (1984, July). A statement on developmentally appropriate educational experiences for kindergarten. *Dimensions,* **12**, 25-26.

SACUS (1986, April). Position Paper on Quality Four Year Old Programs. *Dimensions,* **14**, 29-30.

SACUS (1987, January). Position Paper on Quality Child Care. *Dimensions,* **15**, 27-28.

SACUS (1988,July). Position Paper on Multicultural Education. *Dimensions,* **16**, 27-28.

Sagan, C. (1977). *The dragons of Eden.* New York: Random House.

Schramm, W., Lyle, J., & Parker, E. (1961). *Television in the lives of our children.* Stanford: Stanford University Press.

Schweinhart, L, & Weikart, D. (1986). Schweinhart and Weikart reply. *Educational Leadership,* **43**, 22.

Schweinhart, L., Weikart, D., & Larner, M. (1986a). Consequences of three preschool curriculum models through age 15. *Early Childhood Research Quarterly,* **1**, 15-45.

Schweinhart, L., Weikart, D., & Larner, M. (1986b). Child-initiated activities in early childhood programs may help prevent delinquency. *Early Childhood Research Quarterly*, **1**, 303-312.

Sears, P., & Dowley, E. (1963). Research on teaching in the nursery school. In N. L. Gage (Ed.), *Handbook of Research on Teaching*. Chicago: Rand McNally.

Sears, R. (1975). Your ancients revisited: A history of child development. In E.M. Hetherington (Ed.), *Review of child development research*. Chicago: University of Chicago Press.

Seguin, E. (1846). *Traitement moral des idiots*. Paris: Chez J.B. Bailliere.

Seguin, E. (1866). *Idiocy and its treatment* (English translation of work cited above). New York: William Wood & Co.

Senn, M. (1975). Insights on the child development movement in the United States. *Monographs of SRCD*, **40**, 3-4.

Siberman, C. (Ed.). (1973). *The open classroom reader*. New York: Vintage.

Sigel, I., & Hooper, F. (1968). *Logical thinking in children*. New York: Holt, Rinehart & Winston.

Simmons, C. (1990). *Growing up and going to school in Japan*. Philadelphia: Open University Press.

Snitzer, H. (1968) *Living at Summerhill*. New York: Collier.

Spodek, B. (1982). The kindergarten: A retrospective and contemporary view. In L. Katz (Ed.). *Current topics in early childhood education*. (Volume 4). Norwood, NJ: Ablex.

Spodek, B. (1985, July). Early childhood education's past as prologue: Roots of contemporary concerns. *Young Children*, **40**, 3-8.

Spokek, B. (1990). Kindergarten. *World Book*. Chicago: World Book, Inc.

Synder, A. (1972). *Dauntless women in childhood education*. Washington: ACEI.

Steinfels, M. (1973). Who's minding the children?: The history and politics of day care in America. New York: Simon & Schuster.

Stendler, C. (1950). Sixty years of child training practices. *The Journal of Pediatrics*, **36**, 122-134.

Stevinson, E. (1923). *The open air nursery school.* London: J. M. Dent.

Stewart, M. (1938). History of kindergartens in New York State. In L. Wheelock, Ed, *History of the kindergarten movement in the mid-western states and in New York.* Washington: ACEI.

Stolz, L. (1972). *Living History Interviews: The Kaiser Child Care Service Centers.* Washington: Childhood Resources. (audio cassette)

Stolz, L. (1976). Once more with feeling: Comments by Lois Meek Stolz. *Young Children,* **31,** 345.

Strickland, C. (1982). Paths not taken: Seminal models of early childhood education in Jacksonian America. In B. Spodek (Ed.), *Handbook of research in early childhood education.* New York: Free Press.

Sweet, S. (1990). Private correspondence, dated, November 5, 1990.

Swick, K., Brown, M., & Graves, S. (1984). *A SACUS position statement on developmentally appropriate educational experiences for kindergarten.* Little Rock: SACUS.

Swift, F. (1931). *Emma Marwedel: Pioneer of the kindergarten in California.* Berkeley: University of California Press.

Tarney, E. (1965). *What does the nursery school teacher teach?* Washington: NAEYC.

Taylor, K. (1954). *Parent cooperative nursery schools.* New York: Teachers' College Press.

Updegraff, R. et al. (1938). *Practice in preschool education.* New York: McGraw-Hill.

Vance, B. (1973). *Teaching the prekindergarten child: Instructional design and curriculum.* Monterey, CA: Brooks-Cole Publishing Co.

Vandewalker, N. (1907). The history of kindergarten influence in elementary education. *NSSE Yearbook.* Chicago: University of Chicago Press.

Vandewalker, N. (1908). *The kindergarten in American education.* New York: Macmillan.

Virginia, Department of Elementary Education (1989). *Developmental kindergarten: Definition and description.* Richmond: Department of Education.

Wallis, C., & Booth, C. (1985, December 9). Children having children, *Time*, 78-90.

Wann, K., Dorn, M., & Liddle, E. (1962). *Fostering intellectual development in young children*. New York: Columbia University Press.

Ward, M. (1957). *Young minds need something to grow on*. Evanston: Row, Peterson and Co.

Washington, V. (1988). Trends in early childhood education. Part I. *Dimensions*, **16**, 2, 4-7.

Washington, V. (1988). Trends in early childhood education. Part II. *Dimensions*, **16**, 3, 4-8.

Watson, J. (1928). *Psychological care of infant and child*. New York: W. W. Norton.

Weber, E. (1969). *The kindergarten: Its encounter with educational thought in America*. New York: Teachers' College Press.

Weber, E. (1970). *Early childhood education: Perspectives on change*. Worthington, Ohio: C. A. Jones Co.

Weber, L. (1971). *The English infant school and informal education*. Englewood Cliffs: Prentice-Hall.

Webster, E. (1938). Changes in form of education. In *History of the kindergarten movement in the Mid-Western states and in New York*. Washington: ACEI.

Weikart, D. (1970). *Longitudinal results of the Ypsilanti Perry Preschool Project*. Ypsilanti, MI: High/Scope.

Weikart, D. (1978). *The Ypsilanti preschool curriculum demonstration project*. Ypsilanti, MI: High/Scope Educational Research Foundation.

Weikart, D. (1989). *Quality preschool programs: A long term social investment*. New York: Ford Foundation.

Weikart, D., Rogers, L., Adcock, C., & McClelland, D. (1971). *The cognitively oriented curriculum: A framework for preschool teachers*. Urbana: University of Illinois.

Weil, J. (1986). *One-third more: Maine Head Start expansion with state funds*. Ellsworth, ME: Federal-State Partnership Project Action Opportunities, Inc.

224

Wiggin, K., & Smith, N. (1895). *Froebel's gifts*. Boston: Houghton Mifflin.

Wiggin, K., & Smith, N. (1896). *Froebel's occupations*. Boston: Houghton Mifflin.

Williams, J. (1975). *Origins of the English language*. New York: The Free Press.

Wilson, F. (1967). *The child as artist* (Original pamphlet published in England in 1921). Reprinted in Detroit: The Merrill-Palmer Institute.

Witherspoon, R. (1976). From NANE to NAEYC: The tempestuous years. *Young Children*, **31**, 333-338.

Wolff, M. (1966). *Six months later: A comparision of children who had Head Start* ERIC/EECE. EDO 15025.

Wortham, S. (1985). A history of outdoor play 1900-1985. In J. Frost and S. Sunderlin (Eds.), *When children play*. Wheaton, MD: ACEI.

Yates, J. (1905). Kindergarten and mother's clubs. *The Colored American Magazine*, **8**, 304-311.

Yates, J. (1906). Education and genetic psychology *The Colored American Magazine*, **10**, 293-297.

Zigler, E. (1970). The environmental mystique: Training the intellect vs. development of the child. *Childhood Education*, **46**, 402-412.

Zigler, E., & Valentine, J. (Ed.). (1979). *Project Head Start: A legacy of the war on poverty*. New York: Macmillan.

Zinsser, C. (1988). The best day care there ever was. In *Early Childhood Education 88/89*. Guilford, CT: Dushkin Publishing Group.

Zwicke, O. (1985, October). Laboratory schools: A historical perspective. *Newsletter, Bulletin #5*. National Organization of Child Development Laboratory Schools.

Subject Index

See part II for individual states

227

Name Index

234